PENGUIN BOOKS

HUNGRY FOR HOME

Cole Morton is an English journalist who
writes for *The Independent on Sunday* and other
magazines. *Hungry for Home* is his first book.

Hungry for Home

Leaving the Blaskets:
A Journey from the Edge of Ireland

COLE MORETON

PENGUIN BOOKS

PENGUIN BOOKS

Published by the Penguin Group

Penguin Putnam Inc., 375 Hudson Street,
New York, New York 10014, U.S.A.
Penguin Books Ltd, 27 Wrights Lane, London W8 5TZ, England
Penguin Books Australia Ltd, Ringwood, Victoria, Australia
Penguin Books Canada Ltd, 10 Alcorn Avenue,
Toronto, Ontario, Canada M4V 3B2
Penguin Books (N.Z.) Ltd, 182–190 Wairau Road,
Auckland 10, New Zealand

Penguin Books Ltd, Registered Offices:
Harmondsworth, Middlesex, England

First published in the United States of America by
Viking Penguin, a member of Penguin Putnam Inc. 2000
Published in Penguin Books 2001

1 3 5 7 9 10 8 6 4 2

CIP data available
ISBN 0 14 10.0194 1 (pbk.)

Printed in the United States of America
Set in MT Bembo

This story could stand for the story of emigration from Ireland to America. As rooted as they became in American culture, these exiles never lost a sense of home.

Jean Kennedy Smith, former United States Ambassador to Ireland, on the Blasket story

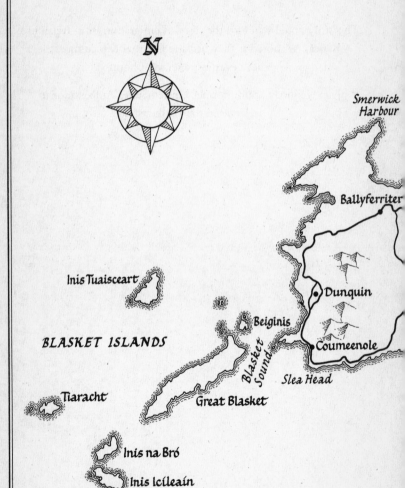

The Blasket Islands
COUNTY KERRY

N

Smerwick
Harbour

Ballyferriter

Inis Tuaisceart

BLASKET ISLANDS

Beiginis

Dunquin

Blasket Sound

Coumeenole

Tiaracht

Slea Head

Great Blasket

Inis na Bró

Inis Icíleáin

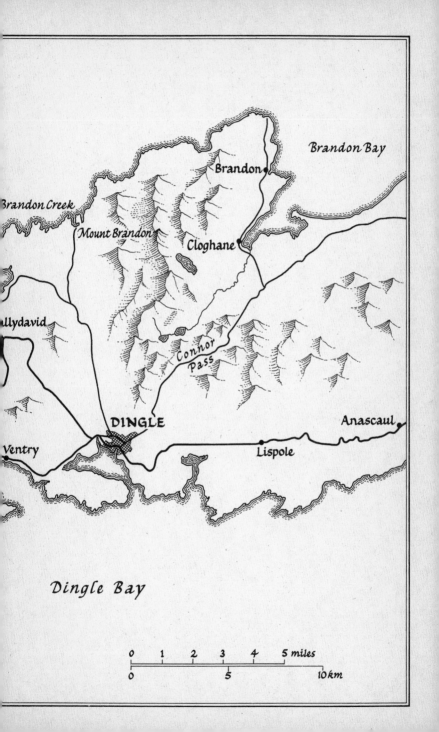

Brandon Bay

Brandon

Brandon Creek

Mount Brandon

Cloghane

Connor
Pass

Ballydavid

DINGLE

Anascaul

Ventry

Lispole

Dingle Bay

| 0 | 1 | 2 | 3 | 4 | 5 miles |

| 0 | | 5 | | 10 km |

Contents

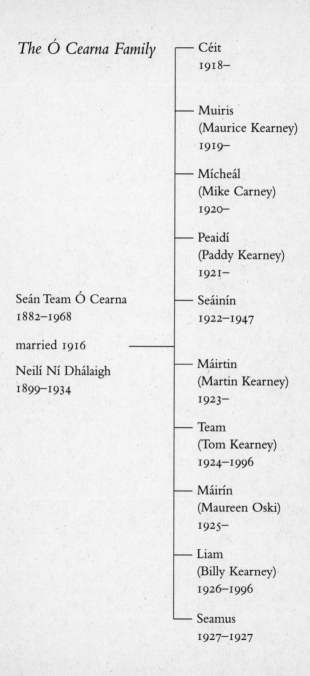

The Ó Cearna Family

Seán Team Ó Cearna
1882–1968

married 1916

Neilí Ní Dhálaigh
1899–1934

Céit
1918–

Muiris
(Maurice Kearney)
1919–

Mícheál
(Mike Carney)
1920–

Peaidí
(Paddy Kearney)
1921–

Seáinín
1922–1947

Máirtín
(Martin Kearney)
1923–

Team
(Tom Kearney)
1924–1996

Máirín
(Maureen Oski)
1925–

Liam
(Billy Kearney)
1926–1996

Seamus
1927–1927

A Note on Gaelic Names

The children of Seán Team Ó Cearna did and do exist, and I am enormously grateful for their cooperation and trust. The material in this book is taken from interviews with some of them, historical documents, other eye-witness accounts, and the customs of the time, although it was necessary to use a certain amount of dramatic licence. This is my own version of their story, imagined from what they told me.

Gaelic names have been used throughout, and some explanation may be appropriate. The surname Ó Cearna can also be written as Ó Cearnaigh; it can be anglicized as Kearney, Carney or in other ways, according to personal preference, and the Ó is usually dropped.

The community of people living on the Great Blasket included five separate families with the name Ó Cearna. As the islanders were closely related and the same first names were used by many different people, it was customary for men and women to be known after their most illustrious predecessors. For example, the head of the household with which this book is chiefly concerned was known as Seán Team Ó Cearna, which distinguished him from others such as Seán Sheáisi Ó Cearna and Seán Philí Ó Cearna.

Seán is pronounced Shawn. I have used the diminutive Seáinín (Shawneen) for his son's name. Mícheál is pronounced Mihawl and anglicized as Michael or Mike. It may help those who do not have Gaelic to read other first names as follows: Pádraig as Patrick; Máirtín as Martin; Muiris as Maurice; Peaidí as Paddy; Peats as Pats; and Team as Tom. For the women,

Céit is Kate, Eíbhlín is Eileen (shortened to Neilí or Nellie) and Máirín is Maureen. The spelling of their surnames varies according to status. Nearly everyone on the island also had a nickname, but the meanings of many of them has been lost.

The great Blasket writers Tomás Ó Criomhthain and Muiris Ó Súilleabháin were published in English as Tomás O'Crohan and Maurice O'Sullivan. The surnames Ó Dálaigh and Ó Guithín can be read as Daly and Guiheen.

Throughout the text, the canoes which were essential to the survival of the islanders are referred to by their Gaelic name: *naomhóg* in the singular (pronounced nay-vogue) and *naomhóga* in the plural (nay-voga).

The names of the islands in the Blasket archipelago are given with their English equivalents when they first occur, and thereafter in the Gaelic version alone. Elsewhere in the book, Gaelic names and phrases are usually followed by an English translation.

PART ONE

The End of the World

The cock is crowing and the dawn is breaking,
And my love, he himself, going home away from me.

A lament for the dead sung on the Great Blasket

I

Christmas Eve 1946

This is the end of the world. The air is full of a terrible wailing. A gale scalps the waves, spilling foam. Gulls shriek as they tumble, caught between the spray, the rain and the low, dark clouds. A mountain stands alone in the sea, its back breaking the wind so that the invisible forces are scattered over its slopes as raiders from the north once were, howling and running down from all directions on to the shuttered buildings of a settlement.

A dozen decaying cottages huddle into the hillside, each long and low and built of stone upon stone, each with a bolted door. The wind worries at the roofs, ripping back felt, and animals sheltering in outhouses bellow and moan in fear. This is a wild and lonely place for any living creature, and tonight there is no escape. The island is surrounded, blinded, by a wall of grey cloud, half a mile out in every direction. Behind it, somewhere through rain and snow, is the mainland, the coast of Corkaguiney, the most westerly tip of Europe. The End of the World, the maps used to say. Beyond be dragons and sea monsters.

A candle burns in the window of one home, its animated light catching on the edge of a long blade which moves across the throat of an animal. The sheep twists its back and kicks out, but its legs are tied together and its belly held down hard against the seat of a wooden chair. Teeth exposed, spittle arching through the air, its head moves in a frenzy. The noise it makes is pitiful. The hands of the islandman are expert and sure. They find the jugular, and slide the blade quickly across the hide, twisting it hard to release a flow of warm blood.

In the half-light, the blood is black. Most splashes into a bowl, some soaks into the earthen floor. Some sprays on to the black fishing jerseys worn by the father and son who are killing this sheep. Both are tall and lean. The old man stoops a little, and there are liver spots on his hands, but his experience makes up for lost strength. His son's young body is hard and strong, with broad shoulders and big hands, but only the effort required to keep the animal from kicking stops his fingers from trembling. Both wear black boots with studded soles, and heavy trousers, and flat caps pushed back from the forehead. They do not talk, but their eyes are on each other in the oil and candlelight, the old man and the youth, as together they hold the sheep down, patiently, and it kicks and shudders. They listen for its gargle to ease into a final, deep sigh.

Just outside the door, a woman wearing an apron and shawl over her long woollen dress leans back on the wall and hugs herself against the cold. 'Oh Jesus,' she mutters, sickened as always by the ritual now coming to an end in her own home. Every year a sheep is killed before Christmas, so that it may be eaten over the festive season. The flesh will be rich and tasty; it's just the crying it makes, like a child, that snakes out from the dying animal, through the air and into her chest, with an icy pain.

The sky is low and heavy. The stars have gone missing. Snowflakes melt in the woman's thin black hair. The fingers that push them away are hard, bony, with nails bitten down. She is the woman of the house, who looks older than her years. Although not yet thirty, she has been caring for a family of nine for half her life, since her mother died. Céit cooks in an iron pot on an open fire, over smouldering turf. She fetches water from the well. There is no electricity here, the light comes from paraffin lamps. Elsewhere they can split the atom, but on the Great Blasket island, life is much as it has been for a century or more. Her father Seán Team Ó Cearna and his sons work the fields, and fish around the island, bringing home potatoes and mackerel for the daily meal. They have a donkey, two cows, some chickens and a few sheep, one of which is now dying inside the door. When it stops struggling, Céit hears nothing but the wind, and the waves meeting the rocks a long way below.

The schoolhouse next door is empty; there have been no lessons there for five years. When Céit was a child, there were a hundred and fifty people living in the island village, and on Christmas Eve a candle burned in the window of every home, in honour of the Holy Family who sought shelter on that night. Now at least half the houses are empty, with nobody to light a wick. There are very few young women like herself among the fifty or so people left on the island, and hardly enough young men to crew more than a couple of canoes. So many of her friends left for America before the war, and now that is over there is talk of the remaining ones being allowed to follow. Whenever the weather allows the island postman to cross to the mainland for mail he always brings back parcels from her cousins, who write that life is wonderful. Céit knows more people in America than are left on this island. Most of those that remain are growing old, like her father. The boys may go. No doubt they will. Perhaps they will send some money home, because she cannot leave him.

The dog barks, and breaks her thoughts. 'Musha, Róisín, what is it?' Out of the night comes another brother, named after his father but known as Seáinín, a quiet, useful man of twenty-four. She is surprised to see the sure-footed islandman stumble as he comes down the hill with a shovel in one hand, and in the other a basket of potatoes dug up from their winter store beneath the frozen ground. 'Faith, you gave me a fright. Are you after finishing so soon?' No response. The returning man pushes past in silence, and seems to fall through the door into the house.

The heat is a welcome shock. Fresh sods are burning in the hearth, where the father kneels, washing his hands in a bowl. 'Come up to the fire, and get yourself warm.' The sheep hangs by a hook on the wall, its blood slowly dripping into the bowl. Seáinín does not reply to the old man, who is startled to see him fall, heavily, into the straw-rope chair with the loose leg.

'For the love of God, be careful. Is there something the matter with you?'

There is. Seáinín's hands are up on either side of his head, the fingers splayed as he rubs hard against each temple. His hair is drenched dark with cold sweat. Sick to his stomach, feverish and shaking, with the kick of a donkey coming down on his skull, the young man bends double, head between his legs. He hits the floor without uttering a sound.

2

The old bus gave a smoky cough, shook itself, and eased forward out of the station at Tralee, the county town of Kerry, in the south-west of Ireland. It was a warm day in late August 1998. We passed a windmill and a steam train on the edge of town, and crossed flat lands with a mountain range rising up ahead.

The driver let his passengers off wherever they wanted, without having to be told. A young mother in a tracksuit and her baby were deposited at a village pub, and the single-decker wheezed to a halt on the open road for an elderly man in black suit and cloth cap, who gave a flick of the hand in thanks as he began the long, slow walk along an uphill path to his bungalow. A bend in the road revealed a wide beach with a bright white beard of surf. Boys kicking a football in the centre of a crossroads stopped their game to examine the bus for familiar faces.

The map open across my knees showed a finger of land pointing out into the Atlantic from Tralee Bay. The Dingle Peninsula, otherwise known as Corkaguiney, was thirty miles long, with the Slieve Mish mountains running right down the centre. The knuckle in the finger was Mount Brandon, named after the saint who sailed west in search of a mythical Land of Promise.

The mountain range followed Saint Brendan westward to the very tip of the peninsula. On the way the northern slopes were sprinkled with villages and solitary cottages as they fanned out into the wide sweep of Smerwick Harbour. Back across the peaks, the southern glens provided a glorious backdrop for the town of Dingle, once a fishing community but now a tourist trap. We stopped for a moment at the quay, which was crowded with trawlers and old fishing boats adapted to take parties out to see Fungie, the dolphin who lived in the bay. His image was painted on pubs, cafés, shops and anywhere else a stranger might be parted from his money. But those of us in search of solitude and wilder beauty stayed on the bus as it travelled still further west, a dozen miles in the shadow of the mountains, through the landscape described by *National Geographic Traveler* as 'the most beautiful place on earth'. The houses separated, bounded by flinty fields where no tree could grow, but where drystone shelters built by pilgrims a thousand years before still stood. The sun broke through, reflected by countless raindrops in the fuchsia hedgerows. On we went, along the coast with the Atlantic lashing against the windows, through a stream that crossed the road, and past the sudden, shocking sight of a life-sized crucifixion scene by the passing point at Slea Head. The Christ figure was a weather-blasted white, with painted blood flowing from his hands and feet.

Around the next bend, rising up between two valleys at the end of the peninsula, was the headland of Dún Mór, the last flourish of the Slieve Mish mountains before they plunged down into the sea, their black heels kicking up foam as they disappeared into the Blasket Sound. This was a treacherous stretch of water that hid its rocks on even the most beautiful of days, eager to add another name to the long list of ships that had been dragged beneath the waves. The undertow ran as fast as a motorway, sucking wrecks and bodies down into the darkness.

And then there it was, the sight I had travelled so far to see. Three miles out, the Slieve Mish range came back up from the depths, returning to the surface in the mountainous shape of the Great Blasket. The village was in ruins, barely visible, but the impervious island stood as it always had, first and largest in a group of six. 'Seen from above you would think them sea-monsters of an antique world languidly lifting time-worn backs above the restless and transitory waves,' wrote the scholar Robin Flower in *The Western Island*. Others had compared the Great Blasket among its neighbours to a whale nursing her young.

Way off in the distance was the furthest-flung Blasket island, Tiaracht, a jagged pyramid of rocks whose name was anglicized as Tearacht and meant 'westerly'. It had a lighthouse, now automated, which was said to provide the last sight of Ireland for ships heading to America. To the south was the long shape of Inis Icíleaín, Inishvickillaune, where the former Irish leader Charles Haughey spent his summers in a solitary mansion. *Inis* is Gaelic for island, but the origins of the rest of the name have been lost in time. Next to it, almost hidden from the mainland by the Great Blasket itself, was Inis na Bró, the island of the quern-stone, supposed to resemble the hand-mill used for grinding corn. Inis Tuaisceart, Inishtooshkert or the north island, was also known locally as the Dead Man or the Sleeping Giant, because it did look like a huge figure laid out on his back in the sea. A low, flat stretch of land just in front of the Great Blasket was called Beiginis, Beiginish, the small island. Like the others, it had never been home to anyone for very long.

An Blascaod Mór, the Great Blasket, was different. It was larger – three and a quarter miles long from east to west, and two-thirds of a mile across at its widest point – and offered both shelter from the wind and fresh water from its springs. The island may have been named by the Vikings after the Norse for a sharp reef, or it could have been that Blasket was derived from the word for a shell in Irish, the only language spoken on the island in its best years.

During the First World War there were at least 176 people living there, in a village at the eastern end, facing the mainland. There was hardly any level ground on the steep mountain slope where the houses were built, but it was protected from the west wind. The village was just above what passed for the island harbour, a small and partially sheltered cove where a canoe, or *naomhóg*, could be brought ashore. The rest of the shoreline was made up of high and dangerous rocks, except for An Trá Bhán, the White Strand, a long beach that led away from the village, below the only fields on the island that were worth cultivating.

Even into the middle of the twentieth century, the people of the Great Blasket lived a life that could be described as medieval. They had no source of power but the burning of turf from the hill, no source of food but the sea and the animals they kept, and the few crops that could be grown on such miserly land. There was water from twenty springs and milk from the cows. Tea and alcohol had to be brought in from the mainland. The work was communal and money seldom changed hands between islanders.

So much for the facts. There have been other isolated communities in remote places, of course, each capable of inspiring horror at the hardships and longing for the simplicity of such a life. The people of the Great Blasket had something special about them, however. They lived on an island of stories.

3

Christmas Day 1946

'We have pills, but they are no good,' Céit tells her Auntie Eibhlín on Christmas Morning as they wait together by Tobar an Phoncáin, the Well of the Yank, a spring at the top of the village. The water never flows in anything more than a steady trickle, no matter how vicious the cold for those who have come to fill their pails. 'I put flour in a bag inside the stove, to heat it up. That's the first relief he got.'

The aunt nods. It is an old remedy for headaches, to warm a sack of flour and lay it on the brow.

Across the Sound, under a stone-grey sky, they can see the mainland. Smoke curls from the chimneys of homes spread across the slopes of Croaghmarhin and Mount Eagle. A bruise in the sky beyond Inis Tuaisceart indicates another band of hail approaching fast. The short hours of daylight are already dying. The wind is resting for a while, but the sea rolls in huge, lazy waves against the rocks, sending spray into the air. No boat can make it to the mainland in this weather. There is no priest on the island to say the Mass, and no shop from which to buy supplies. Neither is there a doctor to cure Seáinín. No help can be summoned, because the radio telephone in the island post office is broken again. This Christmas the Great Blasket may as well be moored in the middle of the wide ocean.

'He was all right this morning,' says Céit as the bucket fills. 'He got up. There was something inside the head all the time

— he thinks it's someone hitting him with a hammer. He was eating with us today, but then he got ill again.'

Seáinín has been vomiting, and has taken to his bed, hidden from sight of the Christmas feast of mutton and boiled potatoes, but not away from the smell of it. There is brandy and whiskey in the house, sent from the bar in Dublin where Céit's brother Mícheál works, and those are supposed to help cure sickness.

'I made a punch and everything. I thought I was curing him. He told me, "You are killing me with this."'

Seáinín plays no part in the rituals of Christmas. The hammering in his head never ceases. To the rest of the islanders the festive season seems forlorn now that there are hardly any children around. They used to go in hordes from door to door on Wren's Day wearing masks and disguises, demanding treats in honour of the bird that defended Saint Stephen. Some of the young men still do the rounds in search of drink, but it is not the same. There is unspoken sadness and fear in the Ó Cearna house on Year's End Night, when the meal is followed by the customary prayers for the absent and the dead.

On the Eve of Little Christmas, the twelfth day, Céit leaves her brother on his own and goes to a neighbour's house to listen to music on the wind-up gramophone that has been brought over from Dingle. It is a marvel, but her heart is not in the dancing. She returns to find Seáinín vomiting again. Even if the weather calms he cannot go to hospital, for fear of the fifteen-mile journey across the Sound and the mountains. Should he get there, by some miracle, how ever would he manage alone without a word of English?

So Seáinín is left to sleep, in the room that his father built on to the side of the house when the children began to grow up. It is just wide enough to contain a double bed, with a wooden cross on the wall above the pillows. The house offers good protection from the wind and rain with its tarred roof and thick walls that are whitewashed every summer. The deep-set windows give little light, so that the door is left open during the day whenever the weather allows. During the worst of winter it is bolted several times, so that the wood does not warp.

There is warmth from the hearth in the kitchen, where a bench and table are pushed up beside a painted dresser. Behind it is another room, with two beds, where the six boys sleep when they are all at home. The father is spending his nights in there with Máirtin, Team and Peaidí while Seáinín is ill. Mícheál is in Dublin, Muiris at sea and young Liam away at school on the mainland with his sister Máirín, who would otherwise lay her head down in the loft with Céit. The beds are wooden, the mattresses stuffed with goose down. The sheets are made from old flour sacks, and covered by woollen blankets bought on the mainland. A patchwork quilt is spread over each one.

Every day there are visits from members of other island families, offering such help and advice as they can. It is a worry. Seáinín is popular, one of the few young men left. Without the likes of him, they wonder to themselves, who will fish, or row to the mainland for supplies? Back in their own homes they talk about his strange illness, and curse the furious sea and the broken telephone. Otherwise, all they can do is pray.

The patient is sleeping, comforted by two hot towels his sister has placed on his forehead. This morning he was well enough to sit up in bed and ask Céit to mend the hole in his jersey, so that he could go fishing. She doesn't know if he was joking. Now he is snoring, loudly, and Céit is in the kitchen boiling salted fish for the meal. She hears him, and smiles. The rest will do him good.

There is no one else in the house; the men are out working in the weak sunshine of early afternoon. From over her head, and on the other side of the walls, comes the sound of dripping, as the ice on the roof and the window-sill melts. The sky is clear. Through the window she sees that it is one of those dangerous days, when the sea is both beautiful and jealous.

Humming one of the new tunes from the gramophone to herself, Céit puts the lid on the iron pot and straightens up. Time to check on Seáinín. Maybe she should warm the towels again. At the door of the room she notices that there is no sound coming from him any more. Must be a deep sleep. He is lying on his back, face up to the ceiling, mouth wide open in a yawn that never seems to end. He does not move. Céit reaches out to touch him. Now it seems as though the world stops turning. She is bound up in this one moment of time, for ever stretching out her hand but never making contact. Water drips from the roof and ice flows inside her. The towels are cold. Her fingers touch dead lips.

'Hush! Come on now, you slow old thing. Is it the stars you want to be looking at?' The father is at the door of an outhouse, encouraging the more ponderous of his two cows to take shelter for the night. The cheerful bullying dies in his mouth as he sees Céit come rushing along the path, hair flying all over her face. There is no need for her to speak, he knows what has happened.

'Seáinín's not asleep at all,' she says, pushing the words out somehow, though her mouth feels like that of a stranger. Her face is hot. The tears hurt. Her brother's soul is leaving his body. 'He's dying away. Oh Jesus. What are we going to do?'

A minute passes, then another. The old man is staring at

the sea, as his daughter stops holding back the tears. It seems so hard, such a painful death for a young man. He looks across the Sound and sees a long finger of smoke rising into the air from the headland. That was how they told him that his wife was gone, her struggle at the hospital was over at last. Now, as then, the end of worry is almost a relief. One hand rubs his white-stubbled chin as the old man says words that his daughter will remember for the rest of her life. She will never really understand what he means. 'Well . . .' His voice is strangely, supernaturally calm. 'Let us look for the grace of God.'

The grace? Well, that would be one thing, but there is no man of God on the island. None can be sent for, with the sea as it is, so there will be no last rites. The father has tears in his eyes and a rage in his heart growing fast, driving out the calm, so that he dare not enter his own home again without the support of his brother and sister-in-law, who hurry down to the house. Eibhlín gasps as she crosses the threshold, and makes the sign of the cross. She kneels by the bedside to stroke Seáinín's head, and starts to speak fast, under her breath: 'O my God, I am heartily sorry for having offended Thee and I detest my sins above every other evil . . .' So it is that Seáinín Team Ó Cearna, the young son of a devout man with a gold-capped tooth, goes into the next world without the comfort of a priest, but with his aunt whispering the Act of Contrition into a dead ear.

4

They could call ghosts through the walls, make angels dance in the fire or cause the roof to shake with laughter, the island storytellers, by means of a well-turned phrase, a facial expression or a gesture of the hand. The islanders were poor and uneducated by the standards imposed on them from the mainland, but some had a divine gift for the spoken word, and an ability to recall the events of ancient times as though they had happened yesterday. There was no wireless, no cinema, and no television to steal away the stories and replace them with new wonders. In the evenings, when the work was done, there was little better to do but gather by the fireside in someone's home and listen as an old man or woman used the skills passed down through generations to tell an intricate and mesmerizing tale. If you wanted to know why the hen laid eggs, how Ferriter's Cave got its name or the way a certain old man was betrayed by his young wife, there was a story for it. The storytellers had enjoyed their golden age long before the printing press, and everywhere else in the world their trade was almost extinct; but the past and the present had always been tangled up in Ireland, and nowhere was that ever more true than on the Great Blasket, where tales of Fenian warriors were still told by firelight as German bombers flew overhead.

The storytellers and their audience had long since died or gone away by the time I went to pay my respects. As the bus left me and dragged itself off around the coast, heading noisily back to Tralee, I climbed Dún Mór to get a better view of the abandoned island across the Sound. From a distance it looked as though a handful of the houses on the Great Blasket could still provide homes, but I knew them to have been gutted by the elements; others had fallen back into the earth and were invisible from the mainland.

Nobody had lived there for more than forty years, but the island was not forgotten. It was known, in Ireland at least, for the memory of its strange people, and for their ways of living and talking which had remained unchanged for centuries until the end. The islanders spoke Irish as it had been in medieval times, before the language was driven west and into the ground by plantation, famine, and oppression. Throughout the desperate years when schoolteachers on the mainland punished children who did not speak English, warning that they would never be able to find work without it, the island community had remained self-contained and relatively prosperous. There was plenty to do, and to eat, and to say, and most of it was untouched by the modern world.

That could not last, of course. As the twentieth century began, the struggle for Irish independence excited a new interest in the Gaelic language, and it was natural that scholars should travel west to hear it spoken properly. The first was a playwright, John Millington Synge, who visited the Great Blasket in 1905 and was captivated by his hostess, the 'young, beautifully formed' daughter of the man they called the King of the Island, who fastened her apron on the window as a blind to help him sleep and laid another on the earthen floor for him to stand on in the morning. She was said to be the model for Pegeen Mike, heroine of his most lauded work, *The Playboy of the Western World*.

Other students of Gaelic imitated Synge's journey in the following summers, and discovered the oral tradition still alive in this remote place. 'The conversation of those ragged peasants, as soon as I learnt to follow it, electrified me,' wrote the classical scholar and Marxist George Thomson, whose name was translated to Seoirse Mac Tomáis on his frequent visits to the Great Blasket. 'It was as though Homer had come alive. Its vitality was inexhaustible, yet it was rhythmical, alliterative, formal, artificial, always on the point of bursting into poetry.'

This contact with the outside world resulted in three books, and it was reading them that had brought me to the top of Dún Mór. The first was *The Islandman* by Tomás Ó Criomhthain, a thin and graceful old fellow who often wore a broad-brimmed hat and a waistcoat. A student from Trinity College in Dublin had shown Tomás the works of Maxim Gorky, to encourage and to challenge the natural storyteller that if great literature could be made from the lives of Russian peasants then why not from those of Blasket islanders? The gift inspired a collective biography, a series of tales and recollections in terse, elegant language that documented the passing of a traditional way of life. It was published in Irish in 1929, and later translated into many languages. Years after his death the author became the first native Irish-speaking writer to be featured on one of his country's stamps.

The second book to come out of this tiny community was written by a younger islander, Muiris Ó Súilleabháin, who had round cheeks, a big smile and dressed like a visitor. *Twenty*

Years A-Growing told how he had been taken to live on the Great Blasket as a child, had grown up there and then left to become a Civic Guard in Dublin. Published in 1933 and translated by his friend George Thomson, it was an immediate success in Ireland, England and America. The novelist E. M. Forster wrote an introductory note that described the book as 'the egg of a sea-bird – lovely, perfect and laid this very morning'.

Peig Sayers was an old lady, the island matriarch, when outsiders began to visit the Great Blasket. She turned out to be one of the greatest storytellers unearthed in any community, and was persuaded to recite her entire repertoire of more than three hundred folk tales into a primitive recorder for the Irish national archive. They ranged from the romantic and the adventurous to the supernatural and the saintly – and included the Fenian cycle of tales learned from her father, which had never been told by a woman before. Some of her stories were funny, some savage, some wise, some earthy; but very few made it in their original form on to the pages of her autobiography, *Peig*, which was published in 1936. The words were originally dictated to her son, then edited by the wife of a Dublin school inspector, and both collaborators sanitized the text a little in turn so that it was homely and pious, a book fit to be taken up as a set text in Irish schools. The image of Peig's broad face smiling out from beneath a headscarf, hands clasped in her lap, became familiar to generations of children, who were bored rigid by this holy peasant woman that had been forced upon them. They grew up loathing Peig, without knowing who she really was and without hearing the stories as they had been intended.

On the pages of these three books I had discovered a place where time moved slowly, and where the rhythms of the sea and the seasons meant more than the ticking of a clock. The people lived without a priest or policeman, sharing the work and the spoils, and settling disputes with rough justice. The big men of the island achieved their status by character or deed; otherwise, there was equality among, if not between, the sexes. There was no leader, but that man whose nickname was 'The King' served as postman and judge. The islanders described in the books had no choice out there on the exposed hillside but to believe that human beings were part of the natural world, not superior but subject to the cycle of the seasons, and of life and death. They danced to a fiddle or accordion in the open air, trusted in the God of creation, laughed at salty jokes and loved wild exaggeration.

When they were first published the books beguiled exiles abroad and those who dreamed of a new egalitarian Ireland in which all work would be for the common good, justice would be natural and ideas would be expressed in Gaelic, a language spoken before Christ walked the earth. Their success brought literary tourists to the island with cameras, money, and treats from the modern world. The isolation was over. Dozens more Blasket books followed – some of them great works, some prosaic guides, some collections of anecdotes in Irish, and some romantic nonsense. Tomás, Muiris and Peig died, and their art with them, but by then it had become an island of stories, true and untrue, in print as well as on the tongue.

All those words written in celebration of the Great Blasket became its elegy. As the fame of the island grew its population shrank, until it was finally abandoned altogether.

The desolation seemed to attract even more people to this most westerly point of the European mainland, to stare out at the empty mountain in the sea and muse on what life had been like there. I, too, had been drawn hundreds of miles by a desire to see that strange, enchanted place for myself, but also by the knowledge that there was one great story yet to be told. It was fascinating enough that anyone could survive on such an isolated island for so long, but there were greater mysteries. What had finally driven them out? Where had they all gone? It was hard to believe that a hardy, intimate community like that would just give up, and disappear. I had two clues, contained in an article from the local *Kerryman* newspaper that I kept folded in my back pocket. It was an interview with an old lady called Céit Ní Cearna, hinting that the death of her brother Seáinín Team Ó Cearna had somehow been the catalyst for the death of the Great Blasket. The writer suggested that there was still a handful of elderly islanders living in the villages at the tip of the peninsula within sight of their old homes. The roofs of those Blasket buildings had long since fallen in and the hearths been torn open by the elements; memories would presumably have failed in places too, been weathered by repetition or embellished by imagination. Peig and her kind understood that the events of the past must always be transformed in the telling so that they could come alive again. The empty island challenged me to find these men and women, who were in their seventies and eighties, and persuade them to talk, so that their stories could be heard before it was too late.

5

That was the worst weather. I tell you, you wouldn't go on the Blaskets that week. The sea was rough, way high.

Patrick O'Connor, of Dunquin

10 January 1947

A low moan is heard on the hillside, as the wind joins its voice to those of women keening by a deathbed. Beside them in the light of a lamp, as the winter lays down its dark skirts for the evening, are some of the last remaining young men of the island, all but silent at the loss of a friend. The old men stand with Seán, grim with the understanding of what it means for him to lose a fine strong son. There is anger among them all that it should end this way.

As moments pass, something else grows up among the tears and mutters: an agreement that things must be done better for Seáinín in death than could be managed at the end of his life. There must be a wake. A coffin is needed in which to carry this body to its proper resting place in the churchyard at Dunquin, where his young mother lies.

Such thoughts are instinctive. Today, however, they are madness. Night has almost come, and the storm that kept them from going for a doctor or a priest is still tearing at their homes. This manic watchman moves from place to place, searching out the cracks in roof and door. The sea below boils with a cold fury, salting the rain. To get a coffin, someone must cross the Sound, get over the mountain to Dingle a dozen miles away, have it made and buy supplies, before bringing the load to Dunquin and carrying it back across the sea. A long, terrible, dangerous journey to make at this time of year.

Grief makes the challenge personal. The dead man's brother, Team, proposes this gamble with the devil, and finds an ally. Seán Pheats Team Ó Cearna shares a surname with the corpse, as a cousin, and like Seáinín he is short but powerfully built, steady on his legs in the canoe they sometimes shared. His eyes, now burning with tears, give a clue to the self-possession that keeps him calm at a time like this. He is an astute man, in control of his life, alert to his surroundings, aware of the danger. The body must be buried properly.

Pushing past the mourners, head full of a rushing sound that is not the wind, he leaves the house and vaults the wall to the schoolhouse next door. There in the darkness is a figure, a young girl with her head bowed. On his knees, on the earthen floor, in the room where he learned his own lessons and where he used to think there was no greater trouble than the wrath of a teacher, Seán Pheats Team looks up at the statue and prays: 'Remember, O most gracious Virgin Mary . . . never was it known that anyone who fled to thy protection, implored thy help or sought thy intercession was left unaided . . . I fly unto thee, O Virgin of virgins, my Mother . . . before thee I stand, sinful and sorrowful . . . do not reject my petition . . .'

An hour is all they need. Half an hour. A lull in the storm to get across. A hole in the cloud. There is no panic in his voice. The words are familiar to him; learned by rote, they come easily. With God's help or not, it must be done.

Climbing the path to his own house at the top of the village he meets another of his cousins, Seán Ó Catháin – Faeili to his friends – and makes a challenge. These are men in their twenties, experienced in the boats but still with hot blood in their veins. By the time Seán Pheats Team has gone off to fetch his oilskins for the journey, Faeili is on his own knees in the schoolyard praying to the Virgin for calm. He is a small, wiry rogue, with a puffin's nose and a fisherman's sense of balance. No one quite knows how he got the nickname he has had since childhood, but it could mean either affable or stealthy. Both apply. Under his heavy eyebrows are the eyes of a man who has seen his own death many times already, and sent it away with a sharp turn of phrase. You would think he was severe, but no one in the island has more fun in them. Usually.

'Has the sense left you entirely?' The question comes from one of the old men standing in the doorway of the Ó Cearna house when the pair return. It is the voice of one who knows the sea, who has seen the storm and defied it himself in high waves. 'It is not worth dying for a coffin. Why would you risk your own lives going out, and the waves white on the rocks?'

Voices rise in agreement. Then another question, more urgent than the others, asked in desperate anger. 'Your souls to the devil, is there not another man here who will join the boat?'

The passion of Team, a sorrowful brother, quietens the crowd. Inside the body lies, and the women wail. Some of the men would like to do the same.

'Myself. I will do it.' Maidhc Leán Ó Guithín, the brother-in-law of Seán Pheats Team, is a giant of a man, as strong as a horse, with a rounded face and a voice as soft as his muscles are mighty. He is at least a decade older than the others, and knows what may be out there in the wild water, but sounds calm, as though they were about to attempt a fishing expedition on a summer's evening. 'I will go out with you.'

Their feet are sure on the way down the hill to the harbour. Down along the path known as the Way of the Dead, past the graveyard where the shipwrecked and unbaptized are buried, taking care on the rain-sodden grass. The people of the village watch from above, behind windows or in the open, as these four men in shining oilskins lift a canoe from its stand. It is perhaps fifteen feet long. The hull, made of skins stretched over a wooden frame and tarred, is upturned. Once underneath the boat they take cautious steps down the concrete slipway, knowing it to be treacherous with weed and water. They cannot see beyond the next man's back, but move from memory, the long vessel approaching the water like a black beetle with eight legs in heavy boots.

They row without words. Eight oars bite the waves together, and pull hard. Each man hears the heavy breathing of the one behind him, the song of the wind and the waves, and the rhythmic clunk of oars rolling on their iron thole pins. Legs pushed out straight along the bottom of the shallow boat, they keep one frozen hand in front of the other. The oilskin coats lie at their feet, discarded with the effort. Usually it is as natural for them to row as it is to walk, but this time there is an urgency. They fight the tide by the shore of Beiginis, hoping to turn once they are past the small, flat island, where the current becomes unbeatable, and ride it across to the mainland. Seáinín is beside them in the boat. Each pull banishes the memory of his dead eyes, for a second.

'Slow down,' pleads Maidhc Leán, 'or surely you will drown the boat.'

They know the truth of it, and breathe deeply to make their rage ebb away, searching for a less frantic rhythm. The canoe must ride the waves; if it turns side on it could be flooded, and each of them drowned. These are not strong swimmers. Any man who falls overboard will be dragged down fast by his boots and clothes, and trying to pull him back into the boat would be suicidal for the others. When the time comes, it comes.

'Jesus. It is black and blue.' On the horizon, out by Tiaracht, the sky is dark with a storm. The eyes of each man go to sea level, where the water itself is black, a sure sign of danger. There is a saying that unless the shower is bright underneath, it is time to go home. Darkness means the sea is not just disturbed by a rainstorm but twisted by the wind into something more dangerous. It is still a couple of miles away, but moving in towards the mainland. This will be a race then, between storm and crew, to see who reaches harbour first.

Way back on a hill overlooking Dunquin a farmer calls his dog and starts for home, to take shelter before the next belt of rain sweeps inland. His eye is caught by a long black shape against the sea, like driftwood on the rolling waves, gone again in a second. An illusion, surely, on a day like this? No, there it is, for real. Seamus Ferriter is a man of the land, not the sea, he is hardly ever seen by the pier, but he knows that something must be seriously wrong for a boat to be out in such conditions. He knows the sky. Cursing the clouds above the Tiaracht, he begins to run down the hill towards the harbour.

The sea is bright. Surf breaks high over the rotten black teeth at the mouth of the cove, rocks that wait under a high tide until the waves drop away, then spear the sky and anything near them. A curtain of hail sweeps across the waves as the *naomhóg* disappears from view again, behind the cliffs. The sea is swelling up, drawing its breath, preparing to rage. No boat can survive that maelstrom. Seamus Ferriter skates down the steep wet path to the pier, clawing at the cliff face for support, his feet sliding from under him. Eyes full of salt and sea spray, he resists the work of his mind, fighting hard not to think of the sorrows waiting below.

6

Whenever an islandman died, the body was carried to his home. The eyes and mouth were closed and the legs and arms pulled down so that he appeared to be at rest. The mother, if she was still alive, or the wife, or a sister, washed the corpse all over and combed his hair, and tied his jaw closed with a white handkerchief before dressing him in the finest shirt available, and his Sunday suit. Over this was pulled a seamless brown cloak, like the habit of a monk. It had no pockets, because the dead could take no belongings into the next world with them.

Every family's most urgent need was to raise a crew for the canoe which must travel to the mainland to fetch a coffin and supplies for the wake. Some men in the island could work with driftwood, after a fashion, but the skill of the coffin-maker in Dingle was respected and admired. A dead body demanded care and generous attention. Tobacco and a box of clay pipes were required for the wake, along with white bread and jam, tea, a barrel of porter and a bottle or two of whiskey. These could also be bought in Dingle, so two of the crew usually hired a cart or car to take them there from Dunquin. Superstition demanded that they be accompanied by a woman, either an islander or a relative on the mainland. The other two set out on foot for Ballyferriter, five miles away in the opposite direction, to fetch the priest.

If it was a fine day, and the sea was calm, the coffin and supplies could be back in the island within twelve hours. In the meantime, the tearful relatives at home continued to prepare the body. It was laid on a white sheet which covered the kitchen table, and a pillow was placed under the head. More white sheets were sewn together and hung over ropes suspended from the rafters to make a canopy covering the body, on to which a cross was tied. Twelve long white candles representing the disciples of Christ stood in bottles around the body, and eleven of them were lit. The twelfth gave out no light, in memory of Judas the betrayer.

Grief could not be private. A father or a sister might turn for a moment to the window, or disappear to the strand for a while, but the house was already filling up with relatives and neighbours, each expecting to help or to offer words of comfort. There were tears, of course, and the tremulous sound of women beginning their keen, an unearthly combination of wailing, groaning and singing that lamented the dead man and praised him. Planks of wood were balanced along the walls as benches, and *punann na marbh*, the sheaf of straw for the dead, laid on the floor beside the corpse so that those who came to pray could kneel by him.

The rest of the village gathered with the family when they saw the coffin being lifted from the returned *naomhóg* and carried up to the house. There was a clay pipe and tobacco in a box by the door for each mourner, the men removing their caps and the women pulling shawls tighter around their heads as they stooped to pass through the doorway, going to the body with a prayer for the soul of the dead man. Some whispered their words, overcome with emotion. Others spoke loud and strong, beseeching the Mother of God to find this soul a bed in heaven.

'The old people here say that if you would touch his hand or forehead when dead, that you would never again be afraid of him to see him or anything,' wrote the islandwoman Eibhlís Ní Shúilleabháin to a friend in 1932. A neighbour had died.

Some kissed the forehead, others wove their fingers around his. 'I felt his hand, dear me, he was as cold as ice.'

Such an act would also banish all danger of being haunted by the dead man. The bravest of children allowed their hands to be pulled out towards the corpse by an elder, but younger ones shied away in fear.

As the wailing abated and the night drew in, the assembled company turned from the body to the hearth and began to tell stories and sing songs about the dead. Faith, he was a fine strong fellow. Never a word of trouble on his lips. By God, it is rare we see the like of him in this life. A thousand tears for the parents that lose such a boy. As the hours passed jam was spread on the bread, the tea made by the women, the porter and whiskey uncorked by the men. Around midnight, the company settled on its knees and the Rosary was spoken: '. . . blessed art thou among women, and blessed is the fruit of thy womb, Jesus,' said a single voice, the leader, reciting the Hail Mary. The room responded: 'Holy Mary, Mother of God, pray for us sinners, now and at the hour of our death . . .'

Several Rosaries might be said during a wake, each one containing more than fifty repetitions of the Hail Mary, as well as the Apostles' Creed, the Our Father and the Gloria. Then, as the men, women and children fought to stay awake in the candlelight, sitting together in the same room as the corpse, they told ghost stories.

Listen, now, while I tell you about a certain young woman who lived on the hill, not so far from here. By God, it was an untidy house she kept, and not a thing in its proper place, but it was the spinning of wool that this wife loved. Many was the night that she sat up late, long after the rest of the family were in their beds, working at her wheel when you might say she would have done better to sleep, or at least to sweep the floor.

The night that I have in mind was very like this one. Her husband and their two sons were where they should have been, and snoring soundly. The hens themselves were resting until the cock should crow with the morning, but in the kitchen the wheel was spinning as hard as ever, and humming as it did so.

Well then, what do you think happened? The door flew open, for it had been left unbolted, and our woman looked up from the wheel for once to see three hideous old hags standing there. The sight of them would make the bravest man cry out in terror; so great was their ugliness that they seemed to be wearing the devil's own horns on their heads.

'Do you need help, woman of the house?' asked the hags together, and she was so scared that she said yes, without hesitation. 'Then you shall have it. Leave the wheel to us a while, and fill the pot with water to boil so that we may have plenty of tea to drink as we work.' There was, of course, no water in the house. The wife had not filled her pail from the well in daylight, so it was now that she went there, in the darkness, and her heart beating fast.

Who do you think that she met at the well of the crossroads but her own dear mother, may God have mercy on her soul, who had entered on the way of eternity not less than a year before. 'Do not be afraid, daughter,' said the maternal vision, 'but listen to me well. The strange women who now sit in your house are spirits who live in An Dún, the old fort that stands up on the hill, away at the back of the island. When you return with water in your pail they intend to fill the pot and boil you alive.'

By now the wife was shaking with fear, but her mother had advice to give. 'When you reach the threshold, twist your arm and let the water spill, as though in great alarm. As you do so, cry out that the old fort itself is in flames, and watch what happens. Then do as I am about to tell you, and all will be well.'

The daughter returned to the house, and when she reached the

33

threshold paused to scream as she had been told. 'Look out! The old fort is on fire!' Hearing her, the hags threw up their arms, ran out of the house and up the hill towards the fort, each crying out in distress, 'My children! My children are there!'

The wife threw all the dirty water out of the house, as her mother had directed, and bolted the door. She laid the broom against it, raked the fire, stood the tongs by the hearth, tidied the room and jumped into her bed. Scarcely were the blankets over her head when the fairy women returned, furious that they had been deceived. Finding the door locked, they called out to the broom to let them enter. 'I am in my proper place, and so cannot let you in,' it replied. The tongs, the chair and the pot were each commanded in turn by the hags, but each in turn gave the same answer. 'I am in my proper place, and so cannot let you in.' The washing water said, 'How can I help when I myself am outside the house, as are you?'

The three hags rattled the windows of the sleeping room and gave voice to their rage. 'It is as well for you, woman of the house, to be so protected,' they cried. 'We would have boiled your bones to jelly and fed them to the dogs.'

With those words they turned back to the hill and were gone. From that night to her last, you may be sure that our young wife made her own house the cleanest and the tidiest in the whole village.

It is one thing to read those words, and it was another altogether to sit within a few feet of a dead man after midnight, watching a practised storyteller bring the old hags to life so that your scalp tingled with fear. The story was told in various forms throughout the west of Ireland, and known on the Great Blasket as *Cailleacha an Dúna*, or 'The Hags from the Fort', because it reflected the belief that the prehistoric settlement on wild common land at the back of the island was a home to the fairies. These were nothing like the sweet Victorian fairies in their tutus, but were spirits that could take human or animal form when they wished, that turned nasty when provoked, and stole children away when they felt like it. Not everybody listening would have believed in that story absolutely, but most would have treated it as a version of the truth about the spirit world, whose people may be wandering in the night outside the house. It also gave a memorable warning that keeping a clean house was the duty of every good wife.

As the mourners kept watch on the body through the night there would be games and music for dancing, as well as stories and jokes. This boisterous partying was a way of letting the departed man know that he was still a member of the community, so that he would not resent the living and return to haunt them. It could also be a celebration of a long life. 'If he is an old man, it will be a funny night, of course,' wrote Eibhlís Ní Shúilleabháin. 'Another man will be telling stories, fairy tales, and young people will be throwing bits of clay pipes on one another and them sort of sport.' If they were mourning someone who had died before their time, however, there were no games and no laughter, only tears and sorrow. 'Of course, when there is a young person [lying dead on the table] there are no fun at all.'

As morning broke the keening would begin again, the women improvising around words and melody whose ancient provenances were forgotten. The sound rose from deep within them and seemed to echo the wind and waves. In daylight the cover was hammered on to the coffin, after the relatives had tied a cap on the dead man's head, kissed him and sprinkled holy water on the body. The sheets were taken down, the ropes untied. Everything that had been brought into the house for the wake must be removed from it before the coffin could leave.

The weeping and wailing grew loud again as the coffin was lifted on to the shoulders of four men, carried out of the house and down the steep and slippery path that led to the island harbour. On the way they passed the tiny graveyard at Castle Point, which was used for children who had died before they could be baptized. The adults buried there were unidentified shipwreck victims, soldiers, suicides, and a few souls whose funerals had been confined to the island by storm. As the men paused and rested the coffin on the grass at the crossroads by the top of the slipway, so that they were free to launch the canoe, the women of the village cried out and banged on the lid with their palms. The older men and women, the children, and the others who could not go to the mainland for the funeral mass because of ill health or duty said their last goodbyes from the top of the harbour, before returning home to close their own eyes in sleep.

The four men lifted the coffin into one end of the *naomhóg*, pushed out from the slipway and gave a few pulls on the oars to take them away from the rocks, where they waited for the other boats to join them. When the island population was at its greatest there were often more than a dozen canoes making their way across the Sound to a funeral, the convoy headed by three abreast, with the coffin balanced in the bow of the middle vessel.

The people of Dunquin waited by the slipway, and relatives from more distant parishes assembled at the top of the cliff. Once ashore, the slow-moving crowd passed people standing in the doorways of Ballykeen township and went on towards Ballynaraha, before turning into another narrow lane known as *Boithrín na Marbh*, the Way of the Dead. This led to a crossroads, where custom dictated that the coffin-bearers should rest. One path led over the mountain pass to Ventry, another around the headland to Coumeenole, and a third down into the heart of the valley, where the river flowed past the parish church and its graveyard.

There were many island names chiselled on the stones and crosses in that field, amongst those of the people of Dunquin. The same was true in graveyards over the mountains in Ventry and Ballyferriter. Each island family had been driven to the Great Blasket generations before by evictions and the need for food, but none had lost the habit of sending its dead back to the ancestral burial ground, despite the difficulties involved. They had adapted well to island life, but in death still felt the pull of the land that had been taken from them long before. Children were also sent to the mainland parishes to be baptized, and later, to be married. The parish priest visited the island with his curate once a year to give the Stations, a great ceremonial day on which he would hear confessions and say Mass in the schoolhouse before enjoying the best food and drink the islanders had to offer, in someone's home. Otherwise he left the community to its own faith, which was as much Celtic as Roman. The men crossed the Sound for Mass in Dunquin on a Sunday morning when the weather allowed it; the women always stayed at home.

For Seáinín Team Ó Cearna to have been buried in a rough wooden box alongside infants and sailors on the island, without the benefit in eternity of a priest having said Mass for his soul, would have added shame to tragedy. Those who had grown up with him were prepared to risk their lives to make sure it didn't happen, despite the advice of their elders. Death was familiar to these people, who worked on narrow ledges or the deceptive sea every day of their lives, and who knew that it would take only a misplaced step or a wayward oar to send a person on the way of truth. It had happened many times before, of course, but by early 1947 the community on the Great Blasket was aged, weakened by emigration and demoralized by the fearsome winter. The death of one young man like Seáinín would break its will for ever, never mind the additional loss to the waves of his four daring friends.

7

10 January 1947

The hailstorm spreads a veil across the harbour at Dunquin, so that the crowd on the ledge above the island slipway cannot see what has happened to the canoe. The valley behind the veil is a shadow, darkening at the cliff edge, where white foam testifies to the gathering strength of the sea. Now there are three more families on the edge of mourning.

They need not weep. The *naomhóg* is in the harbour, having reached there moments before the hailstorm, and the crew is hauling the sodden canvas shell to safety. Each man is weary, wet through, his legs shaking, his hands numb from the cold and red from closing in fists around the oars.

'God save you,' shouts Seamus Ferriter against the wind as he slides towards them, astounded that they are indeed safe.

'God and Mary save you,' replies a breathless Seán Pheats Team, grateful for an extra hand to help lift the *naomhóg* on to a stand. He looks back at the waves, grown bright with cold fury again, and knows how close they came to the end. 'If we were yet beyond . . .'

A few less frantic pulls of the oars across the Sound and they would have arrived later, and been crushed by the renewed might of the storm. The boat would have been smashed and splintered, the bodies swept under and away, for miles. They made it, with every muscle tight, every nerve crazed, every strand of their natural instinct for the sea defied by grief and fury, and a need to do something. It will be called heroic, and insane.

There is nobody willing or able to voice such thoughts as the four men of the sea and the one farmer lean forward with the climb up into Dunquin. There are arrangements to be made if their dash is not to be in vain. At the valley post office, just across from the schoolhouse, a telephone call is made and a motor car hired to take them to Dingle, by way of Ballyferriter, where two of the men get out into the driving rain to find the priest. The others motor on to town and place an order for a coffin with a man called O'Shea, who tells them he will have to make it first, but that he is willing to work into the night. Later, sharing floorspace in the house of O'Shea's cousin, they listen as the wind drops and the rain softens, and wish there had been a coffin ready. 'Faith, we would be in our beds again by now.'

On the other side of Ireland, in the capital city, an islandman walks the streets. Rain pours down on shoulders as broad as his brother's, and drips from the brim of a hat on to the same long chin. The man is Mícheál Ó Cearna, on his way home to rented rooms from the bar where he is a foreman. On the ledge by the bed is a letter from his sister, Céit, sent just after Christmas, that says Seáinín is sickening with the flu, or something like it. Mícheál doesn't know it yet but a telegram, sent earlier today, is waiting for his return from work. His fingers are cold and wet as they tear at the envelope. 'Your brother has just passed away. Please come home.'

Mícheál sits on the side of the bed, and weeps. He does not sleep that night, with anger, surprise and confusion tangled up inside his chest, and guilt at having been so far away from home. The only thing possible now is to return. He packs a bag, catches the first available train and travels all day, through the mid-county landscape to Mallow, down to the first sight of the mountains at Tralee, along the edge of the bay, and, with night fallen again, over the slopes to Dingle.

There is news for Mícheál the next morning, as he eats breakfast with an aunt and uncle in Dingle. 'O'Shea says the lads came to fetch the coffin and are gone back to Dunquin, though there's little hope of them getting into the island today.' The wind and the rain send the dogs of Dingle to the doorways for shelter. Over in the distance there are lumps of filthy cloud snagged between peakless mountains.

Still, Mícheál finds a taxi driver willing to take him out along the Ballyferriter road and round the coast to Dunquin, where the winds are even fiercer and the island has all but vanished in the sea mist. The crew of the *naomhóg* have reassembled on the cliff above the quay, at the place called *Barra na Haille*, 'the top of the cliff', and the greetings are sincere. There are other men in the group also, who welcome the brother home and offer condolences with a firm handshake.

'Well now, my friend,' says Maidhc Leán Ó Guithín, 'I do not think we will ever make it with the weather this way.' The surf reaches out over the top of the cliff to embrace the men. What with the salt spray and the sudden showers that flatten the grass then blow away, they are wet through again. That does not matter in itself, but there is little chance of fighting such a wild sea.

Fitzgerald, the police sergeant from Ballyferriter, is listening to Seán Pheats Team as he shakes his head and speaks solemnly. 'There is nothing to be done. The people inside will be unable to stand it much longer before they have to bury the corpse in the island, God have mercy on him.'

★

'I see a crowd gathered,' says one of two elderly men standing by the Ó Cearna house. He has a telescope up to one rheumy eye, and can just make out the figures on the mainland at *Barra na Haille*. 'They have come from the north and from the south.'

'That may be,' says his neighbour, thinking of the body grown stiff and cold and still on the kitchen table in the Ó Cearna home. The father has been sat in the corner of the room watching the corpse for hours, himself as white as a ghost. The sister has not touched food since the death. There is fear and panic in all the houses. Some of the old women have seen a raven flying over the Ó Cearna home and say it is a sign that there will be more than one end. 'God himself knows, there will be more sadness upon this place if they do not come west, and soon.'

8

It was a beautiful day in late summer. The wind was cold and hard, but it had blown the clouds away to the north. None remained to cast a shadow on Mount Eagle. The sun was warm, and it cast glitter over a sea that changed from aquamarine to bottle green depending on its mood. It looked calm enough to this non-sailor. Others thought so too, judging by the number of cars and camper vans parked up on the cliff above the quay at Dunquin, full of people who had come in the hope of visiting an island that had been abandoned for nearly half a century. A telephone rang inside a wooden shed, which had been tied down with guy ropes against the wind. Maps and posters stuck up in the window offered a ferry service, but there was nobody inside. The unanswered telephone kept ringing. There was no chance that we would be able to get across today.

After three days of waiting for the sea to calm, I was frustrated and angry. This was totally irrational, I told myself, watching the waves blow huge wet kisses at the edge of the Great Blasket. If you're going to write about a remote island that is inaccessible for great swathes of the year, you can't really be surprised when the ferryman won't take you there.

Within half an hour we all knew why. The clouds had come from nowhere, sullen and heavy, pushing a wall of rain before them. Those of us without cars to hide in held ourselves against hedges or walls, glad of even the slightest bit of shelter from the downpour. Along the coast breakers sent foam flying, and the waves dropped suddenly. The island seemed to shrink before our eyes, retreating into the rain until three miles across the Sound seemed more like thirty.

Behind the ferryman's hut was the cliff edge, and sixty feet below that, the sea. The harbour was no more than a tiny cove, its beach covered in debris from the crumbling cliffs. As the retreating waves sucked the water level down, the sea drew back its tongue to reveal a line of rocks like rotten black teeth. Assuming they managed to steer a course between these hidden dangers, islanders weary from their row had then to land and climb. The trace of a narrow path zigzagged across one face, but most of it had been worn away by the weather. That was the way they came up in 1947, before the construction of a wide concrete slope that now wound its way to the jetty.

Down there were empty lobster-pots, a row of upturned beetle-black *naomhóga* and a red rubber dinghy with an outboard motor. The rain came again, slashing into the name of Tomás Keane, painted on to the quayside wall in black letters three feet high. It was a suitably bold memorial to a young fisherman and loveable rogue who had died in a boat accident twenty years before. I had seen his photograph and knew that he was a handsome fellow, with dark hair and fiery eyes. His widow came down to this spot every year, on the anniversary of his death, to paint the name once more.

There was sharp, sudden sunshine, and for the briefest of moments a rainbow stretched out of the sea near the flat island of Beiginis. The black, boiling cauldron became the Mediterranean. The Great Blasket advanced, growing as the mist around it vanished. The guidebook had told me that to walk barefoot across the back of the island on a fine summer's day, with kittiwakes diving over the cliffs and the scent of heather rising from the hillside, was 'as close as you can get to peeping into heaven'.

Tomás Ó Criomhthain, author of *The Islandman*, described

the ecstatic experience of standing at a high point and filling
your lungs with scented breeze. He had grown up on the
Great Blasket and understood its hardships well, but loved the
summer months best. 'For it was inside that all the magic was,
the kind of magic that only a person raised by the water's edge
can understand, who spends his days looking out across it at
the base of the sky. But this magic quickly disappears when
the depths of winter return, and one realizes that it was but a
summer's dream that did not last.'

As I watched, the shadow of a cloud passed over the face
of the great island like a frown, and away out on the western
horizon the shining pyramid of Tiaracht became a satanic
iceberg. The weather changed fast. The sleeping giant was
now a slain warrior, the clouds gathering around his head like
smoke rising from his funeral pyre. A trawler passed through
the Sound, bucking the waves, and the seascape grew vast and
threatening. The surf that burst like a firework against the
Great Blasket rocks sent its white sparks a hundred feet into
the air, falling here and there among the ruined houses of the
island village. It was hard to imagine living in that place, and
we were not even into autumn yet. 'This is a crag in the midst
of the great sea, and again and again the blown surf drives
right over it before the violence of the wind,' wrote Tomás
Ó Criomhthain. 'You daren't put your head out any more
than a rabbit that crouches in his burrow, when the rain and
the salt spume are flying.'

9

A violent storm, with a wind force of eighty miles an hour in some areas and accompanied by torrential rain, swept the entire South of Ireland over the weekend.

Kerryman

12 January 1947

A crowd gathers at Dingle harbour to watch the new lifeboat as it leaves for the Great Blasket. Some shake their head and wonder at the folly of crossing Dingle Bay on a day like this, and as the vessel leaves the shelter of the harbour it runs into massive waves that hit the side hard, drenching the deck and everyone on it. The two islanders allowed to go with the boat have taken cover at the back, Seán Pheats Team finding some protection from the sea and the cold wind with a borrowed overcoat, Mícheál Ó Cearna gripping the rail for dear life. He never was a man who loved the sea. Ahead of them, legs wide and eyes on the horizon, are the volunteers who crew the boat, each man attached to it by a length of rope.

The *St Therese* has only been guarding these waters since November, when she was blessed at the quayside at Valentia, the island across the bay at the end of the Iveragh peninsula. She is forty-five feet long and twelve feet wide, and can reach a speed of nine knots on a good day, which this is definitely not. There are eight crew members, led by the cox

Jeremiah O'Connell, and eighteen more in reserve on the mainland.

'My God, the waves,' says Mícheál Ó Cearna into the wind, but the islandman beside him does not hear. Seán Pheats Team knows about the sea, and knows that his *naomhóg* would be smashed to pieces in such weather. Both men are as wet as seals, thanks to the sea and the banks of rain that pass over them, darkening the sky.

It takes more than two hours for the *St Therese* to fight its way along the coast. As it rounds Slea Head, one of the men on the island sees the boat and shouts out the news in the village. By the time it reaches the tidal stream that races across the Blasket Sound there is a group waiting on the headland known as *An Gob*, calling out greetings.

'Are you after coming home from America?' shouts one man above the storm, making light of the time it has taken Seán Pheats Team to get back. Others laugh, but are glad not to have their fears confirmed; when they saw a lifeboat coming, many of the remaining islanders assumed the *naomhóg* crew had been drowned as well. Some of the fitter old men take down another canoe from its stand and push out to the lifeboat, so that Mícheál and Seán can come ashore with the coffin.

The Dubliner has not seen his family for months. There is so much water around, in the sea and the air, that no one can tell who is crying and who is not. When he finds his brother lying cold in the house, three days dead, with a pauper's coffin roughly made from driftwood by his side, Mícheál Ó Cearna can contain himself no longer. He is tired and cold, wet and nauseous, fearful and horrified that those he left behind have been reduced to this pitiful end. Great sobs burst from him. Céit is in tears, and her father's eyes are red with sorrow. Their swollen throats can barely swallow bread and butter, but she urges her men to take something inside themselves for strength. The tea is sweet, and warming.

They can't stay, of course. The sky is dark enough already, but now evening is coming and the crew of the lifeboat are calling for the coffin to be brought to them. Every nail that is hammered into the lid seems to pierce Céit, and every blow strikes like a hammer at her father's head. His aged arms help lift the young son and carry him, in a filthy squall, down to the sea. In these final moments the weeping and wailing comes flooding in a bitter torrent from men and women alike, as the awful tension of the last three days is released. Mother of God, it is a hard life we have here, washed by the sea and covered in sorrow. Is there no rest to be found, no shelter from this suffering? It is there on the hillside, as the lifeboat guns its engine and turns back into the worst of the storm, that the will of the island people is finally broken.

Out at sea it is so dark you would not see a man who had put his finger in your eye, and the boat is rolling and pitching on waves like mountains. The *St Therese* almost dashes against a rock outside Dingle harbour, but finally makes it to the calmer waters. All the way back to shore Mícheál Ó Cearna watches his father, who suddenly seems so small and frail. For the first time he feels pity for the man, for the trouble he has suffered, first losing a wife so young, then struggling to keep control over a family on his own, and now mourning the son who was meant to have cared for him at the end of his days. There is something else on Mícheál's mind that he knows will only make the old man's pain worse.

On the pier a lady is waiting, with the *gardai*. The policemen speak in English and move towards the coffin to lift it, only to be intercepted by the father, who pushes through them. 'The devil on you, what are you doing with my son?'

'I'm afraid we must be taking him to the mortuary Mr Ó Cearna,' says the lady, who is a doctor, from under a big black umbrella. 'I cannot fill out a death certificate until I know what it was that killed him.'

'By God, it was the government. Write that down.' The words are spoken by Mícheál, red with anger, wet hair plastered against his head and his chin raised in defiance. 'The damn telephone was not working again. Not a thing has been done for these people.'

'I'm sorry, but you must understand, there has to be an examination, to determine the cause of death. Had he any drink taken?'

'Not at all,' says the father, 'unless it was cold water, and that would not be making him drunk. He got sick in the head, so he did, and there was nothing we could do to save him, God give rest to his poor soul.'

Still, the doctor insists, as she must, and the body is taken up the hill to the hospital, to be examined. The islandmen wait, tobacco taking the place of words, steam rising from their clothes as they stand in the doorway of the large cream building, not knowing what is being done to their brother, son and friend. It is very late before the coffin is allowed to make the last part of its journey, over the glens to the chapel in Dunquin, lashed down to the back of a lorry, in the ceaseless rain.

The following morning a Mass is said for the soul of Seáinín Ó Cearna, and his body laid in a grave beside that of his mother, in Ballintemple. The little chapel is full of people, relatives from Ballydavid and Coumeenole as well as Dunquin, but hardly any from the island. There is sorrow by the graveside, but anger as well, at the way the sick man was left without a doctor or a priest. That evening, heads full of a thousand consoling words and tributes they have heard, Mícheál and his father ride on a cart around Dún Mór to the village of Coumeenole, to the house where Céit and her mother were both born, and there they are given a welcome and a good meal, and allowed to be themselves again.

As they sit drinking whiskey by the fire, with the dog asleep on the floor and the Dálaigh family in their beds, Mícheál knows that this is his moment. He has been refusing to consider it all day, for fear of the old man's broken heart and the harm it might do to hear more bad news, but there is no denying the hour of reckoning. He must go back to Dublin tomorrow, for one thing, and will not see the family for a while. 'Father,' he says, and Seán turns, hearing the seriousness in that one word. The son holds out a hand, containing in its fist all the money he has, and looks away into the smouldering fire while the father takes the folded notes. Neither man mentions the exchange.

'Listen . . . I think I may be heading for America.'

There is silence. Mother Dhálaigh snores and the dog's ear twitches, and the sea beats on the rocks below as it always will, but there by firelight a widower who has hardly started mourning one son has just been told he will lose another. Mícheál's eyes are on his father, who looks down at the ground. Will he take it badly, as a desertion, or will he see, as Mícheál does, that there is no future on that damned island any more, and that if one boy can make his way in the States, the others might be able to follow, or at least prosper, on the money he sends back? There is no way of knowing whether the space between the two men is a bridge or a barrier, until Seán speaks.

'Mícheál,' he says so quietly that his voice can hardly be heard. 'My own son. I always thought that you would do the right thing.'

The story of the Valentia lifeboat's spectacular dash across Dingle Bay on Sunday last to deliver a coffin to a bereaved family on the Great Blasket, isolated for three days from the mainland by last week's storm, has captured the imagination.

Kerryman

The old newspaper was bound between hard covers and filed on the shelf at the county library in Tralee. It had hardly been opened in the five decades since Seáinín's death. Dust rose as I turned the pages. The heroes of the day, according to the *Kerryman*, had been the volunteers in their new all-weather vessel who braved 'mountainous seas, whipped by a fierce gale'. There was only one small mention of the initial journey across the Sound by *naomhóg* to fetch help in the first place, and even that said there were two men on board rather than four. Much was made of the state-of-the-art equipment on board the *St Therese*, including 'a modern loud hailer which can "throw" the human voice a distance of one mile under any weather conditions'.

The rest of that week's *Kerryman* gave a sense of the desperate state Ireland found itself in again at the time, despite (or perhaps because of) having remained neutral throughout the war. There was flour and bread rationing in force across the country, a chronic shortage of turf and coal for fuel in many places, and the threat of sugar supplies being cut off. The *Kerryman* lamented the loss of skilled farm-workers to England, where the wages were higher, and the fact that although Ireland had four acres of arable land per head of population it was still short of milk, butter and cheese. 'Bacon and eggs are almost black-market luxuries; fats such as margarine, lard and dripping unknown.'

The food position in the coming year would be the worst in history, said the chairman of the county agricultural committee in 1947. It was a remarkable statement, given the famine of a century before. As then, the people of Ireland were going hungry while their produce was exported to England. This time the reason was that their own government, led by de Valera, believed it was the only way to revive the economy.

An advertisement for cod liver oil featured a bespectacled child whose head had clearly been cut and pasted on to the body of a famished infant from somewhere in the Third World. A cotton mill in Lancashire offered vacancies for girls, with free travel and facilities for religious duties. There were other ads, for tobacco, coffee, nasal drops and day-old chickens, and the chance to win a cash prize of one guinea and a coloured certificate of merit for the boy under eighteen who scored most points in a ploughing match at Castleisland.

'John Kearney (24), single, of the Great Blasket island, died on Friday, January 10, without medical aid,' recorded the *Kerryman*, in a story that took up far less space than the one praising the lifeboat. The district coroner had instructed Dr Elizabeth O'Sullivan to hold a post-mortem, and she had attributed the death to natural causes. The newspaper did not report that Seáinín's family had been told he was killed by meningitis.

On the first day of March 1947, two months after the death of Seáinín, there was an angry confrontation in the Dáil, the

Irish parliament. A General Mulcahy, who represented Kerry, repeatedly asked for an inquiry into how the young man had come to die without spiritual or medical aid. His passion was fuelled by letters from Mícheál Ó Cearna, who knew the general's daughter from the summers she had spent in Dunquin. Although he was back at work behind the bar, Mícheál was also writing in Gaelic for the *Irish Press*. By now the works of Tomás Ó Criomhthain, Peig Sayers and Muiris Ó Súilleabháin (or Maurice O'Sullivan as he was known to his many English-language readers) had made the Great Blasket famous as one of the very last surviving communities that spoke Irish. As members of the Gaelic League, the barman and the general wanted to know what the government was going to do to protect an island people it claimed to hold in high regard.

'The government is not going to set up an inquiry for no purpose whatsoever,' an irritated Minister for Industry and Commerce, Seán Lemass, snapped in answer to the question. There was no point in an inquiry, he said, because it was clearly understood that the radio telephone on the island had been out of order as a consequence of the severity of the storm.

General Mulcahy was fuming. 'Am I to understand that it is not to be regarded as a matter for serious and full inquiry that it is possible for some of the remnants of the Irish-speaking population on our islands to die in such circumstances that for days they cannot get the assistance of either priest or doctor?'

Their exchanges went on for several minutes, the minister repeating that he did not know what other action could have been taken, since the radio telephone had broken down, and the general claiming that requests for the improvement of the landing places on the island and at Dunquin had been ignored.

Nothing was done. On 12 March, General Mulcahy asked another question in the Dáil. This time he wanted the Minister for Posts and Telegraphs to describe the equipment installed on the Great Blasket, to say how many times it had been out of action lately, and why. The answer, provided in writing, was that a short-wave radio telephone had been installed in 1941 to link the island with the post office at Dunquin. It was powered by batteries, run from windchargers, but the wind had often been so strong as to destroy the chargers. When that happened the conditions also prevented engineers from reaching the island to repair the damage. The radio had been out of action for twenty-eight days in the month of January, nineteen in December and fifteen in November. Even in the summer months, a few days were always lost to the wind.

Engineers must have been sent to strengthen the wind-chargers, because in early April 1947 they stood up to storms that brought the town of Tralee its worst flooding for twenty-five years. The bad weather went away but returned with a passion later that month, when a south-westerly gale tore slates from the rooftops, smashed windows, and brought down derelict buildings and trees. The captain of a steamer forced to shelter in Cobh on its way to Limerick told the papers it was the worst hurricane he had ever been caught up in. Three islanders who made it to Dunquin for supplies on a Friday night found themselves cut off from the island. On Wednesday, while the three were still stuck on the mainland, those left on the Great Blasket used the repaired telegraph to contact the Dingle correspondent of the *Kerryman* with the words 'Genntanas bidh le ceithre la' ('Four days without food').

The reporter wired the Valentia lifeboat, but this time the weather was so bad that even the *St Therese* was unable to reach the island. That day the men of the village climbed the hill in a gale to gather at the building nicknamed the Dáil, where island meetings always took place. There were no jokes, the situation was desperate. They decided on drastic action, on an act that catapulted the medieval community into the modern age. Seán an Rí, son of the King and inheritor of his duties as postman, tapped out a cry for help that was carried by morse code and radio wave from this remote island to the highest place in the land. It had a direct emotional appeal that all General Mulcahy's efforts could not match. At 2.30 p.m. on 22 April 1947, an operator in the capital received a message from *An Blascaod Mór*, the Great Blasket station, addressed simply to 'De Valera, Dublin'. It read:

STORMBOUND DISTRESS SEND FOOD NOTHING TO EAT = BLASKETS +

Whether the message would reach the Taoiseach was anyone's guess. The fifty-one people on the Great Blasket knew only that their stores were almost empty because of the repeated storms. If the sea remained hostile, and no help was sent from Dublin, they would surely starve.

Too long have they been ignored; truly they have been left
alone, crying in the wilderness.

Kerryman

14 July 1947

Before sunrise the long silver shape of a naval corvette ghosts
past the rocks into the sheltered waters by Beiginis. This will
be an extraordinary day, on which the leader of Ireland, Eamon
de Valera, will visit the Great Blasket. His ship, the *Macha*,
has sailed overnight from Cape Clear, the previous stop on the
Taoiseach's personal tour of the republic's island communities.

Even here, at the end of the world, the man has a fearsome
reputation. It is only the summer of 1947, but already de
Valera has done enough to establish himself as the dominant
figure in Irish history this century – which is quite an achievement for someone born in New York. The islanders now
stirring themselves to receive him believe de Valera to be a
champion of their language, who wants Irish to be the national
tongue of a free nation. Some have hung his picture on their
wall, alongside the other heroes of 1916. On Holy Thursday
that year, Blasket fishermen saw a German ship called the *Aud*
pass by on its way to deliver twenty thousand rifles for the
men of Kerry. It was intercepted in Tralee Bay, and the west
was powerless to rise up in support of the Dublin rebels. De

Valera commanded a battalion against the British in the capital and was sentenced to death for it. He was allowed to live because the government decided it would not be helpful to execute an American citizen.

This morning, as he prepares to go ashore at the Great Blasket, de Valera is in his fifteenth year as Prime Minister and Minister for External Affairs, during which time he has established a new constitution and guided the country through the Second World War as a neutral. The economy is in deep trouble, and de Valera may lose the next general election, but this island tour is an attempt by the 65-year-old politician to re-establish contact with the rural way of life that inspires his vision of Ireland. Today he has chosen to dress like an islander, in a *báinín* jacket of homespun woollen cloth, black trousers and a round, black fisherman's cap, a *báiréad*.

Maras Mhuiris Ó Catháin, the oldest man on the island, is the elected spokesman for the community today, and the first to see the ship coming in from the north, through the mist. He calls out to other men who are milking their cows, and together they run down through the village, banging on doors and shouting, 'Get up, get up and out, Dev is below!'

Two *naomhóga* are afloat and out to the *Macha* even before its launch can be lowered, and de Valera comes ashore in one of them with his son Rory. The other brings members of his staff, and a journalist with a notebook.

'God save you, great leader,' says Maras Mhuiris when de Valera has made his way to the top of the slip. 'You are welcome in this place.'

'God and Mary save you, noble friend,' says de Valera. 'We are both older since you welcomed me here last. Do you remember it?'

'I do, of course. Why would I not?' It was two decades

earlier, at the ending of the civil war, when de Valera had used the island as a refuge from his troubles.

'Well I remember the soldiers who came looking for you here once,' says Muiris Ó Cearna, an uncle of Seáinín's. 'And you after fighting the Treaty. It was from Valentia they came, and no one that they found, thanks be to God for his mercy. You would have been as safe here then as you are now!'

The Taoiseach takes off his cap and holds it to his chest while greeting the women of the island, who bend to kiss his hand as a mark of respect. With Maras Mhuiris as a guide, although he hardly needs one, de Valera walks up through the village, shaking hands and offering a few words in immaculate Irish to everyone he meets. He is head and shoulders taller than them all. A flag of green, white and orange hangs from a milking shed, which makes him smile. So does a banner made from stitched flour sacks, strung between two posts, on which have been painted the words '*Fáiilte Romhat A Thaoisigh*', 'You Are Welcome Here, Prime Minister'. Outside the schoolhouse, which is empty and shuttered, he places his hand on the head of the one small boy left on the island, and says gently, 'We will have to get you educated, my fine fellow.'

Once inside the post office, with a cup of tea in his hand and only crumbs left on his plate, de Valera begins the serious talk. He refers to the telegram the islanders sent in April, after which a boat containing food, medicine and a few discreet crates of whiskey was sent at his personal request, and is thanked sincerely for that intervention, but then he asks what more can be done? Maras Mhuiris has practised for this moment, and begins to explain. The fishing has been poor this season, the prices at market are low, so there is no money to buy meat. Neither is there enough fish to salt for the winter months, and the ration of flour allowed for each family is not enough to feed them on bread. As for the lobsters, few of the fishermen have sound pots and the *tuigí*, osier branches, with which they are made do not grow on the island. 'If only a way could be found for us to stay in this place and live a decent life, we would not want to leave our beautiful island. Nor can we go on, without some help to build a better place to land the *naomhóga*, and a reliable means of contact with the world.'

De Valera has many questions. He also wants to hear from Seán Team Ó Cearna, the father of the dead boy, and Seán knows what he wants to say. 'It is this way, your honour. The young men and women of the island are after going to America, and those that have not done so already are thinking of it. You see for yourself that there are not many souls left here. The years are upon us, the energies of youth are gone like the flowers in winter, and we can no longer do the things that once fed and clothed our families. We are too old to fish, we are too old to work in the fields, and we are wondering whatever will become of us.'

'What is it then that you would have us do?'

'For myself, I wish to God that I could leave this place. My heart has grown weary, and the life in it is too hard.' There are murmurs of assent from the men sitting on benches around the fire, and sighs from the women standing behind, wrapped in their shawls and headscarves. De Valera now turns to them. His questions are answered with questions. 'Do you still cook in the old way, with the iron pot and the turf?' What other way is there for an islandwoman? 'Is the turf on the hill as good as it was in the past?' It is not, but is anything? 'Will you show me your crops?' We will, of course, why would we not?

The entire village follows as the Taoiseach and his men rise and walk down to the potato fields. The crops are late this year, which is another reason why the islanders need extra flour to keep from starving. De Valera is impressed at the way they make the most of the smallest patch of fertile earth to produce food. 'Well, it is a pity that I cannot bring the rich men of Ireland here, and show them the miracles that are made on the wretched ground.'

There are fifteen families on the Great Blasket, and every member of them is gathered above the harbour when de Valera turns to say his last words to the islanders, after two hours with them. 'Thank you for the way you have received me today. I have heard what you have had to say, and a pleasure it was to hear you say it in the Irish. People of the island, you are keeping the language safe for our country, until such time as it will be heard on the lips of every man, woman and child, from this place to Dublin. Because of this, I promise now to go from here and do the best that I can to lighten your burden, and to relieve the hardships that you suffer. May God keep you in health.'

They wave as he goes, and some are still waving as the *Macha* weighs her anchor and heads out of the Sound. As she does, Eamon de Valera is already below deck in the Taoiseach's cabin, writing in a notebook.

The islanders hear nothing more as the weeks pass. They grow frustrated, and mutter sharp comments about the reliability of men in power. If they only knew it, the future has slipped out of their hands. From this moment on, all the decisions will be made elsewhere. De Valera calls a meeting at his personal office in Dublin and expresses his concern at the deteriorating living conditions on the island, but resists the opinion of his officers that the people should be moved to the mainland. This can only be done as a last resort, he insists. It is agreed that a Mr Ó Gallchobhair from the Department of Lands and Mr Ó Cochláin from the Department of Education should go to the Great Blasket as 'ordinary visitors' in late August. When they arrive on the island, however, the true purpose of their visit is easily discovered. They are easily convinced that the real problem is lack of communication with the outside world rather than poverty, and that the islanders are keen to leave. That being the case, they feel the population should be moved to Dunquin, partly to preserve 'the language of the Gaels'.

While their report is being written, the people of the Great Blasket feel they are being kept in the dark. They are a long way from Dublin, with no understanding of how slowly the wheels of government turn. All they know is that the days are getting shorter, and colder. Finally, on 15 September, they decide on another direct appeal to de Valera, this time by letter. It contains a threat they know will embarrass him:

> Dear Leader
>
> We are sending you these few lines because we want you to let us know what you are going to do for us. Please let us know immediately for winter is coming and if you are not to do anything on our behalf we will have to get some place for the old people and send them to their friends on the mainland. You know well leader that there is a great privation here that no one could stand with twenty years only the islanders. If you can't help us we will have to go across the Atlantic to seek our fortune.
>
> Please Taoiseach send us an answer immediately if you please.
> Yours Faithfully, Islanders.

The grieving brothers and sisters of the Ó Cearna family could not wait for government help that might never come. Death drove them from their home. Having summoned the strength to tell his father that he was leaving for America, Mícheál returned to Dublin and made plans. The obvious thing to do was go to Massachusetts, where his uncle had settled. He would be joined, in time and turn, by all his brothers and one sister. Only Céit was to remain in Ireland with her father as he grew old, but even she could not bear to stay on the Great Blasket with him after Seáinín's death. The sun was shining and the sky was blue on the day her new husband, Paddy, took their belongings down to the quay and loaded a *naomhóg*. It was Easter, 1948.

'I well remember it,' she told me, half a century later. 'As my father said when he came to live with us a few years later, "Thanks be to God that I have my feet on dry land at last. It doesn't matter what I have to eat or drink, we are here."'

They settled just a few miles down the coast, by the beach at Smerwick Harbour. Céit could see the ocean every day, but the Great Blasket was hidden from her by the hills. A great deal happened to the world while she grew old, but most of it happened elsewhere, away over the mountains and plains and seascapes, beyond even Tralee and Killarney. Time passed and the landscape changed as imperceptibly as an ageing face. As the lines grew deep around her eyes, so the building went on – a new holiday home, then another; a wider road for the coaches passing through; a big hotel with a satellite dish –

until there was an old woman in her mirror, and all the houses around had Sky television. At seventy-eight years of age, she still lived on the patch of land to which Paddy had brought her, and in the same house, a low box with a flat roof that could have been a mobile home with the wheels missing.

Over five decades the empty fields around Céit's little lime-green shelter had filled up with bungalows, most of them empty but for the holiday months of July and August. Her garden was overshadowed by the high wire fence around an outdoor court for basketball, a sport popular among the modern young people of Kerry. It could not have stolen their hearts away completely, however, because the words 'Up the Kingdom' had been daubed on to a wall to celebrate the county's success at Gaelic football. The wind danced across the tarmac like Magic Johnson as we ran from the car to the doorway, where Céit was waiting.

'I am the oldest,' she said, filling the kettle for a cup of tea. The white enamelled stove burned coal permanently. She knelt to take a piece from a bronze-coloured plastic bucket. On the mantelpiece above the hotplate were photographs of her brothers and sister. They were all far away in America, but kept in touch. 'I am the captain.' A sound escaped her mouth – it seemed to be a laugh, strangled by permanently pursed lips. 'God knows, I had a tough life.'

The woman herself was tiny, like a sparrow, with wide, bright eyes glistening above a hooked nose that I recognized on the faces of her brothers. Near them on the wall was Pope John Paul II, his hands clasped in prayer around rosary beads. Céit's hands rested on her lap as she talked, palms down on the blue floral apron that she wore about the house, over a blouse and skirt. Her mouth was turned down at the edges, and her eyes were moist, so that when she talked she often appeared to be on the edge of tears. Then something would strike her as funny and she would make that strangled noise again, and throw her hands up. Or she would raise a hand to dab at the wiry hair pulled back from her high, wide forehead. The strands were a deep golden red, the roots grey.

The house was bigger than it had looked from the outside. We had come in through a utility area with a work surface where Céit had been preparing lunch for her son, who drove to her most days on his break from a fish factory. The main room was long and narrow, with a cream-painted dresser, or press as she called it, set into an alcove at the far end. China plates, cups and saucers waited for best behind a glass door. On the wall was a print of the Sacred Heart: Christ of the melancholy eyes and the three-day beard drew back his tunic like Superman to reveal not a golden letter S but a pumping organ. Where his groin would have been was a white cross in a small glass tube, with a red neon ember glowing at the base of it. The electricity wire disappeared down behind the dark wooden frame of a sofa, whose cushions were the same mushroom colour as the lino floor. Little orange and red flowers on the wallpaper seemed to flutter around the burning cross.

Céit sat in an old armchair, which was covered in a throw. The huge black Sony Trinitron television at her right hand dominated the room. On her left a table, spread with a neatly ironed white cloth, sat beneath the window. She had made me a sandwich with thick ham from a waxed-paper packet, to eat with my mug of tea. The knife, the ham, the butter and the bread were left on the table so that I could help myself. A green budgerigar watched me from a cage lined with copies of the *Kerryman*.

'Have you the Irish?' she asked. I had not, to my regret. 'Oh dear. Never mind. I will try.' We had been introduced by a mutual friend, Mícheál de Mordha, author of the article I had read about her in the newspaper. He had come along to act as translator, but despite having warned me that she would struggle to speak English, Céit began to answer each question before he had the chance to repeat it in Irish. Her words were a literal translation of what she would have said in that language, retaining both the Irish sentence structure and the tendency to describe the events of the past in the present tense. It made her thoughts sound less sophisticated than they were. She kept her eyes on Mícheál the whole time, even while talking to me.

'I never go into any pub,' she said in answer to a question about her health. It did not seem diplomatic to remind her that we had first met, briefly, at a party at Kruger's bar in Dunquin, where Céit had been sipping Bailey's Irish Cream with ice. 'I never smoke. I never drink. The old women in the island smoked pipes.'

In Kruger's she had dropped a hint that her mother had not liked living on the Great Blasket. Did she know why? 'She would rather go somewhere else. She was after a man back in Coumeenole, where her family came from.' This revelation was accompanied by a wheezy giggle. 'Oh, dear me, she was always talking about it.' There was a pause, and a smile. 'Well . . . that's the way.'

So how had her parents met? 'Oh, God knows, I don't know anything about that. I wasn't there.' She laughed, and looked away. They never talked about it in her hearing, then? 'No, never!' The idea seemed unthinkable.

Neilí Ní Dhálaigh was still only sixteen when she left her home in Coumeenole to live on the island she had looked out at every day of her life. Her marriage to Seán Team Ó Cearna, who had already been to America and was twice her age, may have been arranged between the two families. Such a thing was not uncommon. Since the Great Blasket community was so small, and families there so large, it was hard to find a husband or wife who was not too closely related. Tomás Ó Criomhthain told the story of an islandman and woman who met in America and married, only to discover that they were actually brother and sister. The woman had been the last of her family to arrive in the States, so did not recognize the brother who had left when she was very young. Such a thing happened 'very frequently' in the old days, wrote Tomás in the 1920s, 'and now and then yet'.

All of which meant islandmen often looked to the mainland for a partner. Seán Team Ó Cearna was a tall, rakish fellow with a house and a bit of money left over from his travels. 'My father went to America twice,' said Céit 'He was sick there. Like myself. The food.' Seán first left the Great Blasket in 1901, when he was nineteen, and went to a railway city called Springfield with his brother Muiris to seek his fortune. Instead they found hard work in labour gangs for low pay, much of which went on rented rooms. After five back-breaking years, Seán returned to the island, while Muiris stayed on in America for good.

Some of his fellow emigrants gave up, swallowed their disappointment and came home, persuading themselves to be thankful for the clean air, wide sky and green fields. Seán returned to find that life was just as hard on his island as it had been in the States. Fishing and farming were not enough for such a strong-minded young man; he was restless, and in 1908 he returned to Springfield. This time there was well-paid work to be had on the railways, and he could enjoy the luxury of a haircut and shave at the barber's, or a pair of new shoes. But still he could not settle. The life was good, but not good enough to soothe his longing for the mountain in the sea. Armed with a shotgun for rabbits and a caseful of suits, stiff collars and silk ties, he made the last trip home.

If Seán thought his booty would impress his fellow islanders, he was wrong. They were, however, fascinated by the gold tooth that glittered in his mouth. In Gaelic it was *Fiacail Or*, and that became his nickname even into old age, when every tooth but the gold one loosened and fell out.

A photograph taken of Seán in America showed him dressed in a fashionable round-collared shirt with a high-buttoned suit, his moustache waxed. He was a very handsome man, I said to Céit. 'Oh. He made that press. Out of old timber. Oh gee, he was wonderful. No complaining. And the roof I have over me is from my grandmother's house. They brought it out to Ballydavid. From the island. In two canoes.' The worth of an islandman was clearly measured by his ability to provide.

'I was born in Coumeenole, at my grandmother's house,' she said. The custom was that a woman carrying her first child would go back to her mother to give birth. Céit arrived in 1918, the first of Neilí Ó Cearna's ten children, which was the same number as Peig Sayers and not unusual at all. After Céit there was Muiris, Mícheál, Peaidí, Seáinín, Máirtin, Team, Máirín and Billy, one a year until 1927 when Seamus came. He did not survive. 'My youngest brother died inside my mother's lap. He didn't take the bottle. It was in the middle of the night, about three o'clock. We couldn't do nothing. He was a nice baby, like Máirín, with big blue eyes. We are very lonely after. He's buried inside in the Blaskets.' She meant at Castle Point, in the graveyard used for unbaptized infants.

'My mother was very good. She was able to do everything. Worked very hard. She died thirty-five. I was thirteen.' The cause of death was probably stomach cancer. 'My mother and father went to Tralee, and the doctors there told him it's no good, to take her to Dublin. He did. He went up to Dublin. She was three weeks up there, then she came back down.'

Neilí died in Dingle hospital in 1934. 'She did not want to

send the sons of her family anywhere, only to keep them together. I remember the day she died. Sunday. Ah, dear me.' A plume of smoke from the headland of Dún Mór was the signal that her struggle was over. 'My father was back in the field, with the oats. I was going to the well with two buckets for water. He came back and told me. My uncle and my aunt made a fire out on the Dún to tell us. There was nothing else to do.'

The coffin was brought to the island before Neilí was buried in Dunquin, but Céit was not allowed to see her mother's face that one last time. 'I didn't. They won't open the coffin. My father don't want to open the coffin at all, because we would be very sad . . .' Her voice trailed away, then returned: 'Well, that's it.'

So then it was down to Céit to give up school and become mother. 'It was June. I won't be fourteen until November. The others were younger. I am the captain, and God knows I have a tough life. It was very hard to cope for boys. They were starving every minute.' Her eyes were tearful. She was almost whispering. 'My father was good. They had plenty tough. There were two donkeys, and two cows, sometimes. He was a good provider.' Peaidí, her brother, went to his mother's funeral without any shoes, but wearing a good suit.

The school did not last much longer anyway, as the number of children on the island made it unworkable. Billy and Máirín were sent to the mainland to finish their education. It was clear that there was no future for the Ó Cearna brothers on the Great Blasket, and as teenagers they followed their fellow countrymen to England, where cheap labour was needed to harvest crops in season. 'Going on the beet', as it was called, provided employment for only a few months at a time, so the islanders returned home afterwards. Seáinín was there the summer before his death, and it was on the steps of a Catholic church in Birmingham that he was startled by a dog and suffered a nasty fall. The blinding headaches that followed soon passed, and were forgotten until he took sick again on Christmas Eve.

Céit's eyes filled with tears at the memory of his death, even after all that time. 'He was inside three days and three nights. We can't get him out. We can't do nothing. Oh, the weather. Gone crazy altogether. Whenever I see it horrible out, that remembers me. He was a strong boy, and he was very good to everybody.'

Céit chose to leave the island as soon as possible after that. 'I can't stay inside. I got fright,' she said, strength returning to her voice. 'I didn't get anything from the Blaskets. I didn't get any house or land like the others, because I came out before them. After my brother died I was very, very, very . . . oh gee, I was very upset. I was scared. I did not want to stay in the Blaskets. Ever so frightened. I had no old woman with me only, and I didn't know that . . . nothing, not too much about dead people.'

She was remembering those terrible few days when the body lay in the house. A grieving father and a sister acting as mother were forced, with the rest of the family, to eat and sleep in that cramped cottage as Seáinín lay there for three days without a coffin. They had no way of knowing when the *naomhóg* would return. In the meantime, Céit had to touch that marble skin and make her brother ready.

'I have to wash his feet.'

There was silence between us.

Despite everything, Céit was sad when they did finally leave the following Easter and moved into what she called her hen house. Although she couldn't see the Great Blasket, the new home did offer a view of the island known as the Dead Man.

'I was crying behind the house, looking back at Inis Tuaisceart,' she said. An estate agent in Dingle had sent word of the house to Paddy, Céit's husband. Seán came across the Sound to help build an extension.

The ties between the father and the daughter who had become a mother to his other children were very strong. Seán stayed on the mainland to help out for a while that summer, but then went back. 'I used to go into the island during the summer and spend three weeks in the place, clean the place and wash the floor,' said Céit. 'I was going to go to England, but I was thinking about my father. Who was going to take care of him?'

In 1953, Seán went to live with Céit and her husband, who had not taken long to start a family of their own. They eventually had three boys and two girls. The house was full, but Céit was still sad at the loss of her first tribe. 'I was very lonely. My brothers are like my own family to me. That's the way I am.'

The brothers grew old, of course. Their visits back to the Dingle peninsula had become rare. The children and grandchildren were more likely to make the journey. It was too expensive for Céit to ring them very often on her widow's pension, but she claimed that they were close still, despite the distance and the years spent apart. 'Team died in America. He was calling me when he was dying. We were very close to each other. He got his wife to send a card with some money every St Patrick's Day.'

In her own mind she had never stopped nurturing them. 'Oh, they're all right. They have their money, and they spend it. I told them several times to put a new cross on my mother, and not to be drinking. I did!' She was smiling, but only half-joking.

After an hour or so, Céit's attention had begun to wander.

Her answers lost their focus, skipping from the past to the present and back again. She had been meek at first but friendly, and eventually charming, but now she was tired. When we left, she came out to the car in the darkness, braving a flurry of wind and rain. I kissed her cheek, which was soft and smelt sweet. She clasped my hand and said something in Irish, a blessing. 'Thank you for spending that evening,' she said through the open car window. 'She's lonely,' said Mícheál as we drove into the night.

A one-eyed sheepdog guarded the pier at Ballydavid, the next village along from Céit's house. It came skittering out from between the beer barrels in a pub yard hoping for a game, but backed off at the sight of a stranger. This was the pier from which Céit's husband had worked as a fisherman, and there were two dinghies moored by it. The dog sat between the prongs of a rusty trailer, under a motorless boat, and gave me the eye. The sea rolled its shoulders as though being massaged by the low mist, and the waves sighed over shingle. The shoreline stretched away to the left in a long, slow curve and disappeared into the haze. Listening to the water lap against the wooden hull of a dinghy, it was not difficult to imagine Paddy pushing out from here with his nets and line, early in the morning. There was no sun, but the sea seemed to shine and the air was fresh, with a salty zest that filled the nostrils and cleansed the pores. The dog growled, shook its coat and gave up.

Somehow, Paddy had managed to catch pneumonia while fishing from this pier in the middle of summer. July. He spent nine weeks in the hospital at Dingle, during the hottest weather of the year, and developed pleurisy. 'Oh gee,' said Céit when she told me about it, the next time we met. 'Bad luck.' No wonder the old lady was melancholy. She lived in a tiny house under a big sky, by a harbour a mile wide, and beyond it the open ocean crashing against spectacular headlands. Sorrows seemed to wash up on her shores like shipwrecked galleons.

For all its natural beauty, poverty stalked the Dingle Peninsula. As the fishing trade died slowly and the agricultural system broke down, before tourism became the main source of income, times were very hard indeed. Even after he recovered from pleurisy, Paddy found it hard to meet the main demand on men in those parts: to provide for the family. 'We can't do nothing. We have nothing. My husband was in and out of the hospital.'

Paddy had been raised in the house behind Céit's on the Great Blasket. 'He was very good-looking. Fine boy. Fine man. It take time for me to get married. I was lazy to get married. I had to look after my family.'

Something made Céit reluctant to talk about her husband or even say when they were married. 'I can't remember now, everything has gone out of my head.' She was clear that she had been seeing Paddy for five years, 'now and then', before their wedding, but it seemed he had been working in England for much of that time to raise money, as instructed by her father. 'I used to go with strangers too,' she said, and she meant while Paddy was away. 'From Dublin. Solicitors and doctors. They were staying in my uncle's house. There was a lot of them.'

How could two people have a romance without everybody in such a close community knowing all about it? 'We don't care.' But where could you go to be in private when you had a houseful every night and the hillside was crowded with islanders and visitors? 'Oh, you can go in the night.' She laughed at that thought.

One of these visitors had grand ideas, she said. 'He wants

to take me to Dublin and put me to college, this man, a solicitor. I can't go, because if I go my brothers have to go to a home. I don't want that, because my mother don't want it: when she was dying she said, "Keep them together." I stay at home. He went away. He was very upset. He married after that. Had three kids. Heart attack. Died.'

So Paddy it was. He wanted to go back to England for another season to raise more money for a house, but after Seáinín died, Céit's father would not let him. 'He spent four years in England. He was a fine man when he came home, and we got married.' He was also a fine singer, apparently. 'There's a tape there now . . .' She pressed a button on a cassette player, and a wavering voice came out of the one speaker, unaccompanied. He was singing *Réidhchnoc Mná Duibhe*, 'The Smooth Hill of the Dark Woman', a lament Tomás Ó Criomhthain was said to have performed at his wedding:

> *Long have I anxiously sought my beloved*
> *In a dark lonesome glen where I am sent astray . . .*

The beach was less than a hundred yards from Céit's home, down a slope, across the one road in Muirríoch, past a sign for shore angling and along a track between two houses. Seaweed, twisted beer cans and bits of plastic crunched with flat purple pebbles beneath the feet; then came the sand, pale and dirty. The foam where the waves met the shore was slick and limp. The water by the pier had been refreshing and energetic, but here it was listless and wan, like a sickly child who never saw the sun. Behind the beach was a road, behind that marshlands, and way off in the distance, mountain slopes. The highest and blackest of them all, with its peak permanently in the clouds, was Mount Brandon. Only a mile or two from

Céit's home, according to legend, Saint Brendan set off from a creek to search for the Land of Youth. He tried twice, and the second time discovered a place that might have been America.

The woman who lived in the shadow of his mountain was neither a saint nor an intrepid traveller. Céit had been to America twice, to see her brothers, and despite their pleas she had returned home. She could not tell me why, except that the food disagreed with her stomach, which was what her father had told his fellow islanders so many years before. The real reason was that she wanted to stay and look after the old man. 'I really loved my father.' By the time he died, at the age of eighty-six, her own children were already settled.

Her suffering was not over. After years of sickness, her husband the fisherman was claimed by the sea. 'He went out in the middle of the night. We didn't know nothing until the morning, the thirteenth of July, a Sunday. They found him down behind that big house. The neighbours saw his coat in the water. He put it on himself. He was a quiet man. Great singer.'

When Céit spoke again, it was the voice of someone who had become accustomed to pain. 'I am here on my own now.'

13

6 August 1947

The islanders wait. When de Valera leaves the Great Blasket they expect him to keep his word, and to show swift, decisive leadership on their behalf. In return for this trust he gives them a committee of civil servants.

When the officials first meet in Dublin to consider ways of improving living conditions on the island they are handed a note from the Taoiseach's office, dated 6 August, that contains some pretty strong opinions on the state of the Great Blasket community. The name of the author is not officially recorded, but it may well have been de Valera himself.

'The Blasket islanders are mostly housed in hovels,' says the note. How would the proud islanders take that description of their homes, if they could read it, after having worked so hard to make their leader welcome? 'They have no church, no priest, no doctor. There is not a single tree on the island, and probably not more than half a dozen bushes. They have not a public house, a cinema or a dance-hall in which to find distraction from their woes. Their land is untillable. They have no cows that I saw, and apart from doles, their only means of livelihood are the grazing of mountain sheep and lobster fishing.'

Then come words that would surely make Maras Mhuiris and the other elderly men and women on the island flinch. 'They are dying out and perhaps it is better for them so.'

The writer believes there should be one last effort to help

before the 'hopeless alternative of shifting the population' is adopted. He urges the committee to consider what can be done to improve communications with the mainland, and to start cottage industries on the island similar to the homespun-cloth and doll-making operations that have been established elsewhere in rural Ireland. It might be possible to work with wool from the island sheep, for example, or to extract vitamin oils from mackerel, or to tin lobsters. A hostel might be established for students of the Irish language and for tourists, since the island is a good place for a holiday for anyone with simple tastes.

However, all the skill and resourcefulness that the men and women of the Great Blasket have used to keep themselves alive in that difficult place during the last hundred or more winters is now apparently useless and outdated. 'A domestic-economy teacher should be sent to the island for six or twelve months to show the people how to make the most of the food they can afford and to keep their houses decently,' he writes. 'And a good handyman to teach them how to do simple building and repairs and to induce them to knock down the loathsome ruins around their houses.'

Confident that his words will never find their way back to the Great Blasket, the writer of this anonymous note from the Taoiseach's office urges: 'in anything that is done care should be taken not to weaken further any spirit of independence there is in the islanders. They will need it all to survive.'

14

Winter closed in, and the islanders survived as best they could, without word from Dublin. Their self-declared champion de Valera had other things to worry about: in February 1948 his government lost the election to a coalition of opposition parties. Afterwards, civil servants continued to deliberate over the future of the Great Blasket, even as a new wave of emigration to America was rising up in the island and the nearest mainland villages. They eventually submitted a report in December 1948, after meeting sixteen times.

Much of what was described in the report could have been found in the books on the island: the Great Blasket was bare, high and unsheltered, except for a slope on the north-east side facing the mainland; it was surrounded by cliffs that made landing difficult; all but sixty of the 1,132 acres of land were wild, mountainous commonage useless for anything but sheep-grazing in summer; and the surrounding sea was frequently disturbed and dangerous.

When the inspection was made the previous summer, there had been fifty-one people on the island, and twenty of them had already passed their sixtieth birthday. The school had been closed in 1941. There were nineteen men under the age of forty who were unmarried, and only four single women. Anybody from the mainland who was prepared to consider marrying an islandman refused to live on the Great Blasket.

Each of the fifteen households had a right to farm up to four acres of arable land on the north-east end of the island, above the beach, although only ten acres were actually cultivated. The same patches of land were worked year after year because they were the most sheltered. It was sandy but fertile soil, spread with chemical fertilizer as well as the traditional manure, seaweed, mussel shells and soot. Each household planted half an acre of potatoes, and in 1947 got an average of just over three tons out of that. Oats and turnips were grown but no other vegetables, not even for visitors. 'The islanders attend mainly to fishing and are indifferent to improving their hold-ings,' said the report, which later suggested that they wouldn't know how to work the land if they were forced to migrate away from the shore. Neither did they want anything to do with government schemes for bee-keeping.

The islanders were treated with suspicion, prejudice and hostility by those who could have helped them. Some applied for home-improvement loans under a scheme for people living in the Gaeltacht areas, but were turned down because the officials didn't trust them to repay the money. They were a race apart, an isolated community with its own rules, whose members were known not to pay taxes or rent to the outside world.

As for food, the islanders lived on fish, potatoes and bread. They were desperate to get bigger rations of flour. Supplies had to be bought in Dingle, and rationing meant they were only able to buy small amounts each time, even though bad conditions might make another journey impossible for weeks. They seldom ate meat, despite having six hundred sheep between them and more rabbits than that on the mountain, which was common land. Everyone had the right to dig for turf, which lay beneath the gorse and heather, to hunt rabbits and to graze animals. One person owned two hundred of the sheep, another owned one hundred, and the rest were divided between nine families, which meant there were four house-holds with no sheep. Apart from being slaughtered at Christmas they were kept for their wool, and transported in *naomhóga*, dozens at a time, to the mainland, where a dealer from Dingle came to buy them.

There were fifteen hens on the island and fifteen male donkeys, one of which was used by each household to carry turf back from the hill in panniers, or sand and seaweed up from the strand. There were only six cows, and during the winter everybody had to survive on tinned milk which was bought along with tea and sugar in Dunquin. An unlicensed bull had been brought to the island; before that, cows in season had to be tied to the *naomhóga* and transported across the Sound, which was a very dangerous business.

The canoes were mainly used for lobster fishing, since the market for salted mackerel had been destroyed by a tariff imposed by the US government. Fresh mackerel was sold at market in Dingle, but that was too far away for the islanders to keep their catch from going off. They did land some haddock, cod and pollock with lines, and salted them for the winter. Fishing with pots for lobsters was a profitable business that brought up to £600 a year into the island. Nine islanders received pensions, while £210 a year in unemployment benefit was divided between twenty-nine people. There was also money to be had from looking after visitors, so the distinguished civil servants meeting in Dublin to decide the fate of these remote people decided that most of the families were 'comfortable'.

It was not poverty but a lack of communication with the outside world that had driven the younger generation away.

The remoteness of the island, loneliness in the winter, the dread of being without food, the danger of not being able to obtain the services of priest or doctor in time of need, the absence of teacher or nurse and the hardness of life in general. As the number of islanders declines these matters affect them more. Loneliness is accentuated and there is a greater feeling of helplessness in times of emergency.

When the radio-telephone on the island was working, which was not often, it could only send morse messages, and only as far as the post office at Dunquin, which was closed after seven in the evening and all day Sundays. The mountains made it impossible to communicate with Dingle or Ballyferriter. The Department of Posts and Telegraphs refused to send a second machine as standby, because it did not believe there was anyone capable of learning to switch from one to another.

What the islanders really wanted, of course, was to be transferred to the mainland. They wanted to be treated as the inhabitants of a similar community in County Mayo had been, which meant the government finding land and building houses for them not too far from the island, so that they could fish and could also continue to graze sheep on the Great Blasket.

The committee did not have the power to recommend evacuation. The strict remit defined by de Valera meant that it could only suggest ways of improving life for the islanders where they were. Nevertheless, the members went as close as they could to saying the unsayable.

The decline in the population has already been so great and living conditions there are so difficult . . . migration from the island will continue . . . it would not be for the people's welfare to disperse them . . . an early decision should be made as to whether the islanders should be migrated to the mainland as they themselves desire.

No early decision was made. The Minister for Lands did not even ask the government to make one until ten months after he received the report. In doing so he noted that the Minister for Finance anticipated problems collecting rent from the islanders if they moved to the mainland – and he also thought that it would 'not be objectionable' to demolish the homes left on the island so that nobody was tempted to go back.

Those islanders who had not already made their own arrangements to leave must have given up hope when another visit to the Great Blasket by two Land Commission inspectors in early 1950 was followed by absolutely no action at all. De Valera returned to power the following year, but showed no signs of keeping his promise to help. That winter the Great Blasket was cut off from all communication with the mainland for a month, and its twenty-eight inhabitants were forced to live on nothing but potatoes and salt.

Once again it was left to the few remaining islanders to make a public appeal, and in September 1952 the *Irish Independent* reported that four of them had signed a memorandum asking for urgent help, 'so that we can be released from our island fortress'.

Enough land had been on the market in Dunquin for the transfer to have been possible, it said, but nothing had been done. 'All we received are empty promises.'

The request was signed by two sets of brothers, Seán and Muiris Ó Guithín and Seán and Muiris Ó Catháin. 'If people at this stage of civilization and standard of living only realized what hardships of mind and body we endure, we are sure that they would raise their voices and rally to our cause,' they wrote. The *Irish Independent* was told by the Land Commission that no decision had been made at that time. Finally, in November 1952, almost six years after the death of Seáinín and five years since de Valera's visit, the order was given to evacuate the island. It took another twelve months for anything to be done.

15

Even the sea that washed this island home and made their
livelihood so difficult and precarious seemed loth to permit
of the departure of the last of the race that had lived, laboured,
loved, suffered and died on the islands for hundreds
of years.

Kerryman

17 *November 1953*

It is just before nine-thirty in the morning, and a fishing boat
called the *St Lawrence O'Toole* has left Dingle harbour bound
for the Great Blasket. On board are two men from the Land
Commission, Seán Goulding and Dan O'Brien, whose mission
is to see that the decision taken by the Cabinet a year ago is
carried out, and the island evacuated. They already know that
such a thing may be impossible today, because the weather is
its usual unpredictable self, but they intend to do as much as
is safe.

Conditions seem ideal until the *St Lawrence* reaches Blasket
Sound, where white foam is breaking on the rocks. The
skipper, Mike Brosnan, shakes his head, and says there is no
way the islanders' furniture can be transferred to Dunquin,
according to the original plan. Two engineers who are also on
board realize they will not be able to retrieve the cumbersome
radio-telephone from the island post office, which closed

yesterday. A *naomhóg* is sent out to the vessel from the island, and its crew warn that any attempt to land could be dangerous, but Dan O'Brien surprises everyone watching by requesting to be taken ashore, despite the sea. Wearing a collar and tie under his overcoat, but no hat, the official has round spectacles that fog easily and make him look like someone who should be desk-bound. Still, he shows an uncommon steadiness on his feet to make it into the *naomhóg* and then out on to the slip, where he meets the head of each family that is to be given a house in the parish of Dunquin, and gets the necessary signatures.

Three times the *naomhóg* returns to the *St Lawrence*, until six islandmen are aboard with such belongings as they can carry in bags and pails. Once he is safely sitting by the mast, O'Brien tells his colleague Goulding that it was indeed dangerous to land, which was a shame since the islanders were ready to leave. 'All household furniture was packed. They realized there was no future for them on the Blaskets.' Since he says it in English, the islanders next to him waving to their wives and sisters pay little attention.

The deck of the *St Lawrence* is crowded as it makes its way back to Dingle in heavy seas, with the six islanders crowded up alongside the crew, the engineers, and the men from the Land Commission. The two government officials look distinctly uneasy, but the islandmen are grinning, glad that something is finally happening. One of them is Seán Faeili Ó Catháin (listed in newspaper reports of the day as John Maurice Keane), one of the four who made the frantic dash to fetch a coffin for Seáinín. He signed the last public appeal for help, a year ago, along with his friend Seán Mhaidhc Léan Ó Guithín (John Guiheen), who is also on board. The other men are Seán Sheáisi Ó Cearna (listed as John J. Kearney), Seáinín

Mhicil Ó Súilleabháin (John O'Sullivan) and Seán Philí Ó Cearna (John P. Kearney). They are all wearing nailed boots, heavy trousers and caps. Over his shirt each man has a typical Blasket jersey with a zip instead of buttons at the neck, and over that he wears a homespun jacket or a long overcoat. The exception is Pádraig Mistéal, known as *Fíogach*, 'Dogfish', who has on a three-piece pinstripe suit and a dapper trilby. When the *St Lawrence* reaches the shore they climb out and walk up the slipway in a line abreast, laughing.

Waiting for them by the quayside is a small man with a notebook, and a Gaelic League pin on his lapel. Walter McGrath has made the three-hour journey from Cork to meet the boat, so that he can file a report for the *Examiner* newspaper. To him, and to many of his readers, the Great Blasket is important because its people have preserved a culture and a language that might otherwise have disappeared altogether. They have become symbols of an old Ireland, pawns in a game between politicians with opposing views of what it means to be Irish.

Walter McGrath has been walking around Dingle for two hours, waiting for word of the *St Lawrence*. Over lunch at Benners' Hotel in Main Street he flicked through *The Islandman*, a book he first read as a schoolboy during Irish lessons. Despite a warning from the barman that the islanders will be uncommunicative, McGrath is sympathetic to them. He believes that more should have been done to allow them to stay, and expects they will have been offended by the government's offer of new houses as an easy way to make amends. Most of all, he expects the six men to be sorry that they have had to leave the island for good.

They stride towards him now in an obvious hurry, carrying their possessions in shiny galvanized buckets. 'Are you glad to be leaving the island?' he asks, notebook out, after introducing himself. 'Yes' is the only answer. Nothing else.

'*Tá uaigneas orainn*,' says Fíogach over his shoulder. 'We are a bit lonely.' Disappointed, the reporter watches them walk away.

16

The evacuation is not the end of this story, although it was the end of many things. The Great Blasket had finally proved unable to sustain human life, and made exiles of the islanders, for ever. There was no going back now, and no point in dreaming about it.

Only the handful of people who were left on the island in 1953 got new homes on the Irish mainland. Where did all the others go? To America, a mythical place of adventure and new beginnings. In his memoir *Twenty Years A-Growing*, Muiris Ó Súilleabháin walks on the empty island of Inis Icíleáin and begins to daydream.

The sky was cloudless, the sea calm, sea-birds and land-birds singing sweetly. The sight of my eyes set me thinking. I looked west to the edge of the sky and I seemed to see clearly the Land of the Young – many-coloured flowers in the gardens; fine, bright houses sparkling in the sunshine; stately, comely-faced, fair-haired maidens walking through the meadows. Oh, isn't it a pity Niav of the Golden Hair would not come here now, thought I, for I would gladly go with her across the waves.

He is dreaming of a paradise that has inspired the Celts since before history: *Tir na nÓg*, the Land of Youth or of the Ever-Young, a place where no one grows old and everything is beautiful. It lies in the far, far west; and sometimes, on a clear summer's day, you can see it shimmer at the rim of the horizon. Once, in the distant past, an enchanting woman on a white horse found the Fenian warriors while they were hunting in the forest, and professed her love for their poet, Oisín. She was *Niamh Chinn Óir*, or Niav of the Golden Hair, who found him willing to be carried off to her home in *Tir na nÓg*. There, in a land without suffering, blemish or worry, they made love for three hundred years.

This was the heaven on earth that Saint Brendan risked his life to find, although as a child of Moses he called it the Land of Promise. He set sail from a creek at the end of the Dingle Peninsula in a leather boat with fourteen monks, and went west for five years before giving up and returning home from Iceland. Unsatisfied, he left again in a vessel made of oak, with sixty monks, and this time got as far as Newfoundland, Florida or the Bahamas. On the way the monks mistook a whale for an island, saw a crystal column and a mountain that spouted flames. They met the lonely figure of Judas Iscariot, who was tormented by demons. After seven years, they emerged from a thick fog to see the promised island, where the trees were full of ripe fruit and where precious stones lay on the ground.

In the minds of the Blasket islanders, and in the mouths of their storytellers, the mythical Land of Youth became associ-ated with America, which also lay in the distant west, beyond the sea. In *Twenty Years A-Growing*, the author stares at the horizon again, and this time his vision resembles the island of Manhattan, known to him through letters and photographs from lost loved ones.

I looked west at the edge of the sky where America should be lying, and I slipped back on the paths of thought. It seemed to me now that the New Island was before me with its fine streets and great high houses, some of them so tall that they scratched the sky; gold and silver out on the ditches and nothing to do but to gather it. I see the boys and girls who were once my companions walking the street, laughing brightly and well contented.

There were very few people from the Great Blasket living in America when Seán Team Ó Cearna booked his first passage in 1901; but the trickle of emigrants grew into a river after the First World War, as the oldest or most adventurous child in each family left the island, found work in the States and wrote home with tales of the great life to be had there. Bad news was usually left out of such letters, which were designed to entice. Dollars were enclosed, so that the next brother or sister could follow. The migration paused during the Second World War, but began again as soon as the fighting was over and the travel restrictions eased. The official evacuation was not a rescue or a noble act, but a final, belated recognition that the community was finished. On the day that the *St Lawrence O'Toole* arrived, in November 1953, there were at least a hundred times more people of Blasket origin in America than on the island itself.

So why did Seán Team, his sons, and all their friends and enemies go west? Niav lured the young with her promises. Weary Ireland had been losing its best to America for a century. But Blasket people were not sheep, and mythology was not enough to explain why most turned their backs on the Irish mainland, and travelled thousands of difficult miles to what they joked was the next parish west. Where did they find the courage and the strength? The answers lay deep in the psychology of a community whose members knew themselves to be set apart from Ireland and the world. The clues to what would happen were always there, in the stories that shaped them.

PART TWO

Island Story

Signs appear of what lies ahead but, if so, small is the notice taken until it comes to pass. That is how it was with us and we living on the Western Island.

Seán Ó Criomhthain, *A Day in Our Life*

A social system which could let such a culture die must be rotten in some way. I now believe that such a civilization is impossible within our modern monetary society. It was money which destroyed this place.

George Thomson, known on the island as Seoirse Mac Tomáis

17

The best place to hear stories was in the pub, and I spent a lot of time there as the last days of summer 1998 passed away slowly. With them went my chances of reaching the Great Blasket that year. The weather did not relent, but the rain blew through the valley of Dunquin, flattening flowers and scattering sheep, giving way to brief moments of sunshine when the hedgerows shone brilliant green. The sea held up its hands to meet the clouds, and everything was wet. Sometimes the storm clouds got trapped between the mountains, and the valley was a dark whirlpool of wind and rain. The devil's stomach.

On such foul days and nights, when the cliffs dissolved into the Atlantic, I was safe in Kruger's, the most westerly bar in Europe. The pub sign swung wildly on its rusty hinges, then flew off into a cow field in the early hours of one morning, and was left there. Only a few lights showed in the houses scattered across the slopes, built with their backs to Mount Eagle and their faces to the Great Blasket, which was lost at sea. The night clouds parted to show the stars, bright and numerous; but anyone foolish enough to pause and look up at them was blinded by the rain. Instead, the villagers of Dunquin set their shoulders to the wind, as they always had, and pushed through the door of the saloon bar.

The brown tiled floor bore the scars of many a wild night. There were scuffed stools, and benches covered in uncertain beige, under a wide picture-window. In daylight you could see the islands; by night the bar was reflected in on itself. Half a dozen men old beyond their years cradled pints of stout and muttered to each other in Irish, a mournful language with the rhythm of the waves. The group was gathered at the end of the bar nearest the door, as though the porch were a source of light and heat. The fire itself was cold; there were no other customers most nights, until just before last orders, when locals who had driven over the pass to Dingle for the evening came by for a nightcap.

The holiday season was over and the timetables had changed, so that the bus called at Dunquin only twice a week. Slowly, the regulars had become friendly enough to nod as I took my usual place in the far corner, where the lights were only half on and the newly mopped floor smelt of disinfectant. My seat was under a set of framed photographs which showed the men at the bar dressed up as peasants as extras on the set of *Far and Away*, one of two films made in the valley. The other, *Ryan's Daughter*, had its own gallery space. There were also a great many photographs of a man in a cloth cap with a wide, beaming face and big ears, who seemed to know a lot of famous people. He was the late Maurice Kavanagh, founder of the pub, a Dunquin man who earned his nickname, Kruger, in childhood re-enactments of the Boer War.

Kruger left the parish as a young man around the same time as Seán Team, but their fortunes were wildly different. According to his own account, readily given to anyone who would listen, Kruger lived a spectacular life. He started as a labourer, then a truck driver, but then joined the US Army and became a commissioned officer, which was the making of the man. Once out of uniform he chose to serve his new country as the press agent to the *Ziegfeld Follies*, a journalist, a film censor, and the bodyguard of de Valera on his American tour. Wherever he went there were girls, cash and flash. The fun came to an end with the Wall Street Crash, which wiped out most of the money he had made. Kruger took chances, but he knew when to quit: so he came home to Dunquin, to run an unlicensed pub.

Above all, America had taught him the value of publicity; and he cultivated his personal myth so successfully that this landlord from an isolated village on the far west coast became famous all over Ireland. Brendan Behan was one of the many writers and artists who stayed at Kruger's guest-house during the height of its fame, just after the Second World War, and he described his host as 'the friend of many Hollywood film-stars, various American gangsters, boxers, politicians and similar sporting personalities'. There were so many signed pictures of stars on the wall that one guest hung up a print of the Sacred Heart and wrote underneath it: 'To my friend Kruger, with love from God.'

He was a rogue and a loudmouth, but he was also loved by the people of the Great Blasket island, who had known him as a boy and who came to rely on him in the years when their community was dying. They needed friends on the mainland. Kruger had a battered old van, one of the few motor vehicles around, and it carried many of the young islanders on the first leg of their journey to America. Even those who did not travel with him knew all about his adventures in the land 'where a man could be a billionaire one day and a bum the next'. Provided there was whiskey or porter on the table he was always willing to tell how, for twenty years, it had been 'a beautiful pasture of green guys from whom I could nibble a living'.

The Ó Cearna brothers had heard the stories, and were told about America by their own father, but they also knew that both men had been compelled to return. If anyone asked Kruger why he had come home, the old tease held his tongue. He didn't want to strangle the hopes of the young before they had even left. They might have better luck than him, after all. But his disappointment was revealed when the famous Kruger Kavanagh narrated his life story to the *People* newspaper in 1955, and told the readers why he had left Broadway behind.

I was seeing some Irishmen to the pier one day and I never saw men so happy. They were going back to the old country. I followed them on the next boat. I came back from America through sheer, downright loneliness, and now I live in one of the loneliest places in the world. The Atlantic roars at night below my window, between me and the Blasket island.

The lonely splendour of the landscape was what attracted the first people to live on the Great Blasket. The tides rose and fell with the moon; the seasons passed, unrecorded, for centuries. Then, one unknown morning more than a thousand years ago, a longboat landed beside the virgin island. A dozen men in rough clothing, carrying sticks and bundles, waded ashore. They chanted a song of praise, whose familiar words quietened their fearful souls.

The men were monks of the Celtic Church, who sought silence and solitude. They found both high on the Red Ridge, where the long, thin spine of the Great Blasket curved down and away from its peak, *An Cró*. Standing on the wild heather, with storm petrels for company, they could see for miles out into the Atlantic or along the coast of Ireland, a landscape of such great scale that settlements became invisible and human beings irrelevant. Creation spoke of the glory of God.

Anyone else would have chosen to live on the grassy slope above the strand, which offered shelter from the prevalent winds and water from springs. The ragged group of holy men ignored these comforts, and struck out for the exposed ridge where the land tumbled hundreds of feet to the sea on either side, but where there was less chance of a glance back at the temptations of home. The coastline around the tip of the peninsula was fringed with the forts and shelters of Fahan, an Iron Age city that offered hospitality to sea-borne merchants from the Mediterranean and pilgrims sailing to Scotland, Scandinavia and beyond in the name of the saints Brendan and Columba.

The first islanders were not tracing ancient stories but looking for an isolated place away from the distractions of society. Self-denial was a sacred duty to them. White martyrdom meant abandoning friends and family, and everything they loved, for the sake of God. There was no surer way to do that than to accept perpetual exile, seeking out the barren places.

The shelters that they built from broken stones stood undisturbed on the Red Ridge for more than a thousand years, and became known as *na Clocháin Gheala*, the Bright Dwellings. The monks were not alone in their wilderness: saints and angels stood by as they used prayer and fasting to wrestle with terrifying demons as real to them as the other brothers. It was easy to believe in the supernatural as they lay awake on the empty hillside, cold, hungry and blinded by the winter night, with the wind howling through the stones of the cell walls.

The belief endured. *An Dún*, the ring fort they built on the edge of a cliff nine hundred feet above the sea, would always be known as the home of spirits.

The monks left, or they were murdered. Vikings raided the coast during the ninth century and used *An Dún* as a lookout post, but their season was brief. The island was left alone again, unclaimed, at the edge of the world. Boats must have landed there from time to time, but written history does not record ordinary lives. It cares only for the actions of rich and powerful men, and none of those paid any attention to the Great Blasket for hundreds of years.

The first to claim legal ownership of the island was a Norman invader, the Earl of Desmond, in the thirteenth century, but it was no more to him than a name on a deed, a remote outpost at the boundary of an extensive empire. He let the Great Blasket out for a rent of two hawks a year to the Ferriter family, fellow Normans who had set themselves up as warlords west of Dingle. They already had a castle with views along the northern edge of the peninsula, and the island allowed them to keep watch on the other side as well.

The Ferriters went native within a few generations, like many of their fellow Norman settlers. They became so absorbed in Gaelic culture, language and religion that the English gentry began to distrust and fear them. By the 1500s, forces loyal to London felt obliged to put down dissent by commandeering cattle, burning down homes and food stores and slaughtering anyone who did not flee to the hills. Those who did get away were likely to starve. Hundreds of thousands of acres of good land were confiscated from Irish Catholics and given to English Protestant adventurers, who sublet them to settlers from their home country. These plantations were protected by force, despite several attempts at armed rebellion.

The bloodiest slaughter of all took place at Smerwick Harbour, a few miles away around the headland, where Céit Ó Cearna would eventually live. The Vatican sent an invasion force of seven hundred mercenaries from Spain, Italy and Ireland there in 1580. Queen Elizabeth was afraid the Catholic nations would attack her from the west, so the new Lord Deputy, Arthur Grey de Wilton, responded fast and hard. A fleet of English ships arrived at Smerwick Harbour on 5 November and fired cannons at a fort built by the invaders. Two days later Lord Grey himself arrived with an army of eight hundred soldiers, including a young captain called Walter Raleigh.

There were enough supplies inside the fort to hold out against siege and bombardment for a long time, but a white flag was raised after only three days. The English could not believe it. The Vatican mercenaries agreed to lay down their arms in return for their lives – but when they had surrendered, Lord Grey sent in a company of soldiers, who murdered five hundred men and some pregnant women. In a letter to his Queen, the commander mentioned the slaughter only in passing, but lamented that some of the munitions and victuals had been wasted 'through the disorder of the Souldier, which in that furie could not be helped'.

Seventeen Irish and English Catholics who had joined the invasion force were tortured, some left to lie in agony for a day with arms and legs each broken in three places by a hammer. They were all hanged on the walls of the fort.

The hundreds of dead bodies were not buried but thrown into the sea. They washed up on the beach and were covered by the sand, until four centuries later the skulls and bones of a few unfortunates began to resurface, to the great alarm of people whose dogs found them as they walked on the windswept beach. Not that the slaughter had been forgotten, in a part of the world where landmarks were still known by the names of legendary figures and their battles. Parents in the villages west of Dingle had always warned their children to behave, 'or Raleigh will get you'. Adults still cursed each other with the words, 'The massacre of the Dún upon you!'

Eight years after the slaughter, the body of a beautiful Spanish woman was cast up on the White Strand of the Great Blasket. This was not one of Grey's victims: she was dressed in sodden splendour, and her stiff limbs were heavy with gold rings and bracelets. The woman had been a passenger on the *Santa Maria de la Rosa*, a merchant ship loaded with twenty-six guns to fight in the Spanish Armada. After being scattered by English fireships and chased into the North Sea, the remnants of the Armada tried to get home down the west coast of Ireland, but storms blew many of the galleons and supply vessels on to the rocks. The *Santa Maria* was dragged into the middle of the Blasket Sound, where hidden rocks ripped out the hull. A cannon was fired as a call for help, but none came. In the last moments the captain was seized with fury and despair, screamed at the pilot that he was a traitor who had led the ship to destruction, and ran him through with a sword.

We know all this because the pilot's son came ashore on Coumeenole beach, the only survivor. He was taken to Dingle to be interrogated and tortured. Not surprisingly, he spun an impressive yarn about the many great noblemen who had been on board the *Santa Maria*, including the King of Spain's illegitimate son, the Prince of Ascoli. That was almost certainly a lie, but a young male body was found and buried in Dunquin, at what became known as the grave of the King of Spain's son. A small memorial of bronze and stone was planted there.

Were there people living on the Great Blasket who heard the cannon and saw the *Santa Maria* go down? Three other Spanish ships were sheltering in the Sound at the time, and one of the captains wrote in his diary that longboats were sent to the island to fetch spring water. This was the first ever written reference to anyone visiting the island, but he did not mention any natives. They may well have been hiding. The legend of the dead *señorita* offered the best evidence of their existence: if she really was washed up, as the oral tradition insisted, then someone must have been on the beach in 1588 to find and bury her. When children still lived on the island they frightened each other at night with the thought of her ghost rising up to chase them from the graveyard at Castle Point.

In daylight they were not so afraid of the place: it was there that they chased and fought each other instead, recreating the deeds of the one great Blasket hero, Piaras Feiritéar.

18

15 October 1653

The legend of Piaras Feiritéar ends on a hill east of Killarney. No fanfare, no pomp, no sack for the head of a killer bound for the gallows. Pierce Ferriter, as his English enemies know him, is a playboy, a poet, a warrior, a rebel, and a dead man alive on a cold early morning, with the mist wet on his beard.

After a hundred escapes, a thousand tales, the man of myth has only just entered his fourth decade. The last leader in Kerry to lay down his arms rocks on his heels, legs apart, easy. The soldiers avoid eye contact, keep their hands on their swords, and wonder again at the confidence of the man. He is not built like a fighter but like a lord, with rolling shoulders and a generous stomach. Is this the flashing blade of camp-fire renown?

He is here to die. A crowd has gathered under a distant tree, behind the falling leaves. The rope is around his neck. Horses stamp and blow out steam. The prayers of a minister whose religion Ferriter does not recognize are spoken without compassion to the empty hill and stolen by the wind. At this moment before death, the poet breathes deeply. The fear he is trying so hard to disguise forces air from his chest and it sounds like sudden laughter. The padre frowns. Ferriter laughs again, for real.

The block is pulled away. The rope swings. The rope stretches. The rope snaps.

Sheep run at the crack of it. Fallen on his arse in the mud, the winded poet wonders if his bones are broken. The soldiers feel the crack of a rope on their own backs as punishment for failure. Not this one, of all of them, for God's sake. They pull the poet to his feet as the hangman throws another length over the wooden gallows arm.

The hanging of Pierce Ferriter – playboy, poet, warrior, rebel, murderer, hero, thief – begins again. And fails again.

It takes a brave man to interrupt the cursing soldiers as they drag the prisoner away from the gallows and argue over his fate, but a brave man is present. He wears the cloth of an alien religion, but knows the executioner's law. If the rope breaks twice, the man goes free. There can be no argument. It is a matter of decency, without which we are all savages.

Exhalted, enraged, embarrassed, the poet does not feel the ropes slide from his wrists, which are raw to the bone. He raises filthy hands to his eyes, and his mouth burns. Under the tongue is a fragment of the Holy Wafer. It was true, then, what the priest promised: that in the final moments, when escape was gone, the Host would offer God's just protection. The Jesuit priest had dressed like a common labourer and had smuggled himself past the guard as morning broke, to whisper a last sacrament for his lord. A remnant, almost dissolved by saliva, remains behind his few black teeth.

The poet in Pierce does not hear the arguments, the fighter in him scarcely registers the shove in his back as the soldiers bring him down the hill, still under guard, fate undecided. They will not contradict a holy man: it is the padre's problem now, his punishment.

Ferriter has been ready for death for years, but he is not ready for this indignity. A red rage swarms behind the eyes, a curse on the minister, a roar at the sky. Whatever is or is not left of the sacrament is swallowed and the bile in his mouth discharged on to the sodden earth.

'I will never live to be called the leavings of a rope.'

They hang him again, despite the padre. This time the rope stays true.

19

Once, when the English cornered him on the Great Blasket, Piaras Feiritéar hid in a cave that could only be entered by a narrow stepping stone over a ravine, with the sea below. He fought the soldiers one by one, as they tried to cross, until all fifty were lying dead below. This feat of strength and bravery was an echo of the legend of Horatius, the Roman who single-handedly defended a narrow bridge across the Tiber by killing his massed enemies one at a time. Traders from the Mediterranean once sailed to western Ireland, and many Blasket tales seemed to owe something to Greek or Roman mythology – but then there have always been men like Piaras Feiritéar in every community: men, and women, whose lives have become legend, the truth of their days cloaked in layers of myth and fantasy.

The story of Piaras's surrender to the hangman's noose testified to the magical power of religion, a powerful source of comfort to those persecuted for their faith. The manner of his dying, with its messianic overtones, kept alive the ancient ideal of the noble warrior, who treasured honour above all. By the fireside, in the hedgerow schools, in bars and behind them, he was a symbol of resistance to English injustice. The maps of the time referred to the Blaskets as Ferriter's Islands, and Piaras was said to have taken refuge on them when his guerrilla warfare became too intense. On the Great Blasket he stood for the wit, cunning and ferocious independence of the islandman.

'When the chase was too near to him he had another place,

a cave in the hill that neither deer nor eagle could come at,' said Tomás Ó Criomhthain. Piaras' Cave, *Scairt Phiarais*, was impossible to find without an island guide, as it lay at the bottom of the steep and sudden drop at Fatal Cliff. There the poet-chieftain was covered by 'a great wide flagstone' with a hole in the middle, from which dripped spring water. Hidden from his enemies by the rock, Feiritéar composed a verse that sang like the words of the psalmist before him.

> *Hast Thou no pity, O God, that I lie this way,*
> *Lonely and cold, and hardly I see the day;*
> *The drip from the heart of the stone never stilled in my ear,*
> *And the voice of the sea at my feet ever echoing near?*

The settlers in Tralee thought of Dingle as the last outpost, where the people were strange, dirty and savage; but the men and women of Dingle town reserved their own suspicion for those who lived over the mountains at the end of the peninsula. The English dominated Kerry for three centuries, using violence to suppress language, religion and culture, but they never quite managed to control the wild tip of Corkaguiney. That was where the poor and the desperate went, the people who would not cooperate with their invaders. They were scorned as ignorant, these Gaelic communities, although their knowledge and traditions were handed down through the years of persecution, by illegal schools held in secret places. Landless peasants could recite classical legends and poetry, discuss the history of their nation, or name the stars.

'As far back as Coumeenole' was a saying that meant something was hopeless, as far gone as it was possible to be, but a few miles even further west than that was an island with seals, seabirds and their eggs to be eaten, seaweed on the beach and fish in the surrounding waters. The island was difficult to get to, but easy to defend against land agents, whose attempts to collect rent were repelled by throwing stones down on them from the cliff above the landing slip. By 1821 there were 128 people living on the Great Blasket.

Most of them had been evicted from their homes on the mainland by Lord Ventry and his agents, including a couple from the actual parish of Ventry, the bay on the other side of Mount Eagle. They were called Ó Cearna, a name found throughout Ireland, but their origins were probably in County Mayo, where the tribe was called after the Irish word *cearnach*, meaning 'victorious'. The other dispossessed families that looked to the island for a new start included Ó Guithín (Guheen in its anglicized form); Ó Dhuinnshléibhe (Dunleavy); Ó Séaghdha (Shea); Ó Criomhthain (Crohan); Ó Conchúbhair (Connor); Ó Shuilleabháin (Sullivan); and Ó Catháin (Keane).

Some of the Ó Guithín family chose to live on Inis Icíleaín, the most southerly island of the group, in a single house that held eight people. A visitor to the island in the mid-nineteenth century wrote that while it was systematically farmed, and sheep were sent there to be fattened up, the living was not always easy.

During one stormy season their fire went out, and, not having the means of relighting it, they were reduced almost to starvation; they, however, supported life for a period of two months by the use of sheep's milk alone.

The Ó Guithín were lucky: they survived, for a while, before giving the island over to the Dálaigh family when one of their men drowned. On Inis Tuaisceart, the north island shaped like a slain warrior, something horrifying was about to happen.

20

Autumn 1848

The worst of the wind has gone now, and the black clouds have moved on. Weak autumn sunshine falls on the stone-grey sea swelling around the smack as it slides in over the water towards the rocks of Inis Tuaisceart. Black-backed gulls dive around the cliffs that cast a shadow over the boat, and the puffins burst from their nests overhead in an agitated swarm. Six weeks of bad weather have prevented anyone from Dunquin or the Great Blasket from visiting this island, where their sheep graze, and the three men now coming ashore are worried. A month ago smoke was seen rising from a beacon on the broad back of the Inis, the signal of distress. Since then, nothing. Not even a wisp from the hearth in the stone cell occupied by Tomás Ó Catháin and his wife Peig, the only inhabitants of the Sleeping Giant.

The climb up the slippery wet black rocks is awkward and slow. The boots of the boatmen slide from under them, despite the nails on their soles, and their heavy, salt-stained trousers are wet through. Animals brought here to be fattened up are hauled skywards on ropes, but breathless humans have to make their own way up to where the turf flattens out, high above the sea. Calling out for Tomás and Peig, the three men pick out a path over the uneven turf, which is covered in rich green pasture sodden with rain and dew. Some way ahead of them is what looks like a circular grass mound, studded with flint. It is actually the Ó Catháin home, an ancient *clochán*, built of unmortared flagstones which have been layered to form a dome over a hollow in the ground, with a hole in the roof for the smoke to escape. The monks who built it a thousand years ago knew that the only way to find shelter from the merciless winds that drove across the flat top of the island was to huddle into the damp earth.

There is no response to the call of the boatmen as they approach the *clochán*. A few sheep bleat. The ghost of a bitch lifts its head to whine, then goes back to tearing at something in the grass. When the first man bends to comfort her with a pat on the head he sees what it is she is chewing, and an involuntary force tears out the contents of his stomach. The remains of a human arm.

A second man has reached the entrance of the shelter, and cannot believe the stench that is coming from it. Whether from cold or fear, he is trembling as his eyes adjust to the darkness. The fire has been dead a long time. There is nothing here but a bundle of blankets. And from under them he hears a whimper, a moan, an inhuman sound. Two eyes stare up at him, and there is madness in them. A skeletal woman, barely breathing, but alive. Now he realizes that the overpowering stench is coming from beside her, where lies her dead husband, limbless.

It is a very long time before Peig recovers her health and her senses, nursed back to her true self on the Great Blasket. Then, one day, without warning, she begins to talk about what happened. The bad weather seemed to last for ever, she says. With the fire alight and the sheep around, she and her husband were confident of surviving until the next supply boat could come, as they had done before. Then Tomás got sick, and after a while he died. He was a big man, strong and burly, and heavy. Weakened by illness and hunger, she did not have enough strength to lift his corpse by the shoulders and drag it up the steep steps of the *clochán* to the outside. So, for long days and nights, she lay by the body as it decomposed. Eventually the sight and smell of it became intolerable. Crazy with grief and suffering, she tore pieces from the decaying man and threw them away, one at a time, through the smoke hole. After the first burst of insane passion had ebbed away, she could not finish the task. So she lay down exhausted and waited to die.

This is the story she tells a man from the Royal Academy in Dublin, Mr Du Noyer, when he visits the Great Blasket a decade later, and it becomes the official version of the tragedy of Inis Tuaisceart. There are others. One night in Kruger's, an old man tells it all again to a stranger, while his pint settles. At first the stranger, who is an Englishman, doesn't fully understand what has been said. Then he doubts its sincerity, wonders if he's missing a joke. But as the old man sips through the creamy head, his green eyes fix on those of the stranger, and he repeats the words: "Twas the wife herself that ate him.'

21

Ireland was full of horror stories during the Great Hunger, but very few of them were told, for shame. Walking skeletons filled the towns and villages, begging for help. Season after season the potatoes they were forced to depend on for food turned out to be rotten and black, and exploded in a stinking mess when cut with the shovel. The survivors tried to forget what it was like to watch a grown man eating grass on his knees in desperation, a baby suckling at a dead mother's breast, or a cottage in flames with the diseased half-alive inside.

A million Irish peasants died in the four years to 1849. Some starved, others were killed by scurvy, typhoid or fever. Meanwhile, food and livestock worth fifteen million pounds were being produced in their own country, but shipped abroad to be eaten in England and its empire. As the suffering spread and the poor could not afford to pay the rent on their tiny plots, landlords chose to use the land as pasture for cattle instead. Their agents drove the starving away, often by burning down their homes. The more generous paid for tenants to be sent to America, on squalid vessels, without means of support on the far shore. Many passengers died on the way. Other families went as indentured servants, granted passage in return for a period of service on terms that resembled slavery. Some picked up their pitiful belongings and their famished children and walked west, looking for more fertile land. This heart-breaking search took them all the way to the coast. People were dying there too.

When a census was taken in 1841, there were ten separate

townships in the valley of Dunquin, with a total population of 1,394. The Famine killed or drove away half of them. One settlement was razed by fire and its ruins shunned because of the disease that had wiped out its people. After ten years of hunger, sickness and emigration, the community was down to 722, and still falling. By the time I reached Dunquin there were less than 150 permanent residents in the valley. The tragedy had left permanent scars on the landscape, like the field markings high up on the slopes of Mount Eagle, which betrayed desperate and useless attempts to find soil that would produce something, anything, to eat; like the scratch marks left on a riverbank by a drowning man.

Nobody died of starvation on the Great Blasket, or so it was said. The census figures question that tradition, showing a decline from 153 inhabitants to ninety-seven in the ten years from 1841. It was true, however, that the islanders did not suffer as badly as their friends and relatives on the mainland. There were two reasons for that great mercy: the missionary, and the shipwreck.

The first Protestant missionary that was ever sent to the Great Blasket ran away again when the islanders threatened to throw him over a cliff. The second saved lives, but got no thanks. Both were employees of the Dingle and Ventry Mission, financed by donations from the Irish Society of London and active throughout the peninsula, where its aggressive pros- elytizing caused a great stink. A Roman Catholic curate who converted was paraded through Dingle one Sunday morning, just as the crowds were spilling out of Mass. The police, the marines and the coastguards all turned out to protect him, in a stand-off described in the newspapers of the day as the 'Dingle Riots', although not a punch was thrown.

Having frightened the first man off, the islanders had a

change of heart. In 1838, they asked the Mission to send someone who could teach their children to read and write Irish. The school was opened in 1840 by Mrs Thompson, the wife of Lord Ventry's land agent and the Mission's greatest fundraiser. After the trip, this formidable but scrupulously civilized lady reported that human nature had been 'reduced to a savage state' in that isolated place. A crowd of women and children had squatted on the floor around her chewing seaweed, 'of which they pressed the long strings into their mouths with their thumbs in a most savage manner, and spat about unceremoniously at will'.

The bare-footed women were fascinated by Mrs Thompson's appearance; the parlour fashions of Dublin, or even Dingle, were alien to the island.

They touched my dress, turned me round and round to look at every separate article, laughed with admiration at my shoes and gloves, kissed and stroked my old silk gown, repeating 'Bragh!, Bragh!', 'nice, nice!', though the reader may believe I did not wear anything very handsome on such an expedition.

When the Famine began, a deal was struck — soup and corn were offered to children whose parents were willing to renounce the evils of Catholicism. Within a year there were fifty-six boys and girls attending the school. The Mission's annual report for 1848 claimed that ten families had become Protestant, a figure representing the entire island community, or close to it. So many children asked for food that the missionary, James Jordan, had to use his own personal store to feed them. He introduced money to the island by paying the adults to improve the landing slip, but took it off them again as rent for farmable land. Seeds were given out free.

Then something strange happened: Jordan's life on the

island fell apart, and very quickly. Within two years he was reporting back to London that the school, the breakwater constructed with Mission money, and his own house were all falling into disrepair. There was no mention of any pupils. His salary was the biggest item of expenditure in 1850, since the islanders were no longer willing to receive his charity. All but one of the families had returned to Catholicism.

The explanation for this mystery, the catalyst for Jordan's fall from favour, was the other reason why the people of the Great Blasket survived the Famine years: they were released from hunger and the shame of taking Protestant hand-outs by a series of shipwrecks.

The *Commerce*, a three-masted ship from Liverpool, sprang a leak at sea on 3 April 1850, and was abandoned just behind the island. The crew made it to the mainland in a longboat, but their cargo of palm oil from West Africa was lifted on the waves. Tomás Ó Criomhthain, a young boy at the time, remembered it as valuable stuff which could be traded on the mainland for corn. 'Those were bad years, and if it hadn't been for that shipwreck, nobody would have survived on the Island. I often heard with my own ears the old hag over the way saying that God Himself sent that ship amongst the poor.'

Coastguards arrived to retrieve the cargo, but gave up when a young island woman threw a jagged piece of rock through the bottom of their boat.

On 19 November that same year, the Genoan brig *Caroline* was driven aground just off the White Strand and split in half. She was bound for Falmouth in England, full of wheat, but the crates got loose from the hold and were seized by a grateful crowd of onlookers. James Jordan wrote back to London that the locals had lost interest in helping the crew when the ship spilled its contents. Nine sailors had come ashore 'naked and distracted', but most of the islanders refused to let them into their houses, he said. Only the missionary himself and two other men by the names of Ó Cearna and Ó Séaghdha were prepared to give shelter and comfort.

At an inquest in Coumeenole a month later, the coroner, who was called Justin Supple, condemned the locals for 'barbarity and inhumanity, not only in the stripping of the corpses of the wretched remnant of the clothes that remained on them after being for days tossed about on the angry billows, but then burying them like dogs in a hole, without shroud or coffin.' Jordan must have given evidence to the inquest, and if his public testimony was as damning as the words he had already written in his annual report then the islanders would have been mortified. His mission to them was finished. The following year the school was closed down, and James Jordan left for good.

The Famine was followed by years of plenty, as the islanders learned to take full advantage of the bountiful waters around their home. Eight-man smacks were abandoned in favour of the shallow canoes called *naomhóga* that needed only a crew of three. Lines could be trawled from them for large fish like halibut and cod, while nets were set for wrasse, bream, and the most plentiful catch of all, the mackerel. It was hard work which often lasted all night, with the danger of swelling seas and nets catching on the rocks, but the high prices paid by traders in Dingle and Dunquin made it worth the trouble.

Everyone worked for each other, since it would have been impossible to manage alone, and returning boat crews had a way of dividing up the spoils which guaranteed fairness. The fish were sorted into portions, then one man turned his back so that he could not see them. His companion pointed to one pile and asked, 'Who is this for?' The man who was looking away named a member of the crew, who kept the pile.

Any fish not sold or eaten immediately were packed into barrels for the leaner months. They had to do that anyway with *ballach* – which had fins that pierced the skin if rubbed the wrong way – because it tasted watery when cooked fresh. After splitting the fish with a sharpened blade from a pair of shears, the islanders would gut each one, leave it in salt for a couple of weeks, then lay it out on the roof of the house to dry in the sun. When winter came, the stiff yellow fillets were soaked in water to remove some of the salt, then boiled and eaten with potatoes and milk.

The bed of the Sound was full of lobsters, but the islanders had no taste for their flesh, although the fishermen sometimes scooped up lobster roe and swallowed it while working. They were amazed that boats from the mainland started putting down lobster-pots, but soon learned how to bring in this particular harvest when they were told how much was being paid for it. Shellfish were easy to find at the shoreline, storm petrels and puffins could be caught and roasted. Life was so easy that islandmen gave up hunting for seals with clubs, although the meat had always been a delicacy, the skins were used as rugs, and seal oil was thought to be medicinal. It was also a source of light, before paraffin, in lamps made with a shell and a cotton wick.

The shipwrecks which had saved the Great Blasket from the worst of the Famine also introduced the island's people to more refined tastes, such as tea, which was a puzzle to them at first. It did not take long for the islanders to become addicted, and soon their twice-daily meal of fish and potatoes was supplemented with bread and tea in the morning and late afternoon. Otherwise they drank watered-down milk to quench a thirst, or porter brought over from the mainland in barrels. When the police took exception to one family selling porter on the island without a licence, the rest of the people took to smuggling it over in sacks. If the priest, during one of his rare visits, ever questioned the amount of drink on the island, he was left in no doubt that the bottles of whiskey and brandy were kept for medicinal purposes only. The truth was that whiskey warmed up the fishermen after a long night in their boats, while porter strengthened the children's bones, kept them going when there was no food to put on the table, and helped them sleep if it was heated and sweetened with sugar before bed.

Island life continued to change as the fishermen went to market in Dingle more often, and earned more money. They had to spend it on something, and shopkeepers in town were ready to tempt them with luxuries like sugar, flour, cutlery and crockery, which then became necessities. By the first decade of the twentieth century the refugee families who had fled across the Sound were members of a strong community which traded with the outside world on its own terms. They were ready to receive visitors.

One fine day in August 1905, a *naomhóg* crossed the Blasket Sound carrying a neat young man with a moustache, in a woollen suit. John Millington Synge, a 34-year-old graduate of the Royal Irish Academy, was a friend of the poet William Butler Yeats and had accepted the older man's advice to study what remained of the Irish language and culture in the most distant parts of the country. Synge had already spent five summers on the Aran Islands and written three plays. He could speak Irish, but considered it his work to reflect the poetry and attitudes of the peasantry in a lyrical new pattern of English.

His host was Pádraig Ó Catháin, the man known as King of the Island, who steered the *naomhóg* from Dunquin, carried the visitor's bags up from the harbour as all the island watched and their 'white, wolfish dogs' barked, then turned on his heels to welcome Synge to his home with a handshake and a speech. Ó Catháin wore no crown, he certainly didn't live in a palace, and his title was more of a nickname than a divine appointment. Most of the men on the island had a nickname, and his was handed down in tribute to a strong and impressive grandfather. Certain duties had attached themselves to the name, however, and it was his task to cross to Dunquin twice a week, if the weather allowed, to collect and send letters at the post office. The King brought a newspaper back with him every time, and the men of the island gathered in the house known as *An Dáil*, the Parliament, to hear the news read to them and to discuss it afterwards.

Ó Catháin was first among the informal panel of elders on the island and acted as a judge in disputes. Although everyone was supposed to be equal in the community, its justice could be rough, as a man called Moore found out when he failed to control a horse which was persistently annoying the neighbours by eating their vegetables. Although a horse was a rare and expensive animal, and presumably an important part of Moore's livelihood, he woke up one morning to find that it had been pushed over a cliff.

Youngsters were allowed to go courting, as they called it, on the quiet slopes at the back of the island, as long as they weren't too closely related and were prepared to take the consequences. As far as the elders were concerned, that meant marriage, unless one of the old women had another remedy. Finally, the King acted as the island's spokesman on the mainland, and when visitors came it was he who welcomed them and offered a bed.

Synge was more impressed with the King's twenty-year-old daughter, Máire, who was 'a small, beautifully formed woman with brown hair and eyes – instead of the black hair and blue eyes that are usually found with this type in Ireland – and delicate feet and ankles that are not common in these parts, where the woman's work is so hard'. Máire began making tea in a metal teapot and frying rashers of bacon 'without asking if we were hungry', an observation which caused the islanders great offence when it was published. Hospitality to strangers was one of the highest duties, and criticizing their hospitality – however mildly – one of the greatest sins. For years after, the Princess, as Máire was called, would protest that the house had curtains from America, so there was no need to tie her apron at the window as Synge had described in his book.

That night, the visitor shared a room with the King and his son. When they woke at six in the morning there was whiskey for breakfast, with a pipe of tobacco, and Synge washed in water from a pan which had been used to knead dough. He dried himself with a towel used by the whole family. Later he showed Máire photographs of families on the Aran Islands.

As she put her hands on my shoulders, and leaned over to look at them, with the confidence that is so usual in these places, I could see that she had her full share of the passion for children which is powerful in all women who are permanently and profoundly attractive.

Back in Dublin, Synge fantasized about spending his days in the house of the King, listening to stories, playing the fiddle and watching the young women dance, but it did not happen. He died before he had even turned forty. When the diary of his trip to Wicklow and West Kerry was published in 1911, it helped to establish the Great Blasket's reputation as a place where the old ways and language were preserved. Many visitors followed, including Carl Mastrander, known as the Viking, a scholar and athlete who declined to compete in the Olympics so that he could spend the summer studying Irish on the island,

and who vaulted over a house using an oar; Robin Flower, his pupil, who laboured alongside the islandmen on new houses and wrote *The Western Island*, a masterpiece; and Brian Ó Ceallaigh of Trinity College, Dublin, who gave the old storyteller Tomás Ó Criomhthain translations of books by Pierre Loti and Maxim Gorky about the lives of peasants in Iceland and Russia, and encouraged him to keep his own journal. The results were *Island Cross-Talk*, published in 1928, and *The Islandman*, which came out the following year. These important works, the first to emerge from an oral Gaelic culture, were enthusiastically received by followers of the Irish language revival in more fashionable parts of Ireland.

Tomás was such a poetic writer that sometimes the English reader could only guess what he really meant. In a chapter called 'My Manhood', he said the girls on the island were 'next door to being half wild', and described how six of them, who were 'just about beginning to ripen, running over with high spirits', had set upon him on the hill as he finished cutting turf. Tomás was young at the time, and what they did may have been some kind of initiation, although he gave no indication that it was unusual among the young people. He certainly enjoyed himself. 'There was many a young man of my own kind who'd rather have them playing their games with him than all the turf on the hills.' It happened again, soon afterwards, at the end of another hard day.

There wasn't one of the six, if I had given her the wink, that wouldn't have gone with me ready and willing for the knot there's no untying; but whoever I had my eye on in those days, it wasn't any one of those six. Never mind – it would do me no great harm to have a bit of fun with them, and I had it all right. If I felt any weariness, it left me then, for those six went for one another again and again, and no sooner were they up than they'd be down again, one overturning the other, and the same with me too. It's long I remembered that afternoon; I remember it still.

As for marriage, his eye was on one of the five daughters of the Dálaigh family that lived on Inis Icíleaín. He found it hard to leave that island after a visit because 'I was leaving behind me the merriest days I had ever known, and, into the bargain, I was turning my back on the girl I liked best in the whole blessed world right then.'

A match was proposed and his Uncle Diarmid worked as the *spéicéirí* or go-between in the delicate negotiations between families which preceded every marriage. The deal was all but done when Máire, his sister, opposed it on the grounds that he would do better to marry into another Great Blasket family who could be on hand to help when times were hard. This argument carried the day, and in the last week of Shrovetide, when weddings traditionally took place, Tomás married his second cousin, Máire Ní Chatháin. Although he never said a word against his wife, Tomás was upset at not being allowed to marry his sweetheart. At the wedding celebration, this man who was usually full of entertainment chose to sing just one song. It was a lament for the broken-hearted.

Tomás and Máire had five sons and two daughters, but their life together was full of sadness. Sickness and death were not unusual on the island, where the only medicine was ancient remedies that did not always work. Tea was made from nettles to improve digestion or dandelions for the kidneys, while camomile was used to make shampoo and to treat epilepsy. Nothing could prevent the whooping-cough epidemic which killed two of the Ó Criomhthain children, and Máire herself died soon afterwards. One son was killed while trying to catch gulls, another drowned in a swimming accident which also killed Eveleen Nicholls, girlfriend of the republican leader

Patrick Pearse. Their joint funeral was the largest ever seen in Dunquin. Yet another son fell while carrying a *naomhóg* and died from his injuries. The youngest daughter did not survive the birth of her seventh child. The youngest boy emigrated to America, leaving Tomás with one son living on the island, Seán Ó Críomhthain, who eventually moved to the mainland and lived in a house near Céit Ní Cearna.

'Such was the fate of my children,' wrote Tomás in the *Islandman*. 'May God's blessing be with them, and with the poor woman whose heart broke for them.' His most famous and most prescient phrase came at the end of the book, when Tomás said he had written everything down as a record because 'the like of us will never be again'. Fleets of trawlers appeared in the Sound, catching far more than the Blasket *naomhóga* could manage. After the Great War the Americans imposed a tariff on all imported mackerel, which caused the market in Dingle to collapse. Prices fell, there were too many fish, the Blasket islanders couldn't get theirs to town quick enough to take advantage of the demand for fresh rather than salted mackerel. The fish themselves then started to become scarce. The fisherman's way of life was over, and there were not many alternatives but to leave. Many of the island girls chose to accept proposals from the boys of Dunquin and other mainland villages who crossed the Sound on summer Sundays to dance. Others had their eye on America.

The wanderer Seán Team had just come back from there, and married Neilí. When she gave birth to her first child Céit in 1919, the island was still well populated, but the exodus had already begun.

Some people had a keen sense of what was happening. Seán Fada, one of the great island storytellers who did not write a famous memoir, told Robin Flower that his memory for tales had almost gone. 'It is Tomás that has done it, for he has books and newspapers, and he reads them to me; and the little tales, one after another, day after day, in the books and newspapers, have driven the old stories out of my head.'

Some of those stories survived because they went west with the emigrants. The further from home they travelled, the more important they became. The teller and those who listened were drawn back to the island, remembering the first time they heard the tale; the tingle in their scalp that night, and the faces of their friends in the firelight. Stories often went with music. Sometimes a fiddler would pause before taking up his bow and tell his listeners how the tune he was about to play came into being, long ago, in that faraway place. The most famous, the one people asked for when they knew a musician came from the island, was the haunting tune called *Port na bPúcaí*, 'The Faerie's Lament'.

22

One Night in the Late 1800s

This is the story of the Faerie's Lament.

Up late with the dying fire, the woman asleep, the wind fussing around, above and beyond, at first he does not notice the sound. Warm in the stone home, high on the back of the southern Inis. The only man on Inis Icíleaín. Nothing through the small, deep-set window but the night, and black it is. Nothing to see, nothing to hear but the fizz of the dying fire, the woman's breath, the wind. And the slow tune he plays for himself, and for her, in this lonesome place, the bow rubbing one string at a time. Angels weeping, the sound of it. Calling.

At first he does not notice the other sound, in the wind, above and beyond. Then it comes, a cold hand on his neck. Outside, in the night, behind the glass, unseen, but heard: a female voice. One long mournful note, then a falling, twisting refrain like the wringing of hands, or a wandering mind. Climbing, climbing, seeking rest, then tumbling down; a cry of bereavement, sorrow, loss. It blows away, on the wind, and he holds his breath until it returns, at first barely, then beside him in the room, as though being sung for this man, in this place, and no one else, ever.

Every part of him is turned to the wall, to the window, although he does not move. Every cell that can hear is straining to do so. He has become a human instrument, ringing with the pure, clear sound. Over and over the song is sung, wordless and wonderful, until the fiddler's arms unfreeze and his fingers feel for the bow. Breathless and alive, he pulls notes from the air – now following, now anticipating the flight of the melody as it glides, then beats its wings, then glides again, in the night and in the room with him, without and within. Again. Again. Until the night begins to lift, and light falls in the scattered raindrops of dawn, and the music grows faint. And stops.

He has it now, in his mind. All through the commonplace struggles of daytime, the common life of man and woman tending sheep on an island, the tune does not leave him. He will not let it. Late in the evening, when the fire is covered and the woman sleeps again, the fiddler shoulders his instrument and plays, hoping that the singer will return.

She never does. One night, back on the great island, he plays the tune and tells how it came to him, embroidering the detail and relishing the attention. Others memorize the melody, take it to the mainland and conjure their own accounts of its origin. One says it was a woman sitting on a stone who heard it first, another that the melody came to an old couple asleep in their bed. There are words, says a third. They do not fit the tune, but this is spirit music, sung by a tongue that had been silent for too long.

I am a woman who has come to you from among the faerie people, who has come by wind and wave. It was by night that I was stolen far away, to live with them. I am wandering this earth again by the grace of faerie women, but it is only for a time. When the cock crows I must leave this world behind, in sorrow.

The tune becomes famous: first in Dunquin, then the peninsula, then Ireland. It is passed on, as these things are, from player to player, session to session, bar to bar, country to country, wherever the Irish gather. It crosses the Atlantic and is recorded by many people; and every time, the tune is a little different, the phrasing changes, the story evolves. The poet Seamus Heaney links the spirit song with the mighty rushing wind of Pentecost and the big music that Rilke heard in the storm, and writes a poem called 'The Given Note'. The tune becomes known as *Port na bPúcaí*, the sound of a spirit mourning the death of another as it is carried for burial behind the impenetrable wall of rocks on that island in the west. Perhaps it is really the sound of a seal weeping in a cove. Or the cry of a hump-backed whale in a school moving under canvas boats. Or, as Robin Flower writes in *The Western Island*, 'a lament for a whole world of imaginations, banished irrevocably now'.

23

If you want to know what it was really like, people said, talk to Seán and Muiris. The elderly brothers lived in a cottage behind hydrangea bushes at the crossroads of *Baile na Rátha* in the valley of Dunquin, within constant sight of the island that was once their home. These two men, whose names were seldom mentioned separately, were born on the Great Blasket when the place was full and the life relatively comfortable, and they stayed until it became unbearable. Seán and Muiris had known Seáinín, and gone to school with his brothers, but they chose never to look for the Land of Youth. As the end of the twentieth century approached, there were only a handful of original islanders still alive at the end of the peninsula, and few were prepared or able to talk about their lives to a stranger. They were the last of the brood, the ones who did not change; and when they died, the last traces of their world of imagination really would be gone for good.

Behind the blooms was a simple cottage, with a curl of smoke coming from the chimney. A black and white cat slunk out of the bushes, padded up the path and waited by the door. The key was in the lock, but it didn't seem right to walk straight in. Fionnán, a young man from the parish who knew the brothers well and had agreed to act as translator, tapped on the window. The room inside was dark, and impossible to see through the old net curtains.

The door opened. '*Conás tá tú?*' The speaker was a small, thin man with a long bulbous nose and startled eyes.

'*Go maith,*' said Fionnán. '*Conás tá tú féin?*'

Muiris Ó Guithín was apparently as well as could be expected, and glad to see a bit of company. He seemed fit for a heavy smoker of seventy-nine, and walked lightly as though on tiptoe, with rounded shoulders. He shook my hand, then shook his head at my clumsy Irish, a grin splitting a face dusted with white stubble.

Muiris led us into the main room of the house, where his brother was sitting on one side of the hearth. Seán rose to greet us, transferring the stub of a filterless cigarette from one shovel hand to the other. He was a big man, with a big, broad face and a tar-deep voice. In his youth, Muiris must have been naughty, nippy, a bit of a rogue, but Seán was five years older, and very much the big brother. Not slow, but solid. When their father died, Seán was just twelve. He became the man of the house. Authority lived in the many folds of his face, and warmth too.

The room was large, with a stone floor and a high ceiling from which the blistered, nicotine-yellow paint was peeling. In the half-light I could see that it was like all the old island homes, with the addition of a small stove in the corner with a gas bottle. A long wooden bench ran along one wall, underneath the window we had tried to peer through. Against the opposite wall was a formica dining-table with wooden chairs, and above it, on a shelf, a plaster statue of the Virgin Mary. A curled print of the Sacred Heart was nearby, and under it a small candle burning in a red glass.

My eyes were drawn to the hearth. Three of the plastered walls were off-white, but the chimney breast was fire-engine red. A little shelf for ornaments or icons displayed a white plastic bottle of salt. The stone fireplace had been painted the same swimming-pool blue that brightened the bench, a cupboard door in the alcove, a tall dresser hung with crockery, and every other piece of wooden furniture in sight.

Seán sat back down on one side of the fire in an old office armchair with a black metal frame and leatherette cushion. Muiris was on the right, on a simple wooden stool. Both men wore cloth caps darkened and shiny with use, island jerseys with the zip at the neck and straight flannel trousers with heavy leather boots. Their hands made shapes in the air as they told us about the games they used to play on the island as children, and their mischievous smiles were accompanied by wheezy giggles. Life had been hard for these two, who had stayed until the very end and never found women to marry, but they knew how to laugh.

Through the window behind Seán's head I could just see the island in the distance. On the wall behind Muiris was a map of it, with the place-names in Irish. It was based on information they had supplied, and their portrait was on the map, a popular seller in the tourist shops of Dingle. Listening to them talk as we sat by the fire, I knew that many other visitors had been there before me, exchanging whiskey and cigarettes for a few tales about the old life. Seán insisted that they never got bored with the subject.

'I love telling stories about the island,' he said in Irish. 'There was great sport there. We thought at that time, when we were growing up, that it was the nicest place in the world, because we didn't have experience of anywhere else.'

Still, life on the island was never easy. 'As you would say, a lot of work followed it. Hard work: going to sea and fishing and then going to Dunquin in winter for messages when there was bad weather. There was another thing – when you would be sowing potatoes and oats and the like, there was no plough there, save for the spade, shovel and a fork. That was the plough we had.

'You couldn't do anything on your own. If you were going to get food, for example, you'd need somebody else to help you put a *naomhóg* down on the water. We were very dependent on each other, yes we were. For certain things, especially with animals – for example, if a sheep went down a cliff, say – you'd have to depend on me to go with you, and the same the other way.'

In December 1953, a month after the official evacuation, Seán and Muiris returned to the island with friends to round up the rams they had left behind. 'The weather broke, so we stayed in the island for Christmas Eve and Christmas Day and the Wren Day. We had no lamp, that had already been brought to Dunquin, and the paraffin. Do you know what we did? We had wax from slabs that had been washed up on the shore so we melted that into a vessel, and used a little cotton as a wick. That was the light we had, and that was the poor light!'

The brothers had known for a long time that their only hope of a secure future was to persuade the government to help them resettle on the mainland. They were two of the four signatories who wrote to the *Irish Independent* in 1952 appealing for the remaining people on the Great Blasket to be 'released from our island fortress'. When that did finally happen, they felt an unexpected sadness, tempered by the need to return to shear the flock in summer. 'We had one consolation: it was very close, the island. You could go to the gate every morning and see it.' They still looked west first thing every morning, without fail, although age and infirmity meant they would never return. 'We used to go in the first week in June. We'd go in Monday and we'd come out on Saturday. Then we'd go in again on Monday. We'd spend three or sometimes four weeks doing that until all the sheep had been sheared. We'd all be helping each other, you understand, that's why it took so long. That's how we used to have it.'

Seán had been doing all the talking, so I asked Muiris if he had any memories of that time. 'The same memories as he has.'

'That was the end,' said Seán.

'You'd feel it,' said Muiris. 'Lonely. When you'd think of the great times we had in there during our youth. Back then, you wouldn't feel any hardship until the winter.'

'It was good from St Patrick's Day till Christmas time,' said Seán, thinking of the days when the island community was still vibrant. 'There wasn't any day that a *naomhóg* wouldn't go into Dunquin if the weather was good. But from Christmas time on, it wasn't too good at all.'

To entertain themselves through the long winter nights, the islanders played chess or draughts, and card games like High-Low Jack, which had been brought back from America. Then there was *poiríní*. 'There were five small rounded pebbles and they'd be on the ground,' said Seán. 'You'd have to take one, throw it up in the air and try and pick up the other four. Somebody else would have a go then. There were a lot of tricks involved in *poiríní* – you'd put one pebble here, and another there, and you'd have to take the three in one go. There was great sport involved in that. *Arra*, they had a lot of games – if you'd call them games. There was one, what would you call it . . .'

'They'd be throwing stones as weights,' said Muiris.

'No, what's the name of that other one again?'

I was listening to a routine, established by repetition over the years.

'*Máthair an áil*, Mother Goose.'

'*Máthair an áil*, exactly. You'd be there with your two hands outstretched and a girl tied to you, and somebody else tied to her, and so on. Another person would be trying to catch one of them and you'd be turning around with the group.'

'Then they had the blindman,' said Muiris. 'You'd put

something over your eyes, and you'd be after the rest of the group, here and there.'

While the adults were in *An Dáil* on winter nights, the younger ones went to Peig Sayers' old house, which was occupied by her daughter Neilí. Both groups told stories and sang songs like *Fáinne Geal an Lae*, 'The Bright Ring of Day', and *Raghadsa agus mo Chaití ag bháleaeireacht*, 'Myself and My Katie Will Go A-Rambling'.

'They also had a gramophone. It was quite late, around the time of the war.' I thought of Céit Ní Cearna, who had just returned from a session like that when she found her brother dead.

'There were certain houses you would go more often of course because you'd be friendly with the household,' said Seán. 'You wouldn't find a lock on any door. You'd just walk in, you wouldn't even rap on the door.'

One of the games they played involved balancing the hearth tongs on their ends so that they stood up straight without support. Seán picked them up as we sat in a half-circle around the fire, and each man tried it, but the pitted stone floor made the trick impossible. Surely no one had ever actually done it? Seán had just opened his mouth to answer when he noticed the tongs balanced at Fionnán's feet. There was astonished silence as we watched them stand unsupported for half a minute or more.

'Well,' said Muiris, chuckling with his brother, 'you must be the man who is blessed.'

Every morning at opening time Seán and Muiris wandered a couple of hundred yards down the road for a glass of stout at Kruger's, where they settled on stalls in the corner of the bar. When there was a crowd, the younger villagers assembled in a protective circle around them, instinctively. This time the two old brothers insisted on buying us pints in honour of the trickery with the tongs. Muiris leant over and shouted into my ear that they used to have to walk five miles into Ballyferriter for a barrel of porter, then carry it down to the boats on their shoulders. As a result there was little porter on the island.

'We drank only water, from the spring,' he said. 'Better than whiskey or porter, the water there.'

Dunquin had changed a great deal since the day they first took possession of their new home, said Seán. 'Aren't there many houses built now that weren't there at that time? Do you see that road coming up here from our house that they call *Bóthar Chéilleachair*, Kelliher's Road?'

I did. The road was named after the man who had been in charge of building it. 'I remember when an aunt of mine was married, there was no house to be seen from the time you left the church until you went back to the post office [about half a mile away], on either side of the road. It used to be so dark at night when you'd be coming home.' The road was now lined with bungalows, and illuminated at night. 'It's a street now. We'll have to call it *Sráid Bhóthar Chéilleachair*, Kelliher's Road Street!' He found that idea most amusing.

In 1953, the roads were still mud and stones. 'Everyone had a horse and cart. We could be standing on the road and no car would come towards you.'

The exiled islanders found that the people of Dunquin had their own version of the common life, the *meitheal*, where neighbours combined to take in the harvest or do some other special job in return for nothing but a little food and drink. 'There used to be two horses ploughing in the spring – you'd have one and he'd have one – and you'd team up. You'd plough for you today, and for him tomorrow. Yes, they were dependent on each other.'

'And when they'd be making a haystack, there would be help,' said Muiris.

'Well, at that time it took a lot more help, the stack would be in the field. There was no tractor here at the time.'

The islanders had maintained a close relationship with the people of Dunquin, some of whom were their relatives. 'Sure, aren't they nearly the same people?' said Seán. 'We were depending on the people of Dunquin always. You'd have to stay over in bad weather.'

'When you'd come out in the boats the people of Dunquin would be on the cliff edge,' said Muiris.

'They'd tell you where the tide was breaking and where you should bring the boat in, that's if there was a swell or it was rough,' said his brother.

'And when Dunquin people would be fishing for mackerel they'd come into the island.'

The old cooperation had been replaced by what the brothers called the *mé féin* attitude, each person looking after himself first. 'That has come to the fore now,' said Seán, whose complaint was that of old men everywhere. 'Especially among the young people. Everybody is looking after his own concern. Ah, maybe, if you needed them, they would help you. But it's not like it was long ago.'

'They have everything themselves now,' said Muiris. 'They have tractors now.'

A few days later I went back to see Seán and Muiris again with a bottle of whiskey, which they accepted without fuss. They invited me to 'come up to the table' and share their supper, which was brown bread with butter and slices of ham, nd fruit bread. They both drank tea with a lot of sugar, in s, but mine was served in a cup and saucer.

ng the china down from the dresser, Seán showed me

four bowls painted with an oriental design. These, he said, were a hundred years old, and had been washed ashore. They were what the family used for drinking tea before they had cups. The previous day an American tour guide who had met the brothers and claimed to be their friend had told me that they possessed a teacup from the wreck of the *Lusitania*, which was sunk off the west coast of Ireland by a German submarine in 1915. When I asked about this, Seán unhooked a tiny cup made of the thinnest china, yellowed by age, with a blue line around the rim and a crack down the side. Yes, it had been washed ashore in a chest, with the rest of a set, in 1916. But there were no marks on the cup to link it with the *Lusitania*. The guide must have been mistaken. Clearly someone had thought it would make a good story.

While we were talking about the winter weather, a neighbour walked in, without knocking. He was a small man who must once have been wiry and muscular, but now he looked pale, and gasped for breath when he spoke. He picked up the whiskey bottle and turned it over in his hands, examining the label, but would not take a drop. 'I used to be an expert,' he said, and the look in his bloodshot eyes told me what he meant.

'You're writing a book then? Did I see you the other night? Now I have you.' Eddie had worked in Islington, thirty years earlier. He looked at the black iron pot hanging over the fire. 'We're in for a big feed.'

It was late in the afternoon, and the room was getting dark. There was no electric light in the house. Muiris told me that he had been in the same class as Mícheál Ó Cearna. They sat exams together that would have given them the chance to become teachers, but neither was sent up for training. Children from the island never were. Maybe that was because they spoke Irish, or because the priest decided who could go to training college and the mainland parents were more able to make donations towards the well-being of the parish. In any case, when Mícheál and their other friends and relations moved to America, or embraced all that a modernizing Ireland had to offer, Seán and Muiris kept exactly the same way of life as they had been used to on the island. They had no car, no television, no gas main, and not even electricity.

'It was too dear at first when we came out of the island,' said Seán. 'We stayed with the open fire, but ah, they have it a lot easier now than it was at that time. They aren't cutting any turf – they don't need it because they have central heating. They aren't doing any work now – unless there's any work I can do for you?' He laughed again, from deep within a barrel chest. 'Oh yes, there was hard work in Dunquin and the island one time, what with sheep and cattle and tilling.'

On the mainland, people had the luxury of a coalman who called to their homes. 'We were cutting turf for as long as we were able to. By God, if they're calling to the door you're paying dearly for it too! We're sorry now that we didn't put the electricity in at that time. We made a big mistake. It's not worth putting in now.' Why not? I asked. 'I suppose it's in the next life!'

'An open fire, a pot-belly,' said Muiris. I wasn't sure what he meant. 'The open fire is the heart of the house. In the island everything had to be cooked on it: the potatoes, the meat, the fish.'

'We boil chicken in it once a week, every Thursday,' said Seán. 'We used to bake bread in it twice a week.'

'And it was better bread than what's around today.'

'It was healthier. The food that is boiled is a lot better for you. We used to have shore food in the island: limpets, dilisk nd seaweed . . . and onions, rabbits, and lamb and sheep. And ' weren't getting any injections or anything.'

'ruger's I had noticed them glancing across to the

television at the far end of the bar. 'You would be happy with that all right,' said Seán. 'It would depend on the programmes. There are certain things on that would interest you, others wouldn't interest me at all. Life has improved greatly if you have the money. The money is a lot more plentiful now than it was.'

The brothers were good company, but they had told so many people about the Great Blasket over the years that their stories had become polished. The raw edges of life had been worn off by repetition. They could reminisce about games, or food, or other matters of historical record, but stonewalled any questions about drink on the island, or the sexual impropriety that must at least have been a possibility in such an isolated community, or even the possibility of anyone falling out. Talking to them through a translator also made things difficult. Although it was absolutely the right and respectful thing to do, and whoever was translating always had the best intentions, the subtleties of inflection and innuendo were lost.

There was, however, one more story that I wanted to hear from them. I knew that in the dying light of one cold afternoon in November 1940, the village had been fog-bound and still when there was a sudden, thunderous noise. A huge black shape came out of the mist and flew over the houses at a very low altitude, terrifying all who saw it. They had seen aircraft before, of course, but this was different: bigger, louder, with three engines screaming, and almost on top of them.

'She was a big one,' said Seán. 'She went down in Inis Icíleáin.'

'She was a sea plane,' said his brother quietly.

'I wonder, was she a sea plane? She had holes from some bullets that was fired at her – but anyhow, she went into the beach in Inis Icíleáin.'

The aircraft was actually a Blohm und Voss Bv138, a strange-looking beast with a hull like a boat and an extra propellor over the cockpit. The Luftwaffe had only been using them for a couple of months, and they were still pretty unreliable. German pilots called the plane the Flying Clog. There were bunks in the fuselage because the pilots usually stayed in the air for up to fifteen hours at a time, searching out enemy shipping and alerting any U-boats in the area to attack with torpedoes. This particular aircraft had left Brest in Northern France early that morning and headed west over the Atlantic, looking for merchant convoys on their way to Britain from America. Unfortunately, the crew had forgotten to have the fuel filters serviced after a long flight the previous day. On the way home, as they flew at fifteen hundred feet looking for landmarks, the engines began to stutter.

The pilot, Feldwebel Willie Krupp, managed to land in the sea near Inis Icíleaín, but as he taxied towards the island the waves damaged a float under one of the wings. There was no way they could take off again like that. The five men on board clambered into two rubber dinghies and landed on the island.

'They took whatever they had in her off,' said Seán. 'You know the pots for lobster fishing? There were piles of them on the beach. They took the tops off, put their stuff inside and brought it up to the house there.'

There was nobody else on Inis Icíleaín at the time, but the house used by the Dálaigh family when they dropped in to tend the sheep did contain some bags of flour and tins of condensed milk. The airmen used their pistols to kill rabbits. They lit a fire, which they hoped would attract the attention of whoever was on the Great Blasket. When no one had come to rescue them after three days, the commander, Oberleutnant Konrad Neymeyer, decided they would have to try and land on the larger island to make contact with its inhabitants.

'That day it was calm,' remembered Seán. 'They came in

two rubber dinghies – three in one boat and two in the other. A *naomhóg* from the island was out and saw them, went to the boat with the three people in it and brought them to *Caladh an Oileáin*, the island pier. They thought the other two would be coming, and they didn't know why they weren't.' Seán himself was out fishing in one of the island *naomhóga* that day. 'We went west towards Inis Tuaisceart and we didn't see any sight of them.'

Willie Krupp and his engineer, Oberfeldwebel Hans Biegel, had lost sight of their fellow crew members as they paddled the dinghy over thickening swells. The surf around the bottom of the cliffs on the north side of the island was ferocious, but somehow Biegel managed to jump safely from the boat on to the rocks, and threw a rope back to Krupp so that he could follow. The jagged black columns of *Faill an tSeabhaic*, the Hawk's Cliff, towered over them, wet and slippery, but Biegel was able to climb to the plateau several hundred feet above. Krupp lost his grip and his footing again and again, smashing a knee against the rockface as he tried. Using his pistol to get a hold here and there he made painfully slow progress, but finally got to the top, only to collapse, exhausted.

Krupp was found asleep in the heather next morning by two young men, Maidh Faight Ó Sé and Peaidí Ghobnait Ó Guithín, who were at the back of the island gathering turf. The pannier and bridle were removed from their donkey and the injured pilot slung over its back to be carried to the village.

'He was a doctor,' said Muiris, 'the other fellow who came up the cliff.'

'Later on a fishing vessel came up beside the beach, and a small boat came in and took the Germans out,' said Seán. He chose not to mention that it was several days before the airmen were taken away. The islanders looked after them in their homes, gave them dry sweaters and trousers, and hid them from Irish soldiers who searched the island. Eventually the five men regathered their strength enough to surrender and were taken off to Valentia before being sent to an internment camp. 'They were put up to the Curragh in County Kildare,' said Seán. British and German fighters alike were detained there, separated only by a barbed-wire fence. It was hardly a concentration camp, since they were allowed to play golf, go to the races and visit Dublin, but Oberleutnant Neymeyer was not satisfied with the prospect of sitting out the war in such comfort. He escaped, and stowed away on an Irish ship bound for Lisbon, not realizing that, like all such vessels, it was obliged to call in for inspection at a Welsh port, where he was arrested. This time it was by the British, and there was no chance of playing golf.

'A few years after the war, two of them returned to the island,' said Muiris. They said thank you to the families who had sheltered them by taking the remaining men out for a meal and a pint in Dingle where, as they used to say in the Blaskets, 'a good night was had for several days'. All night Willie Krupp kept asking Seán Pheats Team Ó Cearna about his sister Eibhlín, who had nursed his wounds and made quite an impression on him. How was she? What was she doing these days? Would there be a chance to see her? He was far too late. Unlike Seán and Muiris, but like most of the island women they grew up with, she had gone to America.

When the whiskey was finished and the fruit bread put away, I walked home through the valley of Dunquin in the rain, with the island invisible in the darkness. You could feel it, though. There were no lights out there, of course, and no moon to shine on ruined houses. I thought of the island at its peak, crowded with children and dogs and chickens, and the youngsters dancing on the hill while their elders watched, chewing tobacco. Muiris would have been a long, gawky boy then, shy, awkward, and in awe of his handsome elder brother. They had long lives ahead of them, but the friends they loved would all disappear in time. Somewhere out at sea in the night was the Ó Cearna home, half fallen to the ground. Thousands of miles away, the sun was still out in Massachusetts, and shining on Mícheál Ó Cearna, now an old man full of memories just like his schoolmates. His brothers were there too, in that so-called Land of Youth. What did they think of the ones who stayed behind, of the life that Seán and Muiris led? Where was home to them now? What had they become? The abandoned island, the lonely old sister and the brothers living in the past were only half the story. The rest of it lay in pieces on the road to America.

PART THREE

The Land of Youth

As Michael was going out the door he picked a piece of loose whitewash from the wall and put it in his pocket. The people filed out after them, down the yard and on to the road, like a funeral procession. The mother was left in the house with little Thomas and two old peasant women from the village. Nobody spoke in the cabin for a long time.

Then the mother rose and came into the kitchen. She looked at the two women, at her little son, and at the hearth, as if she were looking for something she had lost. Then she threw her hands into the air and ran out into the yard.

'Come back,' she screamed. 'Come back to me.'

She looked wildly down the road with dilated nostrils, her bosom heaving. But there was nobody in sight. Nobody replied.

Liam O'Flaherty, *Going Into Exile*

24

27 March 1948

Peaidí Ó Cearna is cutting turf on the ridge at the top of the island. Spring sunshine has dried the ground, and warms the back of his neck as he digs. The donkey waits, panniers empty, shaking her head to be free of a fat, dozy bee drifting by.

It has been three months since the death of Seáinín. Peaidí is twenty-three years old, lean and strong like all the Ó Cearna men, with a long face and angular limbs. There is mischief in his deep-set eyes. He loves being up on the hillside on a fresh day, with gannets blowing in snow flurries over the waves far below and the rabbits keeping their distance. His spade cuts into the short grass scattered with sea pink, and a boot pushes the blade deeper. This is easier and gentler than the endless beet fields of Norfolk, where he spent the last harvest in the company of men from Galway and Kilkenny. That was monotonous work, and no amount of drinking and larking could ease the homesickness he felt then, late at night, sharing a bunk with other men brought together in England by nothing more than the need to earn a few pounds to get their families through the winter. They were all strangers who spoke another language, and he an islandman a long way from his island.

This hillside is where Peaidí feels at home. There are few young boyos around now, and hardly any women, but he loves to fish and take the dog out chasing hares. Róisín is lying on her side, snoozing in the sun.

The sound of coughing carries up on the wind. Peaidí looks back and below to see his own father walking towards him across the mountainside. The old man does not seem well, as though the effort of putting one foot in front of another is too much for him this morning. After a minute or two, as his father comes closer, Peaidí can see his face, the eyes cast down under the cap. Something is wrong.

They exchange murmured greetings. 'You have news today,' says Seán Team Ó Cearna, close now, meeting Peaidí's eyes. There is a folded piece of paper in his hand, and his son knows what is on it. 'Your aunt has written a letter. You're going to America.'

The word has been sent. Peaidí's time has come. His big brother Mícheál quit the bar job in Dublin a few months ago, bought a ticket and sailed to America. The whole family knew the plan, which was for Mícheál to work and save until it was possible to send money home to the next brother. Muiris is already away, at sea with the merchant marine, so it is Peaidí's turn.

The letter in his grip is from Uncle Muiris, who stayed behind in America when Seán Team came home with a trunk full of fine clothing and a mind full of marriage. Muiris got married himself, in Springfield, Massachusetts, and was blessed with eight children. Seven of them were girls, and healthy ones, but the son he always longed for developed a throat infection at the age of twelve, and died. Such things are hard to bear. Now Uncle Muiris proposes that Peaidí go and live with him, and be cared for like a son. There is no question of refusing, and the boy does not really want to anyway. Leaving the island for good will be difficult, but all the Ó Cearna family know that there is no other way for them to survive the years ahead. The death of Seáinín has hurt each one deeply, but somehow cut the family free of the pull of the island. Céit, who took it all so badly, is already on the mainland with her husband and her own son. Old Gold Tooth himself knows that when the last of his children moves away for good, he will also have to leave his home and join her in Muirríoch. The sadness he shares with Peaidí on the hillside today is at the inevitability of parting. Neither man doubts that it is necessary.

25

There was always a big party on the night before anyone left for the States. They called it an American wake, because the whole community stayed up to keep the emigrants company through their last night on the island, just as they would have bidden farewell to a soul beginning the long journey towards eternity. There was almost no chance that anyone present would ever see the departed again. Dust rose from the floor as dancers whirled to the sound of a fiddle or accordion, and the old folk watched on, thinking of their own sons and daughters across the Atlantic. An uncle rose on unsteady legs and gave a boisterous rendition of a familiar song, with a chorus that everyone sang. An aunt quietened the room with a lament. There was as much food and drink as the extended family could afford, treats like cake and porter, and the young people who were not dancing were leaning against the wall, making eyes at each other. The father who caught himself filling up with tears stole a sideways look at his son, wondering how to say goodbye. Thinking of him asleep on his shoulder as a little boy. The daughter comforted her mother with an arm around the waist and a few soft words, as though it were the older woman who was sorry to be leaving, and all the while cherishing secret thoughts of the adventures to come.

The small cardboard suitcases were packed and ready, the travelling clothes hanging by the door. Childhood sweethearts watched it all, helpless and lost, wondering where the money for their own tickets might come from. There was so much to say, and so little of it said. Better to dance, or step outside for a moment to watch the clouds slipping under the stars. As dawn came the revellers caught their breath, shook hands with the emigrants or stole a final kiss before wandering off to bed, leaving only the close family to eat breakfast together one last time.

It was such a long goodbye. There were chores to do, as there always had been, but when the cow had been milked, the water fetched, and the tea drunk, the time was right for leaving. 'Come now,' the father would say, causing his wife to take a sudden sharp breath. She brought down a bottle of holy water from the shelf and sprinkled a little of it on the head of her son, speaking out a prayer of protection; then dropped soot from the fire into his pocket to keep the faeries away. Going out of the door, he pulled a piece of whitewashed wall away from the family home, as a keepsake. Down at the quayside the women of the island gathered, twisting their shawls and crying out words of love and sorrow as the *naomhóga* were taken from their stands and lowered into the water.

'Musha, my lovely child, however will we stand the cold winter without you?'

'My heart, the island will be sad when you are gone.'

The boys and girls who were leaving sat in the canoes with their knees tucked in and the stiff new clothes rubbing their joints, and they tried to see it all, and feel it all, and remember it all, for the day would come when this island and these people would be nothing more than memories to them. Their throats choked at that thought. The words of the women faded on the wind as the canoes slipped out from the quay and into the Sound, riding the waves, so that the travellers were left with only the sight of their mother, or sister, or beloved, waving from the shore. Nothing then, but the movement of the sea, and the quiet encouragement of the oarsmen, and the journey to come.

★

Sometimes, on a calm day, every island canoe was lifted into the water and the families of those who were leaving crossed the Sound with them. Then there was a procession: men and women, boys and girls, laughing and weeping, climbing up from the harbour at Dunquin and walking through the lanes that wound across the valley, past cottages owned by relatives and acquaintances. They were heading for *Carraigh an Ghiorrai*, the Rock of the Hare, a place on the high pass between Mount Eagle and the peak known as *Cruach Mhárthain*, the Stack of Martin, where the travellers could turn back and see their island for the last time.

I walked that way myself on a cool evening in September 1998, from the harbour to the pass, in their footsteps, thinking of them. Beside me was a man born in the valley who had lived all but a few years of his life there: Mícheál de Mordha, who had seen the last of the islanders walk past his house. Mícheál was a Gaelic speaker who had left Dunquin for university then lived in Dublin as a journalist for a while, before returning to the valley to work among his own people, first as a broadcaster with Raidió na Gaeltachta, then as manager of a heritage centre dedicated to the Blaskets. He was a modern businessman, an entrepreneur who could be sharp and witty, but also a devout man, who had the melancholy streak and the thirst of a poet, and a passion for the old ways.

We began on the cliff above the harbour, where half a dozen hire cars were parked. This rutted common land was known as *Móinteán*, 'the peaty place', and it was bounded by a drystone wall built by local people during the Famine as one of the strange relief schemes which paid men a few shillings to keep their families from starving. 'This was Céit Foley's shop,' said Mícheál when we reached a two-storey farmhouse at the end of the wall. 'Whenever a party would come past here, they would stop and go in to buy tobacco.'

There was a crossroads. One way curved up and away to the right, towards the cliff edge and Slea Head, but we turned left, inland, and down a dip towards *Báile an Ghleanna*, 'the town of the glen'. It was overgrown with wet brambles, and we could only pass through what had once been a tidy settlement by using slippery planks and stepping-stones. This was where the Dálaigh, Keane and de Mordha families once lived, close by each other in stone cabins, before they built new homes further up the hillside in the 1940s. The old ones had tumbled into ruin and had almost disappeared beneath the wild hedges. Fuchsia thickened the air with its sweet smell.

We passed the schoolhouse, and an old grey cottage by the road that was the home of an elderly and reclusive islandman called Peaidí Mhicil Ó Súilleabháin. 'Stay here a moment and talk with me,' said Mícheál, and we stood by the gate. The old grey net curtain shivered at the touch of an unseen hand, and in a moment, to our great surprise, the front door opened. A tiny old man in dark clothes shuffled out, stooped and ancient but sprightly. He wore a cap, of course, and one of the island jerseys. His hands were thrust into the pockets of dark flannel trousers which were tied up at the ankles, as islandmen did to stop their trousers snagging on bushes, which might have upset their balance and sent them tumbling over the cliffs into the sea. Peaidí Mhicil's family was the last to leave the Great Blasket, a year after the official evacuation. He did not stay outside in the evening breeze with us for long, but nodded in my direction, said something in Gaelic, squeezed a high-pitched laugh from his shrivelled chest and disappeared. As the door closed again I asked Mícheál what had been so amusing. 'Oh, he said you were a big fellow who'd be good in a canoe.'

The walk through the townlands took the emigrants and their families a long time, as they stopped to talk to friends and relatives along the way. We were moving briskly compared to them, but it was still half an hour before we passed the house of Seán and Muiris Ó Guithín at the second crossroads and headed uphill. Above us on our right was the golden-brown peak of Mount Eagle, and to the left the land fell away into another little glen, with a hidden river running through it. Beyond was the grey-stone parish church, and the graveyard where Seáinín Ó Cearna and his mother Neilí were buried. Beyond that again, where the land rose steeply, was what looked like a modern cathedral, its grounds landscaped to ensure privacy. It had been built by a rock star as a country hideaway, but was now empty and for sale.

We stood in the ditch to let a car pass. The wind grew stronger as we walked uphill towards *Mam Clasach*, the mountain pass, where a television aerial stood beaming down pictures into the valley. 'We did not have the television in our house at all until 1986,' said Mícheál. He stopped and pointed to a large stone with a cleft in it: the Rock of the Hare, the place for goodbyes. We looked back, down into the wide valley of Dunquin and out to sea, where the Great Blasket stood apart. Sunshine broke through the silver clouds and fell like a spotlight on the ruined village. The whitewash on two of the houses shone as the light intensified, then faded. From a distance it looked as though they were still inhabited.

Turning again to face the road ahead, we saw the Slieve Mish mountains fall away to a coast on either side, with Dingle far away on the right and Mount Brandon black against the sky on the left. The road fell sharply towards Ventry harbour, where caravans were arranged like pebbles by the strand. The King of France once arrived on that beach with a mighty fleet to claim back his wife and daughter, who had both eloped with Fionn Mac Cúmhaill, leader of the Fianna, the legendary army charged with protecting Irish ports against invasion. The battle that followed went on for a year, the legend said, until every warrior was dead. The King of France lost his mind and fled over the mountains.

It was also said that an islandwoman who had never left the Great Blasket before came up to the pass where we were standing and was astonished by the view. 'What a wide, weary place is Ireland,' she exclaimed, before turning on her heels in a panic and going straight home, to the closer fit of her own landscape.

Many of the men and women who had stalled on this mountain road and let themselves be blown by its high winds never saw the island again. Here they said their last words to anyone who loved them enough to have come this far. It was such a desolate place, high above everything green and growing, with not a scrap of shelter from the elements. The clouds huddled closer to the mountain as we stood there in the gathering dark, the two of us, trying to imagine. Mícheál had a son and two daughters, each old enough to be thinking of leaving home. My own son was only months old, but on that mountainside the knowledge grew in my bones that he would go his own way one day, in a future that no longer seemed so distant.

Wherever he went, I would probably see him again (flights to the other side of the world being quick and relatively cheap) but that comfort was not available to the mothers and fathers who had wept on this spot in the past. The parting was final. It was a lonely place then, although crowded with people hugging, kissing and crying. There were promises to write, promises not to forget, promises to send money for a ticket. Nervous laughter, chatter. Then quiet, as the moment that had been anticipated, hoped for and dreaded, for months or years, finally arrived.

★

Within minutes the pass was empty again. Only the sheep or a bolting rabbit felt the wind. The parents were already on their way home, walking slowly back down one side of the hill, heading for the island, arms around each other in consolation. The travellers were on the other side, swallowing hard, thinking ahead. At last, they were on their way.

26

10 April 1948

There is no wild wake for Peaidí Ó Cearna. His mother is dead, both his sisters are on the mainland. The neighbours come by for a slug of whiskey, but there are fewer of them than ever. So many people are leaving the island that American wakes have lost their novelty. Only the old, the infirm and the very poor stay, or those who refuse to abandon the place until the end, which they know full well is coming.

Peaidí leaves the island quietly with his father after breakfast, and at Dunquin he bids farewell to the old friends in the boat crew. Fred Sheehy is waiting above in his taxi, ready to drive around the coast to Céit's house. At Smerwick Harbour they are joined by a gaggle of young men and women, all heading for the States. The next stop is Dingle, to pick up more passengers. Everyone bound for America used to catch a train from the town, but post-war coal rationing has closed the Tralee line to passengers. Taxis and charabancs are the only way to travel down the peninsula and across country all the long way to Cobh in County Cork, where the liners wait.

Near Holy Ground in the centre of Dingle, Sheehy stops the engine and waits for latecomers. It is time for Seán Team to say goodbye to his son. Neither man has spoken much this morning. Both men have trembling legs as they climb out of the vehicle, but that is surely the cramp. It is a cold day, and they both shiver.

'Well, then.'

This is it. Seán is a proud man, but he loves each of his sons deeply. They embrace, and as Peaidí's chin rests against his father's shoulder, he feels the wiry old body under the jacket convulse. For all his efforts, Seán is overcome by tears, and when that happens Peaidí cannot help but be swallowed by the same sorrow. The people in the taxi watch as the two men stand by the roadside in each other's arms, crying their eyes out.

27

'If you are not an Irishman, what are you?'
'I am a Blasket man, my boy.'

Muiris Ó Súilleabháin, *Twenty Years A-Growing*

Every step towards Dingle took the islanders out of their familiar world and into an alien place, as the young and naïve Muiris Ó Súilleabháin found when he slunk away from the Great Blasket in 1927 with dreams of joining the Irish police force. Only a few miles inland, he met a cowman dressed in tatters with a pipe between his teeth, who greeted him in Gaelic with courtesy and care. They shook hands, and a grateful Muiris was sent off along the right road.

After walking a long way, he saw a settlement in the distance unlike any other he had known, with 'big high houses packed together and many trees growing in their midst'. Feeling a little unsure of himself, Muiris was glad to see another traveller on the road, a well-dressed gentleman who wore a watch chain across his waistcoat and carried an umbrella. This meeting was very different to the last, however. The elderly farmer had been at ease with physical exercise, but the town man wiped his brow, sweating from the effort of the walk. He did not understand Irish, but made it perfectly clear that he considered Muiris to be the ignorant one. The burgher's manner was abrupt and impatient, in contrast with the elegant conversation of the poor farmer. The warmth with which total strangers greeted one another in the far west was entirely absent, and the only language that Muiris spoke was despised. He was only a dozen miles from home, but it may as well have been the other side of the world.

Dingle was the biggest town that many Blasket men ever saw in their lives. Women seldom left the island, but if they did it was to go into service at the house of a merchant or landowner near Dingle, or to be treated at the hospital. There were only half a dozen or so streets behind the quay, but the shops and houses were crammed together and a couple of thousand people lived in the immediate vicinity. More came into town from the country with their children and livestock on market days, when crowds filled the place. The town became a pit of suffering during the Famine, and the Board of Guardians was so overwhelmed by poverty and destitution that it paid for some of the inhabitants to be clothed and sent abroad to avoid starvation; but even after such devastating times, the broad and enclosed natural harbour meant Dingle remained an important fishing port. The islandmen carried their sheep and cattle across the Sound in *naomhóga*, then drove them to market, with salted fish and lobsters. They could spend the proceeds in town, on quantities of drink that were just not available on the Great Blasket, or by backing losers at the Dingle races.

Some shopkeepers were keen to maintain good relationships with the strange, Gaelic-speaking men from the far west, and it was in Dingle that islanders sold bolts of shipwrecked copper to a trader under the noses of the coastguards; but others were wary or tried to take advantage of them. Tomás Ó Criomhthain was outraged when a shopkeeping cousin offered him inferior braces, because she did not think her simple island relation would know the difference. When he was first brought to town as a boy, his eyes had grown 'as big as two mugs with wonder' at the sight of huge ships laden with goods from France and Spain. The people dazzled him then, too – everyone was equal on the island, but that was clearly not the case in Dingle. 'I saw gentlefolk standing there with chains across their bellies, poor people half-clad, cripples here and there on every side, and a blind man with his guide.'

On John Street there was a travel agent called Galvin who sold tickets for the transatlantic shipping lines, and his record book preserved the names of the thousands who passed through on their way to America. They included Seán Team Ó Cearna in 1901, and again seven years later. Once the tickets had been signed for and thrust deep into some safe corner of a pocket or purse, the emigrants walked with their tied packages and cases down the Mall to the railway station. Hats were held as the little engine blew off steam, and hurried goodbyes were said as farmers from the surrounding countryside herded livestock off the freight carriage to sell at market. The train whistled – a long, lonesome sound that would be remembered for ever – and the wooden carriages creaked and groaned as they were pulled out of the station, along the narrow track towards Castlegregory and Tralee. Progress over the mountain range was slow and dangerous, with seventy gates to cross and sheep on the line. All but the most fearless or foolish looked away from the seven-hundred-foot drop as the train passed above the wild landscape of *Gleann na nGealt*, the Valley of the Mad, where the King of France had fled after being driven insane by the slaughter at Ventry. Another time, more recently, the wind blew so hard that the engine and carriages were derailed and people died.

The line closed to passengers in 1939, having been outpaced by motor buses that seemed to fly over the new roads. They were never short of passengers – fishing and farming were not sufficiently lucrative to keep people at home in Dingle, and for decades the town was as depressed as the rest of rural Ireland. Its fortunes changed in the 1960s, when the film director David Lean decided to make *Ryan's Daughter* in the mountains west of Dingle. The effect was dramatic: many of the hands he hired to look after animals, act as extras, or guard the fibreglass village that was built on the pass above Dunquin were subsistence farmers who had never been paid for a day's work before. They were astonished and appalled to see cats and dogs being fed the cakes the cast did not eat. The star of the film, Robert Mitchum, hired Milltown House, a guest-house on the edge of Dingle, and there were dozens of other actors, technicians, support staff and hangers-on to feed, water and entertain. When one of the film crew took exception to the noise two locals were making in a pub, he bought them ten pints to share. There was silence for a long time after that.

The money flowed for a year. Then, when the movie was released, the tourists began to arrive from all over the world. With a little paint and a few scrubbing brushes the terraced buildings tumbling down Main Street were made to look as they had a hundred years before, dressed in bright hues of pink, blue and yellow. In time, fancy seafood restaurants and souvenir shops opened, their owners surviving in the winter from what they earned in summer. Europeans and Americans began to visit the town in great numbers, some staying in relatively smart hotels like Benner's, others putting their heads down in hostels. Naturally, their presence was a boost to the pubs, some of which were also shops, as they had always been since the days when a nip of whiskey helped a regular customer to feel appreciated. By the time I got there you could hear live music every night of the week in Dingle town, and there were more than fifty places to buy a drink.

★

Stars were set into the pavement outside Dick Mack's bar in Green Street in honour of the famous people who had allegedly drunk in the pub, including Robert Mitchum, Julia Roberts and Paul Simon. The walls were blue and red, the shop windows decorated with dusty old whiskey crates and a pair of green wellingtons. Inside was the sort of old-fashioned Irish bar that breweries spend millions trying to recreate: on the right of the dark, narrow room was a counter, lined with pump handles; a bucket, a model *naomhóg* and a tuneless old fiddle hung down from the ceiling, which was the colour of mustard phlegm from an old smoker's lungs; and from a second counter on the left you could buy boots or belts, in theory. People came to Dick Mack's to get lathered, not to buy leather. The shelves were stacked with stiff brown shoe-boxes warped with age, and a receipt from 1908 was framed on the wall. A blackened oil painting of the late Dick Mack watched over the bar.

His son Oliver understood that a pint of stout was sacramental. He held the glass at just the right angle so that three-quarters of a pint of milky brown liquid ran down the side, then he put it down to settle. You could watch the sun set, romance a stranger or grow a beard while waiting for the creamy head to separate itself from the bitter black. Oliver could tell who had ordered Guinness for the first time, or who was used to the brisker ways of city barmen, because the customer would shift from one foot to the other and try to catch his eye, imagining that the drink had been forgotten. When it did come, at last, the fat cream clung to the side of the jar.

'So where are your people from?' The woman beside me in the snug expected an answer. She was short and wide, an earth mother in her late fifties, wrapped in a shawl, with hair up in a bun, fastened with a Celtic clasp. 'My people come from Connemara,' she said, in a soft and mannered New

England accent. 'Originally, that is. We moved down to this part of the world five or six generations ago. Now we're in Vermont. Where are your people from?'

The truth was I had no idea. Camberwell, maybe. That was where my father spent his childhood, climbing over bombed-out buildings and swimming in the Thames. As for where his father was born, that was a mystery to me. No one ever talked about it. It wasn't the sort of thing one suburban Londoner asked another, unless they had different coloured skins. Then again, I had been attracted to Dingle in the beginning as a possible balm for the constant feeling of home-sickness that I always felt, without ever knowing where home was.

It was a place of escape, as far west and away as you could get, which I discovered when a friend from London who had once lived in a caravan on the edge of Dingle took me there for the summer, a long time ago. The wide open spaces, the distant mountains and the unfathomable sea were all liberating to a teenager who had grown up with the sound of traffic always in his ears. The people were welcoming to the friend of an old friend. They made me laugh, they bought me pints, they played music full of passion, and they knew who they were.

I was a gauche city kid bowled over by the romance of it all, and that was mostly Emma's fault. We met at a dance on the edge of town and I fell for her, like a skydiver with a fridge for a parachute. She was beautiful, with eyes to drown in and corkscrew curls. Or maybe she wasn't like that at all – I remembered her one way, but there were never any photo-graphs to prove me wrong.

The enthusiasm was all mine, it transpired. Other boys holidayed in Dingle that year and were as well received. She agreed to visit me in England, but when the day came the doorbell never rang. I never heard from her again. Strange how the smallest pebble can cause so many ripples.

In those days I knew nothing of the people who lived over the mountains, in the far west, but it was the attempt to understand what the islanders felt as they took each difficult step towards America that brought me back to Dingle fifteen years after Emma, my heart hammering as if I had come looking for her. Everything was familiar – the statue of the Virgin by the church, under whose cover we kissed, *An Café L018eartha* where we used to meet for coffee – but different. Dingle was less beautiful, the weather more savage. There were couples everywhere and I was on my own. The people I knew had all gone. This place that I had adopted as a spiritual home turned out not to be mine at all. Emma had moved to New York long ago, although in my mind she was still one of the convent schoolgirls who walked down Green Street at lunchtime. Those slight, awkward teenagers were barely aware of their power over the boys who watched them from the other side of the road. I recognized her in them, and the myth died, right there on the pavement.

It was still true, though, that life was well defined for people in Kerry, in a way that had once seemed so attractive. They looked at the landscape and read its meaning, knew the suffering of which it told, and where they stood. Returning, I understood that for some it was too well defined, and it drove them to leave for some unfamiliar city where history could not hold them back. In the city there were no villages left – there might be quarters dominated by the rich or poor, black or white, African or Asian, but the boundaries between the names on the map were blurred – and in cramped, crowded urban streets, personal horizons could be endless. To leave Dingle you had to walk under a big sky and cross miles of open country before the next town – but each life was fenced in by untameable nature. No matter where they went or what they did, anyone who came from such a landscape would have to work very hard to forget it. The people of the Great Blasket looked back at their island from a boat, from a mountain pass, or in a picture if they were far away, and saw a mountain defined by sea.

'That,' they could say with confidence, or dread, 'is where my people come from.'

The sign in the window promised set dancing at nine, but the Small Bridge pub was half empty. People knew better than to be prompt; there was time for a walk in the rain, and a bag of chips. An hour later the place was stuffed with hot bodies in damp clothes, and half a dozen musicians sat on benches, on three sides of a square, under the window near the door. Every eye was drawn towards the burning heart of the room, a briquette fire in the big brick hearth. The walls, floor and ceiling were close and dark; and in this musical grotto liquid gifts of black and white were handed out by smoky firelight. Guinness posters and St Patrick's Day streamers still hung from the ceiling, months after their time. The season was over, and no one was a tourist. A straight-backed woman in her forties wore a purple velvet shawl and a white blouse with a lace collar. She had come for the dancing.

The piper flexed his fingers and began to explore a tune. His elbow squeezed air from the bag, and his eyes met those of an accordion player, who nodded and found a counter refrain. A guitarist, thin with a young face, picked up the rhythm, dampening the strings and cutting across them on the off-beat. An older man, stocky and red skinned with a white moustache and an intent look, let the stick in his hand trip across the skin of a bodhran.

Conversations were left unfinished as people turned in their seats to face the session. There was no room to move, and barely enough to stand. Men, women and children all watched and bobbed their heads in time, tapping a foot or drumming a glass with their fingers. Other musicians climbed aboard the tune as it passed: a second guitarist who had watched his friend's fingers on the fretboard; another piper; another bodhran.

A signal passed through the crowd and eight dancers were on their feet. Part of the floor cleared. Each held a partner and they were off, turning tight patterns within small circles, bodies mad and free yet never colliding or stumbling into a space where they should not have been. They moved as an eight, into the circle and out, stamping their heels to accentuate the beat. It was ancient but vital, an impressive movement performed here and wherever there were Kerry people. The public, collective courtship could have been taking place on the hill of the Great Blasket, in the hull of a transatlantic steamer, or at a social club in Massachusetts. They might have been dancing to a wind-up gramophone, a one-string fiddle, or an amplified band. The dancers were a spectacle, but in another time the whole room might have been spinning and reeling.

It was like that at the dance in Dingle on a Saturday night in 1943, when a young islandman called Muiris Ó Cearna met a beautiful red-haired girl called Joan. He walked her home, under the stars. The next day Muiris left for England, to join the Merchant Navy, and they did not see each other again . . . until six years later, when he had joined Mícheál and his other brothers in America. Among the thousand Irish on a dance floor at the Tara Hall, thousands of miles from Dingle, Muiris saw Joan's flaming hair again. They danced.

'What the devil are you doing here?' she asked, laughing.

'The very same thing as you.'

They were married in 1951.

The crowd applauded as the dance ended. Beyond the arch, away from the music, in a second bar at the back where there was more light and a pool table, a young man sank the black and a courting couple leant against the wall, kissing. He was watching the pool game from behind her hair. She had one eye on the dancing.

28

11 April 1948

Peaidí Ó Cearna kisses his father goodbye, then disappears
back into the crowd. The old man is left alone on Holy
Ground, remembering what it feels like to leave behind all
that is familiar. In his mind he sees his fellow emigrants sitting
together on the wooden-slatted seats of a steam train in 1901,
nervous and excited, waiting for the world to change. His son
will see Ireland through a window, slipping past, for the first
and last time. The land will grow flatter and meaner with
every mile. The green slopes and wide open spaces will narrow
into crowded carriages and chaotic booking halls, but Peaidí
and his friends will have their minds on the future, not the
present or the past. The arrival, not the leaving. The memories,
and the longing to be home, will not be real for weeks.
Their letters will never mention what it was like to cross the
south-west to Cork, and with good reason: there will be
extraordinary tales to tell from America. But first they must
make this journey among strangers, who will look on them
as foolish paupers and mutter insults in a language they do not
understand. These boys and girls from an island of storytellers
and poets will learn to be silent and watchful. They have left
behind a community that knows them by name, and by the
deeds of their grandparents, but before the day is over they
will learn to value the anonymity of the crowd. Like his father
half a century before, and like so many other islanders since,
Peaidí is being gathered up into a great sea of humanity heading

west. He has caught the last wave, and will not be seen by another eye that recognizes him until America. The waters part for a second, and from a distance Seán Team watches his son climb back aboard Sheehy's bus. Then the crowds close in again, and the boy disappears from view.

29

Following Peaidí's cold trail to the harbour proved difficult. The railway platform at Tralee was empty and the ticket office abandoned. All the luggage lockers were full or broken. Even the shops seemed to turn their backs on the traveller, presenting car parks, service bays and overflowing dustbins. There were faint signs of life from behind the door of the Bus Eirean office, in which I was the only enquirer. A young woman with long, straight hair tied up loosely looked up at me from her desk for a moment, then turned her back. I shuffled through the coloured pieces of paper on the counter. None of the timetables made sense. It was too late to say hello.

'Yes?' she said, turning to face me again at last. 'Can I help?'

Was there a bus to Cork soon, I wondered?

'You'll need the four-fifteen.' She looked away. It was just past noon.

'Really?' I said, peering down at the schedule, which was slowly beginning to make sense. 'Isn't there an earlier one? What about the two o'clock?'

'Oh sure. Hang on . . .' She disappeared into a side office behind a frosted-glass door, and I heard murmurs before she re-emerged. 'Yes. That's the bus to Mallow that usually connects with the one to Cork. It usually waits. There is one at twelve-forty but you wouldn't be better off, because it goes out to Killarney and comes back again, you know?'

To be honest, I didn't. 'Look,' she said, 'the bus you'll get at two is actually the one that leaves here at twelve-forty, right?'

'Really? How does that work then?'
'Don't ask,' she said. I didn't.

The train arrived first. It was filthy, the windows opaque with grime, and it took twice as long to get to Cobh as a car would have done. We left late, easing past fossilized freight bogeys and modern houses covered in grey pebble-dash streaked with rain and grime. Everything about Tralee seemed to be wrapped in a gritty film that bled away all colour. It was a fine place to be leaving.

The view changed and we passed field after field of rough pasture, with cows standing vacant in the rain. At Farranfore, a tiny country station with its own airport, the waiting-room and ticket office were boarded up, their walls and windows covered in graffiti. Nobody got on or off.

Just past Killarney the horizon lifted and formed itself into the peaks of Macgillycuddy's Reeks, great black canines in a gummy landscape. Suddenly the clouds separated, a brush-stroke of blue sky appeared, and across it shone a rainbow, rising from a forest of pine trees to arch across a stone cottage. A river slipped over rocks, and sheep marked with blue dye grazed under a tree. For a brief moment this was the tour-guide Ireland, the one in the movies and on the calendars, the Emerald Isle where the leprechauns laughed as they stroked their little ginger beards, and wild-eyed colleens danced through the fields. Then it was over, the sky dark again. We moved on, away, past a car abandoned by the roadside and into a rainstorm, a reminder that the Isle was indeed Emerald only because everything was so well watered.

An old man got off and left behind a copy of the *Irish Times*, folded at a photograph of the current Rose of Tralee. Her name was Luzveminda and she was half Filipino. Anyone of Irish descent could become the Rose by entering a beauty contest that had adjusted to more enlightened times with tests for personality and social awareness. Besides advertising a Catholic aid appeal for the Sudan, Mindy, as she was known to her friends, was pictured with the reigning Conchie of the Year, the winner of a competition that apparently set out to find the man most like a village idiot.

The rest of the paper was filled with a scandal involving the American president, including the information that one of his infidelities had taken place while the First Lady was visiting Ireland. Whatever else would be said about Bill Clinton in the fullness of time, the *Irish Times* that day was certain he would always be welcome in its country. On a recent visit, the President had been met by huge, adoring crowds everywhere, from the bombed-out city of Omagh to the golf course at Ballybunion. The goodwill was in recognition of the part he had played in trying to bring peace to Northern Ireland, including going against British opinion to grant the Sinn Fein leader Gerry Adams a visa to visit the US. 'Bill Clinton has been important for this country, and the Irish people like him,' said the editorial. The visit had been 'probably the last bit of peace and approval the poor man is likely to get for a long time'.

Cork station was a long walk from the centre of town. I hauled my heavy bag up the platform to the bar and buffet, but it was closed. Cold, tired and feeling unwell, I was also hungry and thirsty after three hours on a train that had no facility for food or drink. Fifty pence was expensive for a small cup of instant coffee from a vending machine, and even more so when it poured the liquid without offering a cup. The Coke machine kept my money but did not dispense a can. The cold-water tap in the toilet was scalding hot. Miserable and uncomfortable, I slumped on a bench and looked around, at a steam engine fenced off in the corner of the station and a statue of Mary in a glass cabinet erected by the staff of the Kent Coach Company, with two pale-blue electric lights shining at her feet in perpetual devotion. After a trip across the Sound by canoe, the long goodbye on the Classach, the journey by road or rail to Dingle and Tralee, the train to Mallow then Cork, the Blasket emigrants must have been exhausted and disorientated. Religion would have offered consolation to some, and doubtless the railway taverns provided the same to others, but as I sat alone in the deserted station at just after eight in the evening, I understood why they always chose to travel together or with others from the peninsula. As the islanders themselves said, it was a wide world in which to find yourself without a friend.

30

12 April 1948

'Help with the luggage at all there?' Cobh station is crowded with bodies: sweethearts, hawkers, pickpockets and porters, all waiting on the platform as the train doors open and the emigrants step out, in their hundreds. Bags, boxes and suitcases are lifted down, and there are always willing helpers. 'Let me get that for ye now,' says a ferral man in a flat cap as he grabs for the handle of a pretty girl's case. She can't see him clearly in the half-light but they are almost cheek to cheek, and he smells of tobacco, whiskey and sweat. His gap-toothed smile is just a little too wide, his other hand on her arm a little threatening. 'Will you be wanting a place to stay now?' The girl is tired, her head is reeling from the journey on a rattling, smoking train to places that she did not know existed, and she barely understands a word. She has lived on the Great Blasket all her sixteen years, and was never beyond Dingle until today. Nothing in her life has prepared her for this terrifying crowd, full of towering men and bodies pressing close to hers. My soul, where are the others? Three girls and four boys, put together for the journey by Galvin the travel agent – but they have all disappeared. The man with the strange, smooth hands is even closer now, in the breathless dark, saying something about 'a good house, clean and respectable?'

She does not reply. It is not her language, and thank God and Mary, two of her travelling companions have appeared. Island boys, big lads, with strong arms and calloused hands that can twist the neck of a goose. 'Ah, to hell with ye,' mumbles the rook, but his smile never fades, and before the words are dead on his lips he has moved through the crowd as smoothly as a swan on a lake, to another innocent. 'Madam! Allow me . . .' The three Blasket teenagers keep close together now, and push their way on under the station arch, looking for the offices of the White Star shipping line.

'Sure,' says the clerk in their own language. 'We have you on the next sailing, no need to worry yourselves at all.' He checks their luggage, and explains that a tender will take them from Deepwater Quay to their ship, early tomorrow morning. 'Now listen to me well, there will be no help to those who miss it, and no compensation.' The warning registers. They would not dream of compensation, whatever it is. There is one more trial to face now before departure: a visit to the American Consulate, back up the hill above the station, where papers are inspected and each passenger subjected to a thorough medical. This has been compulsory since the Famine, when thousands of sickly people fled Ireland but died on the open sea. The 'coffin ships' that carried them then were crowded, unsafe vessels, some of which had been used for the transportation of shackled slaves. A law was passed, making the shipping lines accountable for anyone who was too ill or infectious to be allowed into America, and demanding that they be carried back to their country of origin. It fell to the medical officer in Cobh, who examined emigrants under a bright lamp, to make sure that only the fit were allowed on board. Those who passed were given a red label. A yellow one meant you had to be 'disinfected, fumigated and bathed in hot salt baths'. The liquid in the baths turned your hair white temporarily, if it hadn't already been shaved off your head. The medical officer wore rubber gloves for his own protection. Some patients were sent to quarantine camps, where they waited for weeks. Others did not get better, and died in Cobh.

The companions face no such indignities, having proved themselves fit enough to travel by canoe, cart, bus and train to Cobh. Neither is it hard for them to find a place in one of the many lodging-houses, despite their fears. Letters home from America have warned them about landlords who employ musicians to get emigrants out of bed in the middle of the night for a dance – 'While you're swinging around having a fine time the devil sells your bed again to some other soul, so that when you get tired and go back to lay your head a stranger is there inside!' – but that doesn't happen any more. We're nearly in the fifties, and the world is changing. There are fewer emigrants than before the war, and they are usually treated fairly. The travellers climb the stairs to a pair of rooms in the attic of a house called Sea View, and force open a window to get a better look at the lights out in the harbour, shimmering in the water with the stars. One of the ships is theirs, but it is impossible to tell which. They fall asleep quickly but sleep lightly, dreaming not of home now but of America.

31

The night had grown dark and cold by the time my train arrived in Cobh, so there was no one to meet any of the four passengers as we walked into town past Deepwater Quay. The ornamental gardens on the waterfront were in the grand English style, with a bandstand and stopped-up cannons standing guard across one of the largest natural harbours in the world. Nautical brass gleamed outside the Commodore Hotel, and in the windows of pubs called the Admiral and the Ship's Bell. On my right was the boundless yawning sea and sky, but tall Victorian townhouses were stacked high on the hill to the left, shoulder to shoulder, some brightly coloured and beautifully kept, others shabby and blistered. Behind and above them all, the floodlit Cathedral of St Colman hovered over Cobh like a Gothic spacecraft, its tall, thin spire a golden rocket spiking the night sky. Unearthly music trailed from it as a carillon player sent the sound of forty-seven bells down through winding streets and out across the water. It was the most extraordinary building that anyone from the Great Blasket had ever seen. The wonders of New York were yet to come.

Out in the harbour a tanker waited for the tide, and blue welding torches flashed from the naval shipyard on Haulbowline Island. Between 1815 and 1970 more than three million people emigrated from the town, usually to America, on famine ships then steamers then luxury liners. Cheap transatlantic flight took all the passengers away, and Cobh never recovered. Its heart was republican but its body, the look of the place, still belonged to the age of the Empress.

Until 1849 the town was called the Cove of Cork because it was the first port of call in the estuary, a dozen miles upriver of the county capital. The name was changed at the height of the Famine, while thousands of starved and disease-ridden men and women were in the harbour begging for passage to America. Against the wishes of her own advisers and the politicians in Ireland, Queen Victoria insisted on a visit to see conditions for herself, an announcement which set off an unseemly scramble for the honour of receiving her. The landowners of Cove won by offering to rename the place Queenstown, although they did not bother to ask or even tell the people who lived there.

Cannons gave a loud salute, crowds lined the quayside and bonfires lit up the grounds of the big houses on 3 August 1849. 'The day was grey and excessively "muggy", which is the character of the Irish climate,' the royal visitor wrote in her diary. Prince Albert went ashore in the morning but Queen Victoria stayed on the royal yacht, writing and sketching. In the afternoon the couple boarded a tender and toured the harbour, with naval vessels firing rockets over the trailing steamers.

We then went into Cove and lay alongside the landing-place, which was very prettily decorated; and covered with people; and yachts, ships and boats crowding all round . . . to give the people the satisfaction of calling the place Queenstown, in honour of its being the first spot on which I set foot upon Irish ground, I stepped on shore amidst the roar of cannon (for the artillery were placed so close as quite to shake the temporary room which we entered); and the enthusiastic shouts of the people.

It is hard to imagine how enthusiastic those shouts were, given the desperate state of many local people, but no doubt the starving rabble was kept well away from the royal visit. Victoria never did see much of the suffering that her own government had caused by neglect and incompetence. As for Queenstown, most of its ordinary folk were completely surprised by the gracious bestowal of a new name, and not altogether pleased. Her Majesty spent no more than a few minutes on shore and was gone again, to Cork.

The people of Queenstown showed what they thought of the name change as soon as the Irish Free State was created in 1921. The town council renounced it as a reminder of British imperialism, and opted for a Gaelic version of the original. The two main squares were renamed after Sir Roger Casement, the former British diplomat who converted to the cause of Irish nationalism and was hanged in 1916, and Pádraig Pearse, leader of the Easter Rebellion in Dublin that year, who preached that bloodshed was better than slavery. Queen Victoria would not have been amused.

By the time Her Majesty risked stretching a dainty foot on to the quayside, Cobh had become known as the Harbour of Tears, because so many people had boarded vessels there in hope of a better life abroad. The Irish who had already settled in America heard the cries of their former countrymen and women and sent help in the form of the USS *Jamestown*, a three-masted sailing ship which entered the Cove of Cork in April 1847 with 800 tons of food from the people of Boston. A couple of months later, the city joined with New York to despatch the USS *Macedonian* with more supplies. The aid was kind, but worth little more than teardrops in the ocean. Since nobody knew how to cook the imported Indian meal, the government had to print leaflets advising that porridge could be made with water or a little milk. It could be rolled up into mush, which the official documents described as a lump like moist bread. 'It is a great thing for all classes of persons, but particularly for the labourer.'

The Famine did strange things to some people's minds. While lavish preparations were being made for the visit of Victoria, and the death toll was rising, the local bishop decided it would be a splendid idea to spend a lot of money on a great big church. After eleven years of planning this turned into a cathedral, the foundation stone of which was laid in 1868. When bishops and archbishops finally gathered to consecrate the building in 1919 it had cost £235,000, the equivalent of millions now, of which a good part was donated by people in the United States. The result was a tall, dark and joyless enclosure that must have been a strange and distressing place for Blasket islanders to kneel and pray, used as they were to contemplating God in the wide open spaces of creation.

Perhaps it was right for the cathedral to be so miserable, given the sadness that hung over Cobh. Along the harbour-front were memorials to ships that had sunk after leaving or passing near the port, including two of the most famous wrecks in history. The *Titanic* was on her maiden voyage in April 1912 when she called in at Queenstown on the way from Southampton to New York. One hundred and twenty-three passengers joined the ship, all but ten of them travelling on third-class tickets. Tenders brought out fourteen hundred sacks of mail bound for America. The few hours that the *Titanic* spent in Queenstown harbour were enough for enterprising locals to go out in small boats and board her, selling lace, linen and souvenirs. Colonel John Jacob Astor, one of the richest men in the world, bought a lace shawl for his wife and paid $800 for it. No doubt an exact replica was available at a much cheaper price to less wealthy customers on shore soon afterwards. Colonel Astor had no need of all that money where he was going: three days later the unsinkable ship struck an iceberg off the coast of Newfoundland and went down, with the loss of fifteen hundred souls.

Eighty-six years later, the *Titanic*'s brief visit again provided locals with an income, thanks to a blockbuster movie about the disaster. The film did not actually mention Cobh, but the hordes of Irish men and women whose wild jigs and passionate laughter lent ethnic charm to the scenes in steerage class must have boarded somewhere. There were references to her all over town, from the Titanic pub to the gift-shop selling T-shirts, and a big black metal gate at the site of the old White Star ticket office, with 'Titanic' stamped on it in brass letters for no apparent reason. Behind was an alleyway leading to an empty space where the pier used to be.

Across the street in Casement Square, two men were racked with pain and sorrow. An angel stood over them, anxious to give comfort. This statue was a monument to the huge Cunard liner *Lusitania*, sunk off the Old Head of Kinsale after being struck by a torpedo from a German U-boat in May 1915. She was lost in less than half an hour – the bow was stuck in the ocean bed while the four propellors at the stern stood out high above the water – and nearly twelve hundred people died. Every available vessel was sent out to bring home the survivors. The American Consul watched a ghostly procession of rescue ships arrive out of the darkness to discharge 'bruised and shuddering women, crippled and half-clothed men and a few wide-eyed little children'. Reading his words, I remembered a delicate bone-china teacup I had seen on the dresser in the home of Seán and Muiris Guithín in Dunquin. It had been washed up on the shore of the Great Blasket just after the wreck occurred, as an outraged America considered joining the war against Germany.

★

The journey from Cobh to New York took weeks and sometimes months on the slow and dangerous Famine ships. Steerage-class passengers were crowded into every available space. They slept in makeshift bunks less than two feet wide, and were rarely allowed on deck except to cook up meagre rations of gruel to go with their ship's biscuit. The steam engines that came later cut the journey time dramatically and were much more comfortable. When Seán Team Ó Cearna made the first of his two trips across the Atlantic at the turn of the century, the transatlantic speed record was held by the *City of Paris*, a steamer from the Inman Line that made it from Cobh to Sandy Hook, fifteen miles outside New York, in just under six days. Allowing for weather and stops, it took most ships twice that time. Seán Team slept in a metal bunk, under a blanket emblazoned with the crest of the shipping line, and washed from a basin in the room he shared with three other men. Public rooms were provided for third-class passengers as well as sleeping quarters. The smoking-room was nothing like as comfortable as first class, where they listened to string quartets and relaxed on sofas, but it did have wooden benches and tables. There were tablecloths and napkins in the dining-room, with jugs of water and bowls of fruit.

Life was even better for Seán Team's sons, who travelled just after the Second World War when liners were glamorous and even the cheapest cabins were reasonably well appointed. The posters in the office of Galvin, the Dingle travel agent, featured beautiful women in fashionable outfits waving from the deck as these floating cities docked in front of the glorious skyscrapers of New York. Getting there was half the fun, the shipping companies suggested (with some desperation, as their business was already under threat from the airlines). Peaidí Ó Cearna sailed from Cobh on the USS *Washington*, described in a proud White Star advertisement as the largest liner ever built in America. 'The Washington offers such ocean luxuries as smart shops . . . a beauty parlour . . . sound pictures . . . gymnasium and swimming pool . . . spacious comfort in every cabin, and in every cabin real beds – not berths!'

Máirtín Ó Cearna took the *Georgic*, the last ship ever to be built by White Star before it merged with Cunard in 1934. It was constructed at the Harland and Wolff shipyard in Belfast and weighed nearly 28,000 tons, with accommodation for up to fifteen hundred passengers. But it was Mícheál Ó Cearna who got the best bargain, from a travel agent near the bar where he worked in Dublin. Mícheál travelled by ferry and train to Southampton, where he boarded one of the most beautiful liners of them all, the *Queen Mary*. The King and Queen of England had launched her from Clydebank shipyard in 1934, but by the time Mícheál boarded the *Queen Mary* she was a war veteran, having served as a troop carrier. His journey from England to New York took less than a week.

The gift shop in Cobh was stuffed with little plastic leprechauns brandishing shillelaghs, unplayable bodhrans with Guinness logos stamped on them, and baby romper suits proclaiming 'I've Got Irish Roots'. I watched the queue and wondered if the Blasket survivors I was pursuing had the same estranged relationship with their place of origin. This cheery fantasy was how a certain portion of the Republic's population wanted the outside world to see them: it was a smokescreen, an illusion, just like the glossy calendars full of beautiful photographs of Kerry that gave no hint of the sodden grey banality of an industrial estate on the outskirts of Tralee. The writer Pete Hamill once described how immigrants to America, alienated and rootless after breaking away from the centuries-old narrative of life at home, invented new personalities for themselves. 'The Stage Irishman was the creation of people who needed masks,' he wrote, and this was where they bought them, on raiding trips back to the Auld Sod. At a hotel in Dingle I had seen a storyteller in an Irish cabaret, wearing a turned-up hat in conchie fashion and speaking in a thick brogue. 'Is it yourselves who are all there?' was his opening question to an audience of returnees. 'I'm only 50 per cent there meself.' It was like watching Bill Cosby put on white make-up and sing 'Mammy'.

Outside, a bright-red tug took welders across to the steel-yard. There were very few jobs to be had in Cobh. More out of respect than in hope I made some enquiries about the possibility of getting a berth on a ship heading west, hoping that in this great harbour where freight vessels still called there would be some way of emulating the journey of so many emigrants; but after days of calling it became clear that there was no chance. Ships were heading for Russia or Brazil, but none to New York in the foreseeable future. The historic route to America taken by the Ó Cearnas was barred for good.

32

19 April 1948

Manhattan looks so peaceful from the sea. It rises from the horizon purple in the dusk, a stone circle alone on a plain. The East River and the Hudson throw their arms around this simple construction, pushing back the flat shorelines of Brooklyn and New Jersey. As the ship approaches, a few elegant columns become distinct, gathered in wait or welcome, giving no indication of the human swarm in their shadows. America begins to boast while its new arrivals are still in the open ocean, as a playboy with an Errol Flynn moustache, returning from some disastrous adventure in the East, spins his thin knowledge into a routine.

'See that needle there? Just behind the first row of sky-scrapers, a little faded, higher than all others? The Empire State Building, my friend, wonder of the world, tallest on the planet. Built by an Irishman, sure. And there, on the starboard side, by the water's edge? The Wonder Wheel, tallest Ferris ride on earth. Star attraction of Coney Island, great pleasure-dome of the working man. OK, so the place is a little sad since the fire got to all that wood, but you should see the Snake Woman. On the beach? They are the crowds, my friend, the crowds. Yeah, just like ants.'

The deck also becomes crowded as the liner moves through the Verrazano Narrows, with Staten Island close by on the left, a green and quiet place detached from the city, for now. The wide Upper Bay still feels like the Atlantic as seagulls fly alongside, hurdling the slipstream. A naval destroyer lies sleek and low in the New Jersey docks beside cranes and container vessels, invisible against the gun-metal-grey water but for the soft peach of sunset making its rust scars burn. There is no sound but the ponderous throb of the liner's engines, the sigh of the waves, the lonely clang of buoys bobbing in the wake, and the awe-struck mutterings of passengers. A skinny Polish teenager in a trenchcoat sucks air between his teeth as the Statue of Liberty emerges from the grainy light of dusk, gliding up to meet him on the port side.

Now adults jostle for position on the guard-rail and hold their children up to see that sight, as millions have done before them. 'The tomb of Columbus,' says someone, but she's kidding. An intense man with a pale beard seizes the moment. Opening a small black book at a well-thumbed page he begins to read, in his second language after Greek or German, Latvian or Lithuanian, Irish, Italian, Arabic or Yiddish, or some other tongue from some far place, the words inscribed on the base of the statue:

> Here at our sea-washed, sunset gates shall stand
> a mighty woman with a torch
> whose flame is imprisoned lightning,
> and her name Mother of Exiles.
> From her beacon-hand glows
> world-wide welcome.

Perhaps the reader is a rabbi or a cantor, a mullah or a priest; maybe a teacher, a student, an actor, or a farmer with a love for learning. The words are by Emma Lazarus, written to raise money for an unwanted statue which became the most potent symbol of America after its flag. Liberty holds out her golden torch, glittering brighter for the falling dark, and the weather-worn copper-green of the statue herself also shines. Close up, she is a vibrant, surprising green, the colour of grass or the deep, salty sea under a sweating sun. This bold beauty stands to one side, not towering over the ship but ushering it through.

Growing in confidence and volume, breathless, the reader goes on with the poem, as others around him still their own tongues to listen:

> 'Keep, ancient lands, your storied pomp!'
> Cries she with silent lips.
> 'Give me your tired, your poor,
> Your huddled masses yearning to breathe free,
> The wretched refuse of your teeming shore.
> Send these, the homeless, tempest-tost to me,
> I lift my lamp beside the golden door!'

The euphoric sight of Liberty is followed by a sudden stab of fear and worry. Stomachs tighten at the name Ellis Island. Eyes go to a short stretch of land with trees on its shoreline, protecting a brick-and-limestone building that could be a factory or a palace. Every immigrant has heard stories of the indignities and confusion faced by a relative or a friend in that vast registry. Some were turned away. For the first time since leaving port, they cannot help but consider the possibility of failure in this new country.

But then Manhattan looms, demanding attention to its Olympian skyscrapers with their angels and gargoyles built so many floors up that only the birds can see them. If cathedrals point upwards to God, then these commercial equivalents built by ambitious white men before empire was a dirty word point towards human achievement. Look at us, they say. Look at what we can do, and how stylishly too. Anything can be achieved here.

The waters grow black in the shadow of the financial district, spangled by its lights. The Hudson is crowded with transatlantic vessels, pilots, tenders and barges. The shoreline is busy too, as people say their goodbyes, haul cargo or wait for the new arrivals. Some have dark intentions. The passengers are all on deck now, gazing up at the towers or down on the quayside. They still remember who they are and where they have come from. Some know where they are going, into the reality of America. Others know it as a place of myth and money, where you can make a new life. Everyone is equal there. A few still believe you can pick gold off the streets. The sides of the ship hit one of the piers strung out along the West Side with a sudden jolt. There are many more of those to come.

33

I looked west at the edge of the sky where America should be lying, and I slipped back on the paths of thought. It seemed to me now that the New Island was before me with its fine streets and great high houses, some of them so tall that they scratched the sky; gold and silver out on the ditches and nothing to do but to gather it.

Muiris Ó Súilleabháin, *Twenty Years A-Growing*

Few of the letters home to the Great Blasket mentioned the sentry standing by the gateway to the Land of Youth. One hundred million Americans can trace their ancestry to a man, woman or child whose name was transferred from a steamship manifest sheet to an inspector's record book in the Registry Room at Ellis Island. The process took up to eight hours on busy days, and ended in rejection for a thousand people a month.

Seán Team Ó Cearna waited in line there when he first tried America in 1901. The new inspection centre, built of brick and limestone in imitation of the grand buildings of the French Renaissance, had only been open a few months. Seán was one of 389,000 people who climbed the slate steps to the Registry Room that year. Most of them never went home again, but he did, only to return in 1908, by which time a million people a year were passing through.

Ellis Island was being wound down when his boys arrived in

New York after the Second World War, and it was eventually turned into a museum which attracted at least as many visitors. The queues for the ferry from Castle Clinton, on the south tip of Manhattan, started early in the morning. First stop was the Statue of Liberty, inside whose hollow metal body the temperature was already climbing towards one hundred degrees. The school parties got off there, emptying the ferry of all but a dozen other people, most of whom were retracing journeys taken by parents, relatives, or themselves. I wanted to see what it would have been like for Seán Team and other Blasket islanders to be processed there – and to get a sense of the many who had queued alongside them, from places they had never heard of and could not imagine. Having been absorbed once into the flood of humanity heading west from Ireland to America, at Ellis Island they were forced to appreciate how many thousands were travelling in the same direction from all over Europe and the wider world.

Most of the immigrants wore their best clothes, the ones they had kept in storage throughout the journey, in order to impress inspectors and relatives. Often these were their national or ceremonial dress. The rancid rags they had worn every day for two weeks were thrown away and their owners regained the dignity of the black-and-white photographs of themselves, taken before departure, which they had carried to America and which were eventually donated to the museum. The poses were stiff, but most of the subjects looked at ease with themselves, full of a reassurance that was surely lost or challenged in the new country. Most were not victims or refugees at all but voluntary immigrants, although the museum seemed to nurture a myth of rescue.

Everything they owned in the world was with them, in cases, bags and trunks which had to be left at the entrance to the depot while they registered. Their valuables were later displayed in glass cases: rosary beads from Ireland, a shawl used by a Polish Jew during his prayers each morning, a pewter sacramental cup from Lithuania, a fragile little pink china figure dressed in lace – the Christ child used during a traditional family Christmas on an island of the Azores. A Swiss-American woman had donated the teddy she brought with her as a girl. There was a mandolin carried to America in 1909 by Barnett Chadekal, a six-foot-nine soldier in the army of the Czar who had been photographed, massive in his army greatcoat, next to his son Hyman. With their wife and mother Jenny, they fled a pogrom against the Jews in Lithuania, reached Hamburg and boarded a liner for New York, where they lived on the Lower East Side until Barnett managed to buy a small farm upstate. He became a citizen in 1926. Spread out next to the mandolin on which Barnett played folk tunes for Jenny's dancing feet was an embroidered sheet from Denmark, 'used only during births to show the doctor something beautiful brought from the homeland'.

Whoever they were before, everyone who entered Ellis Island was identified by a paper tag with a number on it that corresponded to their ship's manifest sheet. 'You may have heard that people had their names changed here, because the inspectors didn't write them down properly,' said a tall guide in brown uniform. 'That is a myth. They filled in the information themselves at the point of departure, so if someone was illiterate or put down their occupation by mistake, it was they who got it wrong.' Two per cent of applications were refused. There was a right to appeal, but without a lawyer. 'This was not a violation of your constitutional rights. You were not a citizen. You didn't have any.'

In comparison to what they had been through, the long wait I had experienced at JFK airport after my flight from Shannon now seemed like nothing. It must have been terrify-

ing for anyone who had fled political or military persecution
to be herded into lines by guards in uniform, shouted at in
a language they didn't understand, and separated from their
family. Men, women and children queued separately. As they
shuffled forward, a step at a time, from the quay to the baggage
hall, up the stairs and finally into the vast Registry Room, all
were inspected without their knowledge. Those who walked
awkwardly, who coughed, sneezed or were short of breath
were marked with a symbol in blue chalk on their shoulder
and led away. What was that mark? Who could explain what
was happening?

There were translators, of course, fluent in forty-four languages, but they were very busy. Each inspector saw four to
five hundred people a day. The doctors were most worried
about cholera, a scalp-and-nail fungus called favus, and
insanity. If Seán Team Ó Cearna had been epileptic, suffering
from tuberculosis or physically disabled when he first came to
America, he would still have been let in. The second time, a
year after new laws had been passed in 1907, he would have
been barred. The other main worry was trachoma, a contagious
eye infection common in parts of Europe but rare in America,
which could cause blindness and death. The test involved
turning the eyelid of each immigrant inside-out with a finger,
a hair-pin or a buttonhook. It didn't take long, but hurt like
hell.

An X chalked on the back meant you were suspected of
having a feeble mind. In a side room that resembled a police
cell you were asked questions and told to complete tests. Those
who could put a square peg in a square hole were allowed to
rejoin the line; those who could not, or who were physically
infectious, were sent back to their country of origin.

At the end of the queue was the Registry Room itself, a
crowded place and noisy with people speaking in a thousand

tongues all at once. The island of Manhattan was visible through the long windows, waiting. Every queue led to a legal inspector in a starched collar and serge jacket, who stood behind a desk and asked questions. He took only a few minutes to decide whether you were socially, economically and morally fit to enter the country. If nerves or anxiety at the fate of your wife and child gave rise to a slip of the tongue, you were in trouble. After such a long wait, during which the mind had no choice but to drift, this was the moment to be alert. A European woman was asked whether she would begin to wash a set of steps from the bottom or the top and replied, 'I did not come to America to wash steps.' She was let in.

America's open door closed a little in 1917, as the nation entered the First World War. Political radicals, most non-whites and almost all Asians were unwelcome as anti-immigrant feeling grew. Those who were most hostile to the newest wave of arrivals included earlier immigrants or their descendants, such as the Irish, who had begun to achieve political influence. Theories of racial superiority were spreading and the Ku Klux Klan was booming. Quotas were imposed. The law was changed to require all arrivals to be able to read a passage in English or their native language, most often from the Bible. The Serbs, for example, who had been driven out of their jobs and homes, were told to read from the Book of James: 'Your riches are corrupted, and your garments moth-eaten. Your gold and silver is cankered and the rust of them shall be a witness against you, and shall eat your flesh as it were fire.'

The quotas were reduced in 1924 and inspection transferred to the country of origin, so that Ellis Island fell out of use until it was refurbished and reopened as a memorial to the many who had passed through its gates. Mícheál Ó Cearna and his brothers were allowed to enter the States as a crack opened in the Golden Door just after the war, because they had close relatives who were US citizens and who would vouch for them. The last batch of willing Blasket island youth finally came to America then, along with their contemporaries from Dunquin and the villages west of Dingle. Three decades later, out of gratitude and a sense of a debt that needed paying, Mícheál Ó Cearna contributed to the appeal for the restoration of the Statue of Liberty, and ensured that his father was one of the 400,000 listed on the American Immigrant Wall of Honour built outside the Registry Room. This monument to survival shone in the sun but it had the solemnity of a war memorial, since the sight of name after name stamped into the reflective metal was deeply moving. Seán Team Ó Cearna was listed in his Irish form alongside men and women called Carney, Kearney and dozens of other variations on the family name.

See the United States most famous landmark so close
you can almost reach out and touch her!
Liberty Helicopter Tours Brochure

'Caution,' warned a sign in big red letters. 'This area is subject to high winds created by operating helicopters.' Tiny cyclones sucked rubbish into the air, and children held their ears against the noise. Some were queueing with their parents for the forty-dollar 'trip of a lifetime', a ten-minute whirl around the skyscrapers in one of the two choppers operating from an old pier on the West Side. A man in an orange boiler-suit raised his arms and another half-dozen paying customers were lifted into the air as a luxury liner moved into view out in the river between the landing pad and New Jersey. Other children had their faces pressed up against the link fence a few yards away, waiting to see who the next arrival would be at the Manhattan

VIP Heliport. They knew it must be someone special because there was a black stretch limousine with dark windows waiting by the kerbside, and a Range Rover behind it full of men in white shirts and black ties. 'Maybe they're secret-service agents,' a father told his son with a wink, thinking of presidents and men of power. The number plate was F7. 'Maybe it's Michael Jackson,' said the boy, living in a different world.

A radio crackled inside the limo, the uniformed chauffeur sat up and folded his paper. A white flash in the cloudless sky grew larger until it became a shuttle helicopter from JFK, bearing down on the pier, getting bigger and louder, landing. A secret-service man unfolded a black-leather wheelchair from the back of the Range Rover and pushed it towards the door of the helicopter, crouching as he ran to avoid the rotor blades and their down-draft. The door opened, the spectators squinted in the sunlight and saw that it was nobody they recognized. A very old man, thin and pale as a wisp of smoke. His travelling companion was young and beautiful.

The black cars moved away, downtown, and the crowd dispersed. I looked around, at the bus station across the street, the abandoned overhead railway, the garbage trucks lined up in their depots, and the tenement blocks. Behind them was the Empire State, fabulous and futuristic, still as extraordinary as it was when the VIP Heliport was Pier 69. The black stumps at the water's edge had been where Peaidí Ó Cearna first set foot on American land almost exactly fifty years earlier, in the summer of 1948, six days after leaving Cobh on the USS *George Washington*.

Peaidí was met at the pier by his Auntie Bridget, who called the boy Paddy and led him on a fifteen-minute walk through the busy streets to the railway station, past luggage handlers, lodging-house runners, thieves, taxi drivers, street vendors, and shoppers. The crowds and buildings of Dingle had been disconcerting the first time he ever saw them, those in Cobh were impressive, but New York was absolutely overwhelming. It was alien and dangerous, noisy, aggressive, dirty and confusing. Whatever else Paddy felt like on that day, turning circles in that place before the liners gave way to the pleasure flights and airport shuttles, it wasn't a VIP.

34

If I had been made to live in New York City I never would have stayed in America.

Patrick O'Connor, formerly of Dunquin

20 April 1948

Walk. Don't walk. Run. Twenty-Ninth. Steam from the streets and the metal train screaming. Pistons firing. 'Hey boy, get outta the goddamn way.' Salt sea dying, car fumes filling nose and throat. Lights changing. 'D'ya ever see that kid Robinson play?' Ninth to West Thirty-Fourth, less crowded. Time for breath catching. Open windows, strung-out washing. Shouting: 'You're as much use as the damned Spruce Goose!' Babe Ruth, Orville Wright, both of them gone. Israel born, and Candid Camera. Outside the Square Garden, hot dogs fizzing. 'Jersey Joe's a no-hoper, no kiddin'.' In the dark of a bar, an orchestra playing; for a nickel in a jukebox, someone singing.

Hold my hand. Wouldn't want to lose you now.

Don't walk. Look up, the sky grown dark, the towers closing in above. Macy's, the biggest store in the world. A thousand neon wonders glowing. Jesus, the traffic. Walk. Don't run. A drunkard laughing. Empire State, a thing of beauty. Here now, Fifth. 'How you feeling? OK? Hell of a place to be living, eh?' Treasure of the Sierra Madre. No words left, no words for this. Shuffling, balancing, swerving, nervous, getting through. Just getting through. 'Beware the Red Menace is Coming.' Black man in a suit. Man in a black suit. Shoeshine boy, shouting and running. Heavy red-neck fellow sweating. Chafed. This tie. How much further can it be? 'Hey, fella – better watch out where you're stepping!' Forty-Second, right, Grand Central. Heart hard pumping. Into the shadows, footsteps falling.

Who'd have thought there were so many people in the world?

35

Grand Central Station used to be the gateway to an undiscovered country, the terminus from which pioneers were carried to the ends of the fast-expanding railway system. The vaulted ceiling was painted with stars, a canopy for dreamers; but the trains had been re-routed since Paddy's day and were only heading for the suburbs. I wanted to follow him north across the city boundary and beyond to Springfield, Massachusetts, which meant hurrying back nine streets to Pennsylvania Station. This lauded Belle Epoch building was demolished in 1963 to allow more room for the rebuilt Madison Square Garden, first and ugliest of the world's modern arenas, and passengers were sent underground to the modern station beneath the stadium. The weak blue light from an oppressively low ceiling made everyone look, and feel, nauseous.

There was barely time for a glass of Harp in Houlihan's before hauling my baggage down an impossibly narrow escalator to the waiting train 56, the 'Amtrak Vermonter', a big silver beast which had begun its journey very early that morning in Washington. After the squalid Irish trains it seemed so roomy and clean that I stepped outside for a moment to be sure I was in coach class – then stretched out, reassured, on a reclining seat with the air conditioning easing away the hot temper of the streets.

We emerged from tunnels somewhere in the Bronx, with a view back over factories and apartment blocks to the skyline of Manhattan. For half an hour the train gathered speed alongside flyovers and freeways, passing through an urban industrial landscape punctuated with billboards advertising staples and cockroach killers. 'Bugs – Eat This!' I took out the little green plastic Statue of Liberty I had bought at the station, and shook up the snowstorm in its plinth. What did they make of it, the people who had put this together in a Hong Kong sweatshop? At $2.95 it was a bargain, even if the torch had already snapped off.

An hour out, past Westport, Connecticut, the scenery flattened and turned green. Deep forest bordered the tracks on one side, and on the other marshy banks led down to an estuary where yachts and dinghies rested on their hulls in the low tide. After the ocean and the city, it would have reminded the travellers of what they had left behind.

The emerald idyll ended at Bridgeport, where the road swept over the railway and a block draped with pipes and gantries turned out to be a lightbulb factory, among refineries and docks. As the 56 zigzagged along the route of the Connecticut River, the view alternated between scenes of pastoral beauty, wide stretches of water, and small towns where the site of greatest historical and architectural interest was an abandoned mill. Brown and green were the colours of the journey, blending before sleepy eyes. Green for the grass, the trees, the river reflecting them. Brown for the rusting railway equipment and old freight wagons left in a siding, for the dusty earth and vegetation burnt away by the sun, for the buildings on the city limits, the undersides of bridges, the uninhabited warehouse yards. I dozed, listening to the radio.

'I'm Leah, and I clean windows. I'm a Scorpio and . . .' She was advertising a new unisex fragrance available in a special Back-to-School pack, with moisturizer, for only forty dollars. Even with my eyes closed I could hear the landscape changing, as the radio stations fizzed in and out of range. The soca, salsa and ragga of the black and hispanic DJs in New York City gave way to white noise, and then white music. 'One great light song after another here on Light 100.5 WRCK.' Berlin, Connecticut, had a battered but cute little brownstone station, with the Berlin Steel plant blocking out the light behind it. Buddy Holly sang 'That'll Be the Day' on The Big D 103 as the train accelerated again. The frequencies were close together, and the songs came fast, in fragments. An unidentified, tearful yodel on Country 92.5. The melting-pot of New York was separating itself into lumps. We'd just been lovin' too long as we entered Hartford, past another abandoned factory with grass growing on its forecourt, and it was no use cryin', the tears were all done, as we left town. A stately building set back in parkland, with a golden dome, flew past the window. My mind seemed less receptive to architectural wonders since Manhattan. Someone called Jack Carney on WDRC was offering the chance to win a lobster. I wondered how he spelt his name.

The Blasket travellers were almost at the end of their long journey when they reached these flat lands of New England, this quiet America that had been settled by the pilgrims, scarred by the industrial revolution, and was just about getting on with life. How did they feel as the bell rang on the crossing and their steam train gave a warning? After Hartford it was almost all green, like home, until the edge of the next city.

'Welcome to Springfield. Someplace Special.' A sign suggested a visit to the zoo in Forest Park. We slowed down alongside the canal, under the freeway, past a glass tower and the blank, flat faces of the Marriott and Sheraton Hotels. 'Legal Problem? Let me help you.' Attorney Rich Iago looked like a small man although his photograph was thirty feet high. Shrewd, though, in his little round glasses. I could have used a friend to meet me at the station. The islanders usually had relatives waiting for the train, with an Irish greeting and a thirst for news, ready to walk a block to the John Boyle O'Reilly Social Club for a glass or two. You'd find a dozen familiar faces there, or names anyway, playing poker or propping up the bar. 'God be with you, son.' 'God and Mary with you.' Someone had a room or a piece of floor if you needed it. There were jobs around for those who knew the foreman, and this was the place to find him. A beer on the bar for the greenhorn. 'Heard you play football OK. There's a game Sunday.' An hour after arrival and the warm feeling inside was not only coming from the drink. Here, at last, after all these miles, were your own people.

36

I was a stranger to the John Boyle O'Reilly, however, and nervous as hell about it. The club had moved from its old rented premises in the centre of Springfield to a low modern concrete building on an industrial estate at the edge of the city. Progress Avenue. An Irish tricolour flew beside the Stars and Stripes, above brilliant flowerbeds. Only members were welcome. The bar was in the basement, at the bottom of a gloomy stairwell past an advertisement for a benefit evening in memory of three Catholic boys who had been killed by Protestant arsonists in Northern Ireland. Wooden doors decorated with shamrocks opened to reveal a long, low room, lit by wall-lamps with green glass shades.

A dozen eyes looked up at me from the faces of men, old and young, who sat at stalls around a rectangular bar. 'If you're drinking to forget, please pay in advance,' said a sign above the barman's head. On the wall between a painted leprechaun and an illuminated photograph of the Skellig islands was a roll of honour for the club's biggest fund-raisers. At the far end of the room, where the lights were brighter, I could see elderly couples playing cards while they listened to a band. A tall, bearded man in a Guinness T-shirt hit a bodhran, and a small woman with a boyish crop strummed a guitar. They sang about being broad-backed members of the IRA.

I cursed my English accent. Somewhere in this dimly lit place was a man I had travelled thousands of miles to find, with no idea about how I would be received. As president of the club, he had built its membership up from fifty people to more than a thousand. This was his natural environment, the home he had made for himself so far from his birthplace. He was resting his elbows on the bar, an old man with white hair swept back from a long forehead, and a straight nose that looked familiar. A man born on the Great Blasket island in September 1920. The brother of a brave, tiny woman who lived by Smerwick Harbour in County Kerry. Here, at last, was Mícheál Ó Cearna, the first of the brothers to emigrate to America, and the first to agree to see me. Not quite smiling, he shook my hand and pulled back a stool.

'A drink?'

The question was friendly enough but the tone careful. There was a stillness and authority about him. The other men around the bar watched us without breaking off from their own conversations. I spoke quietly, uneasy at the band's choice of song, although by this time a bullish man in a baseball cap was singing 'Dirty Old Town' in an Irish accent that was clearly not his own. A glass of Harp was put before me on a mat, and a vodka for Mr Carney, as the barman called him. No money changed hands.

We talked about the letter I had sent. He asked what I was trying to achieve, and made it clear that he was dubious. 'I don't really do this sort of thing any more,' he had already told me on the telephone, meaning talk to writers about the island. The last had been a man from Dunquin. His caution was understandable, I knew that, particularly when the person who wanted to rummage around in your family history was an Englishman half your age. Then I mentioned Céit, and what she had told me about the family, and his voice softened. The thin, moist lips were hers, and the accent similar, even after all this time.

'I don't forget what she did for us.'

Our tentative conversation was interrupted by wellwishers,

who wanted a quick word in the Ó Cearna ear. They didn't have much to say, but just saying something seemed enough. We did not go thirsty. A younger man in the corner stared for a while, then sent a round over with his compliments. Mr Carney nodded, and touched his forehead in thanks. After a while he suggested I come over to his house on Hungry Hill the next day, and ask my questions there. He didn't know if he could help, but he would tell me what he knew. My audience ended when another person stepped up to shake his hand, and it was then that I realized he kept using the same phrase to introduce me. 'This is Cole Moreton,' he said. 'He's an Englishman, but he spends so much time in Ireland they're thinking of making him a citizen.'

It wasn't true. I hadn't told him that. At first I took it as some kind of joke, then I began to realize what was going on. The club was named after John Boyle O'Reilly, a Fenian. For most of his life he believed in the use of force to end the British rule in Ireland. O'Reilly enlisted in the Hussars with the intention of recruiting other Irish members of his regiment to rise up and fight when the signal came, but it never did. He was convicted of treason and sentenced to death by the English, but sent to Australia on a prison ship instead. A priest helped him to escape to America, where he took up the cause of Irish freedom again as a journalist, orator, poet and publisher.

'He didn't have much use for your cousins over there, anyway,' said Mike Carney. There was no malice in his voice but I wasn't sure that everyone else in the bar felt the same way. His introduction had sounded flippant, even awkward, but it was more artful than that, a way of telling his people that I was OK. He was protecting me.

37

The dead of New England were gathered in limbo at the Southern Inn, an out-of-town motel in a service area just above the Massachusetts Turnpike. At least it felt like they should be. The saving grace of this stopping-off place for the long-distance traveller was its closeness to the Fifties Diner which hid behind a gas station across the road. From its shocking-pink-and-black sign to the tiled floor, chrome fittings and the long counter at which truckers sat eating huge burgers after midnight, the diner was the America I had seen on television and in the movies. It was hard to contain my excitement, as a stranger, at what must have been a mundane scene for everyone else there. The waitresses wore white uniforms, their hair pinned up and their faces cynical but kind. Behind glass in the corridor a paunchy man in a baseball cap wearing jeans and cowboy boots spooned quarters into a telephone, his elbow raised in the air as he leant against the wall. Trucks as big as houses stood silent outside. This was the set of a thousand road movies. There was even a pair of Harleys in the stand.

Unfortunately, I had forgotten the script. It was a big mistake to grab one of the photocopied pink menus from the counter myself. After that, every time I caught the eye of a waitress she would smile and nod as if to say hi, then carry on doing her thing, which was serving other people. Anyone but me. What was I doing wrong? How were you supposed to behave here? There would have been diners like this all over town when the Ó Cearna brothers first arrived in Springfield at the dawn of the real fifties, a prosperous decade which would bring the shock of rock & roll and invent the teenager. The disorientation the Ó Cearnas felt must have been constant. If I was this agitated and frustrated when I knew the scenery and had seen the moves acted out a thousand times on screen, how had it felt to come to such a place without much of the language, and none of the instinct? How long did it take to stop feeling panic?

She came over, of course, just as I was about to leave. Late thirties probably, her eyes brim-full of a lifetime spent serving the strange, the difficult, the mad, the love-lorn, and no doubt the lonely.

'What can I get you, honey?'

A squeeze of the hand maybe, I thought. An unprofessional smile, a friendly chat over a milkshake? No, make that a long, rambling confessional with a bottle of something red, a warm bed on which to lie and be held all night, and a huge fried breakfast in the morning, eaten while you sit on the porch and blow smoke rings. Please.

'Pattie melt.' She did not. 'Thanks.'

'You're welcome.'

I worked my way through a medium burger with Swiss cheese on rye bread, fries, coleslaw, battered onion rings, a visit to the salad bar and unlimited refills of Diet Coke, with a guide to Springfield propped up on the salt cellar. I wondered about shooting some hoops at the Basketball Hall of Fame, dedicated to a game invented at the local YMCA so that beefy young Christians could spend their energy in winter, but it was far too hot for all that. I felt way too fat now, anyway. I could have gone to the Armoury where the Springfield rifle was invented, or maybe looked for Mulberry Street where Theodor Seuss Geisel was raised. He became Dr Seuss, author of *The Cat in the Hat*, *How the Grinch Stole Christmas* and other children's books, many of them inspired by life in Springfield, which sold in millions. Then he cleared off to California and made it big in the movies. Walking back to the motel across vast empty forecourts after midnight, watching the cars wait on the Mass Pike, I could hardly blame him.

A couple were having fun in the next room. The Puritans would never have allowed it. Too full to sleep, I slumped back on my bed to read about Springfield, a city they founded. The pursuit of holiness was obviously exhausting, because they soon felt the need for servants. The cheapest and easiest to acquire were the Irish, who could be treated like slaves once you had paid for their passage. Any Catholics who would not submit to the Protestant creed were convicted of witchcraft or persecuted through a colonial justice system that seemed to operate on the rule that a man was innocent if the rope broke when you hanged him. After ten years in service the Irish were free of their indentures, and many of them started small farms. They obviously didn't bear grudges, because when the revolution came in 1775 many of these freemen and women fought fiercely alongside other Americans of Puritan descent.

The second wave of immigration from Ireland began fifty years later, as crops failed in the years leading up to the Famine. The industrial revolution had seized New England and there were roads, dams, factories, then railroads to build. Such heavy labour required a workforce that was large and cheap, and Irish farmers and labourers fleeing from starvation were glad to do anything for a pittance, which initially seemed to them like a fortune. Wives and daughters were taken on as domestic servants in the homes of the managers and developers, then later went to work in the factories their men had built.

As the immigrant community grew larger, the Yankee

citizens of Springfield began to resent and fear their new workforce. The Irish were wretched, drunken creatures, who lived in filth and were to blame for their own poverty, said the bosses and civic leaders. It was true that they lived in the poorest part of town, where rain turned dirt paths into ankle-deep mud and there were no sewers. True too that they were doing work no one else would touch, and it hurt. Whiskey took the pain away, but it also made men rowdy. A cholera epidemic brought panic, but nobody knew what caused the disease, so they blamed the Irish and their dirty habits. Some Protestants who believed Catholicism was incompatible with American ideals were prepared to burn down churches to make their point.

The Irish fought back, secretly and also legitimately in the polls. Over time, using their natural eloquence and ability to organize resistance, they mobilized the vote, infiltrated the political system, won control, and made sure their countrymen got the best jobs in City Hall, in the police and in the judiciary. They were white, they knew how to play the game, so they got out of the ghetto. Grand Catholic churches were built by subscription, with schools and hospitals attached, providing a structure to the Irish community. There were secret associations too, like the Ancient Order of Hibernians, who believed in mutual support and a free Ireland. Their backing for the Republican struggle back home was loud and generous. It was happening all over America, this shaping of the Irish into a political force, with a voice that would ultimately shout all the way to the White House.

'There boy, see that? They got a nigger. You gotta remember this.' A white woman with smoke on her face uncovered her son's eyes so that the flames danced in them. She held his hands against his cheeks, a firm touch but tender, loving, caring, forcing him to watch the body of a black man twitch on the end of a rope. The man was still alive, past caring about the pain but screaming at the utter, filthy humiliation of it all as the boy's father cut off his ear and held it up, blood running down the sleeve of his shirt. There were torches burning, and men in white hoods. It was only a movie, on a television in a motel room in the early hours of the morning, but it was based on real life, a massacre that took place in the South in 1923. In Springfield that same year an Irishman was city marshall, the chief of police. In every society, there are some immigrants who fare better than others.

38

The Carney home was a sea-grey clapboard bungalow behind an immaculate lawn, on a wide and leafy road. A painted plaster seagull squatted between two pots of blazing red flowers on the front porch, and in the driveway was a two-tone 1985 Buick automatic with the registration plate BLASKT. The brilliant-white front door opened and Mike Carney stepped out in striped Bermuda shorts and a checked blue tennis shirt with a vest underneath. He was also wearing sunglasses, and white socks with sneakers. Just behind him was his wife Maureen, an animated, snow-haired woman dressed almost identically, who looked as though she could have run a marathon. She had a dazzling smile.

'My earliest memory would be when I was four or five, running around with hardly any clothes on, playing,' said Carney when we had settled in the living-room, with cold drinks and the fan on at full speed. 'It is muggy. You know that word, muggy? It's an American word.'

There was an aerial photograph of the Great Blasket on the wall above his head as he sat in a high, straight-backed armchair, rattling ice around a plastic beaker. 'I was sent to school when I was about five, just to keep me quiet.' The schoolhouse was just next door to the Ó Cearna home on the island, but the children were required to be out of bed by seven in the morning. 'You had to be ready and dressed. You washed in the big basin outside the door. We had no running water, of course. In the winter, same thing.' I wondered why those skinny, half-naked children washing outside in the snow never froze to death. 'The weather wasn't very cold there. It was warmer than the mainland. Oh, it was windy as hell though.'

For breakfast they ate bread, and shared a big pot of porridge. There was always tea to drink. 'Maybe you had to go and get the cow in the field and bring it home to be milked. Everybody had a turn to do every day. That was laid out to you by your father or by your mother, or by the oldest of the family. You respected the eldest very much, you were always ready to listen to advice, and you believed it. My sister Céit was the captain of the ship. If Céit wasn't home then Muiris qualified, and if Muiris wasn't home I qualified. It went down the whole family, *ó ghlúin go glúin*, as they used to say, from knee to knee.'

Lessons began in the school at nine and finished at four. 'In the winter time we all had to bring a sod or two of turf, to light the fire.' There were two classes, upper and lower, on rows of benches back to back in the same room. The teachers, both women, were strict. 'They had the stick. And the belt too, sometimes. Today you can't even touch a kid in school. Fortunately, maybe – I don't know.'

Everything was taught in Gaelic. 'That was all we knew. We had a pretty good education, the only thing that hindered us when we left the island for the mainland was the English. We didn't know that much.' It should not have come as a surprise to hear that the lessons on that island included American history and geography. 'All the rivers, all the towns, all the cities. We had a fairly good idea where Springfield, Massachusetts was. Most everybody on the island had relatives over here. They used to send home those beautiful parcels at Christmas time.' The younger islanders looked forward to receiving toys, but the adults hoped for dollars. 'That's the first thing they used to check for. "Oh yes. Great country America," they'd say. We felt that it was a great place for money. We took it for granted.' Years later, he found himself posting cash back to Ireland. 'We wrote home, to tell 'em how good it was. Christmas time, sending the letters home with a couple of dollars in. Money is very enticing, you know.'

When school was finished for the day, the barefoot children were free to run about all over the island. Their favourite place was the headland called *An Gob*, where the sea wind was at its strongest. 'We used to jump up in the wind like seagulls. It was a play for us, we thought we were birds. As kids we used to pee against the wind, see which one would go the furthest.' He was the champion. The deadpan face he had maintained until that moment cracked and he laughed like a seagull swallowing a fish, gulping it down. 'Ah yeah, well, it was a pastime. A natural thing. We got it back in our face again. We had to create our own amusement. Later on, we were fishermen without going in the ocean.'

I thought he meant that they fished with a line from the rocks, but that was not it at all. 'We used to bring barnacles home to cook them and eat them, and we had an empty shell, OK? So we used to appoint three young fellas to a boat, as if they were fishing lobster, then they used to fill up their little shell with water, go round to where the cows walked and stick it in the manure. Naturally the flies used to follow that, and we caught them in the water. So then we would count how many flies we had. Isn't that something now? We were fishing for those yellow-type flies. This happened, this is not a bunch of baloney or anything. Then we had one guy come around to buy the flies off us, like the Frenchmen bought fish from our fathers. The more you had, you were the champion.' He was laughing again. 'That's a story I thought of the other night. I don't think it's ever been told. I don't think there's anything wrong with it. It was cowshit, you know? What the hell, it's only a natural thing. It's a lot better than what they do today.'

He told me to call him Mike. The caginess of the previous night was gone. Whatever had caused the change, I was glad of it. This man telling stories in his own front-room was a kidder, a charmer, who kept looking across to re-establish eye contact, so that I could see the twinkle behind the glasses. His father always told him that he left America because the food there upset his stomach, but Seán also missed his friends on the island, and simple pleasures like hunting wild birds. 'He was staying with my uncle Mike, who was trying to get him work as a ganger on the railroad, but Mike came home one day and he says to the wife, "Where is John?" She says, "You know what he did today? Went back to Ireland." His friend, one of the Keanes, had gone back. In them days all you had to do was go to Boston, pay five pounds and you were on the ship. So he took off. But he came back again after that, and got a job on the railroad.'

It was during his second spell in Springfield that Seán acquired his famous gold tooth. 'That was a great thing in them days, in this country, but you don't see too much of it any more among the Irish. My father used to pull teeth on the island anyway. You know what he did? Put a rope on the tooth, tied it to the bed and then made you walk. They had no dentist and if you had a rotten tooth that was the only way to get it out. Or else he used to get the pliers. They had a great sense for pain. A lot of people can't bear pain sometimes, but on the island they did. They could take it. There was no other way out, either. There was no doctor, there was no nurse, so what were you going to do?'

Mike remembered his mother as an easy-going woman who loved to sing. 'They thought she had a heart condition,

and evidently she ended up with a blood clot. The last time
I saw her was coming from the doctor in Tralee. She didn't
look too good to me. She was pretty drawn, as you would be
after having nine kids, one year after another.' Céit took on
her mother's duties while she was in hospital, and when she
died. 'I give great credit to my sister for the job she did. I do
respect her, and I do take good care of her when I go back.
At least I hope I do.'

As he talked, I thought of Céit alone in that bright-green
house that could have fitted into the Carney's backyard, by
the beach where her husband was found; then of her life on
the island before that, moving busily around the stone cottage
caring for the young ones who were like her own children.

'She was extremely patient with us. She stayed home from
school in order to do that. She couldn't finish her education.
She was our hen mother. She was the commander-in-chief,
trying to bake and wash. Everything had to be done by hand.'

His mother Neilí was buried in the old graveyard at Dunquin, but Mike was only twelve, too young to attend the
funeral. When the time came he looked out across the Sound.
'It was a beautiful day in June. I thought I could see the glare
of the casket in Dunquin, in the sun.'

Two boys from the island travelled to Ballyferriter in 1935 to
sit an examination that would determine whether they were
suitable to become teachers. If either was sent on for training
it would change his life completely. One candidate was
Mícheál Ó Cearna, the other his schoolmate Muiris Guithín,
who was the same age. 'In them days, unfortunately, the parish
priest controlled the schools. He had the right to select who
was going to become a teacher. My father couldn't take care
of the priest like some other people could, he couldn't give
him any money.' Both boys passed the exam but neither was

recommended. 'I said, "To heck with it then, if that's the case." Maybe I was just as well off, I dunno. I don't regret it.'

It was only a few weeks since I had seen Muiris and his brother Seán, an ocean and a lifetime away at the crossroads in Dunquin, pulling on cigarettes by a peat fire in a house without electricity. 'Do they ever go anywhere, those two?' asked Mike. 'Into Kruger, maybe?'

As a child he was determined not to become a fisherman like his father and grandfather. 'I couldn't see any future in it. I almost used to cry for the poor fishermen when they would go out and get caught in the storm, trying to battle them waves, and the wind, and the salt water. They used to come home drowned to the skin. Their hands would be busted from the oars, trying to row, and their back used to kill 'em for the rest of the week. It was not for me.' Muiris Guithín stayed on the island to fish but Mike went to work on the mainland, at a farm. 'I was glad to get the opportunity. You see, on the island you never got paid for what you did. It was a struggle. I was always ambitious to get out of that place.'

The farmer's brother was a member of parliament in Dublin, and he sent word that a pub there was looking for country boys to take on as apprentice barmen. 'I said, "Oh my God, go to Dublin? The big city?" He said, "They're looking for an apprentice up there in Molloy's, Talbot Street. You'll get paid five shillings a week, kept and fed. The second year you'll get ten shillings a week. The third year you'll get a pound, and then you're a junior barman." He bought me a suit and put me on the train, in 1937.'

The boss and his son picked him up from the station in a car. 'My God, the traffic. I said, "I'll never make this out. I'll be back in Kerry in a week or two."'

He was not. There were Gaelic speakers around him, and the attractions of Dublin included the All-Ireland football final, the first of twenty he would see over the years. The bar work involved bottling Guinness from a hogshead and colouring pure whiskey. 'Whiskey used to come five hundred gallons at a time, and it looked like water. Clear alcohol. The owner had to have a licence to get it from the druggist, then you had to colour it. You had a tester for it. I never cared for whiskey after that.' After four years he joined the staff at Davey Byrne's, the pub made famous by James Joyce in *Ulysses*, where the young islandman was required to wear a bow tie and mix cocktails. 'I was never suited to that myself, I thought, but you had to do it. Painters, actors, writers, they all used to come in. I used to get tickets for the Abbey Theatre and go to see the good plays: *The Plough and the Stars*, *The Shadow of a Gunman*, all those.'

The city life stimulated his mind and he took to writing articles in Gaelic for the *Irish Press* and the *Kerryman*. All three of the major Blasket books had been published by then. 'The island had become very prominent. To say you were from the Great Blasket uplifted you, if I may say so. People were glad to meet you. Their eyes used to pop out. People used to come into the bar to meet Mícheál Ó Cearna and listen to his Irish.'

Every summer he returned to the island, but he was increasingly aware of the limitations of that life. 'If the weather got bad you were anxious to get out of there. We had no movie house. We had no dance hall. You couldn't meet the young females and dance with them. On the island we all knew one another. We used to sing a lot together, you know. We had a set dance. Somebody had an accordion, and a violin. We used to create our own atmosphere, but it was nothing like the mainland.'

Back in Dublin he went to dances whenever he was off duty. One evening at the Teachers' Hall a fellow Kerryman introduced him to a sparky beauty called Maureen from Roscommon. 'We went to several dances together and got along well. That was almost two years before I left. I was sorry to leave her behind me.'

The death of Seáinín made up his mind that it was time to go to America. All his brothers and sisters were grieving and wanted to get off the island, but it was up to one of them to go first and prepare the way. 'Somebody had to lead the field. I said to myself, "If I go over and pay my way, and then talk to my uncle or aunt to bring out my brother Muiris or Peaidí, that would help." Since the war had ended America was starting to open up, but you had to be claimed by somebody here. You had to sign a document stating that you would not be a burden on the State. My uncle sent the affidavit that he was willing to sponsor me. You'd have to stay with him until you got a job. You had the option of staying here for five years then becoming an American citizen if you wished, which I did.'

The air fare was expensive, but the travel agent in Dublin had a fine alternative: the *Queen Mary*, one of the great liners, leaving Southampton for New York, with cabin-class berths available at reasonable rates. 'I thought, "Jesus, that sounds good. The *Queen Mary*? I'd love to go on that." Big sensation. Big ship. They had it remodelled, after its service in the war. It was a beautiful time. I ran into a lot of people on the ship there, coming to America like myself. We had a ball – dancing and singing, and everything else that goes with it.' His memory of the journey into Manhattan was vivid. 'My God, what a sight, coming into New York harbour. The Statue of Liberty. Everybody went up on the deck – maybe twelve hundred people, all on the left-hand side. It's a wonder the ship didn't go down. Everybody wanted to see the Statue of Liberty. It looked beautiful. It was a good hot day. I felt that the statue had her hand out to greet us, with the torch. Then again I looked at Manhattan and said to myself, "Oh my God, who the heck built all those big buildings? What in the heck is the idea?" Today you have double that amount.'

His immigration papers had been checked at Southampton, so there was no delay before he stepped off the pier and was met by his Uncle Tom, a bus driver. The streets of New York were ten times as frantic as the ones he had found so confusing in Dublin. 'Crazy, crazy traffic. I thought, "How in the hell am I going to put up with this?" I couldn't understand the accent all that well.'

The train from Grand Central to Springfield took four hours. 'They had a big feed ready for me when we got here. They wanted to hear the news about home – how this fella was doing, and that fella. What amazed me was that I had more relatives in Springfield than I had back in Ireland. I had five aunts and three uncles here, and they all had big families. Daughters and sons, they all came to see me and they gave me money. I thought it was great. I said to myself, "My God, I don't have to work at all." But that doesn't last very long.'

One of the family found him a job as a clerk in a grocery store. 'Oh, the stuff they had. Today it's quite a lot different, they got supermarkets of sixty thousand square feet, but it was a lot to me. I never went to a supermarket before I left Ireland.'

Mike used the anglicized version of his name in America, like all his cousins – but instead of spelling it Kearney as they did he settled on Carney because it looked closer to the Irish. After a year, when he was feeling more sure of himself in this new country, Mike wrote to ask Maureen if she would be willing to join him. 'She wrote back and said she'd like to. She didn't like it when she got here, either. It was August and the weather was extremely hot. But the two of us got along well together, and decided to settle down. You could do anything here: you could have a car, you could have a home.' They were married after two more years and Maureen went to work for the same grocery company, in the warehouse. They rented a third-floor apartment on the corner of Carew and Liberty Street. 'After that I got a nice four-room, first-floor apartment not too far from my uncle. Then I bought myself a two-family house down on Armoury Street, and rented out the top floor. Of course, in them days we were young: we went out and did our jobs then went out painting houses in the evening, myself and my brothers.' At weekends they played Gaelic football in Van Horn Park. 'We had a team here, and I got involved in the organization of it. We had a good club, it used to keep us together, company-wise. On a Sunday we'd be invited down to Hartford for a game, or to Bridgeport, New Haven, Holyoke. There were other teams. They were all coming out then, from Ireland. We had a dance hall downtown too, mostly on Saturday nights: the Tara Hall, on the second floor.'

The halls began to close during the mid fifties. 'That was the beginning of staying home and watching television – the fights on a Friday night, on *Cavalcade of Sports* at ten o'clock. We used to have a barbecue, myself and my neighbour, we'd have a couple of beers and sit down and watch the fights.' The Ó Cearna brothers had arrived in America at a time of great prosperity, when the austerity of the war years was over, the Great Depression a distant memory, and it was time to enjoy the comforts of life. The cars were big and beautiful, the clothes bright, and the homes increasingly full of luxuries that no islandman could have dreamed of. A few years earlier Mike had helped his sister fetch water from the well – but in America there were washing machines and launderettes, steaming baths and fridges with ice. His entertainment on the

Great Blasket had been stories from the old folk or dancing to a fiddle, but here were the jukebox, the wireless, the cinema and eventually a screen that brought the world into his home. 'I got my first television in 1954. Black and white. Look at the one we got now – twenty-seven inches.' It was indeed enormous, and dominated the room. 'That's on a swivel base, you can move it any which way. And of course, it's stereo. We've got another one in the bedroom, nineteen inches. So we have come a long way.'

He broke off from his stories to show me around the house. The boiler, the air-conditioning and the basement room he had built with his brother Muiris were displayed like trophies, and why not? This was a man born into isolation and material poverty, who took a genuine pride in comforts that signalled his place in the great, wealthy, civilized community of Irish America. He really did believe in his adopted country as a land of opportunity, and in himself as an example of what could be achieved. There was a photograph of John F. Kennedy on the basement wall, and a plaque from the Irish Tourist Board commending Mr Carney for his contributions to Irish culture through the John Boyle O'Reilly club. He showed me his entry in the *Who's Who* of Irish America, and a certificate marking his contribution to the Statue of Liberty preservation fund.

He had made something of himself at the A&P grocery company by taking a diploma at night school. 'It was all about business: American techniques of ordering, and money and cash registers and cashing up and money, and percentages and money and all that stuff. Very helpful.' Not least because it helped him become a store manager, which meant he could buy his neat little clapboard house. When the A&P started to close small stores he had to leave, after twenty-seven years' service, but a fellow countryman helped him out with a job at the new Hall of Justice. 'I got in touch with a county commissioner,' he said. 'I knew the guy, he came from Ireland. Nice man. Great singer. "Michael," he says, "we'll keep you in mind. Maybe we need security officers down there." I was fifty-five years of age. Working on the court-house system for the State you start on the bottom again, and you have to build yourself up, getting pay rises and so on. But I did eighteen years with them.'

Among his papers was a certificate signed by the Mayor of Springfield, declaring 26 February 1991 as Michael J. Carney Day. That was the day he retired from the Court House. The citation said, 'His bright Irish smile will be missed by the hundreds of men and women who have come to know him for his sharp wit and proud brogue.'

The last souvenir he showed me was humbler than the rest. 'This is the oven that my mother – Lord mercy on her soul – used to cook with.' The small black iron pot would once have been surrounded by smouldering turf. 'She used to bake the bread in it, and put the lamb in there. It came out beautiful. You don't see anything like that any more, I guess.'

39

The next time I saw Mike Carney was early in the morning at Our Lady of Hope, a vast Roman Catholic church built in the Florentine style with a bell tower 145 feet high. The interior was cream and gold, so full of space and light that it seemed empty despite the five hundred people at eight o'clock mass on Sunday morning. Families dressed in their smartest casual wear sat silently, at respectable distances from each other in the echoing church, as an elderly priest mumbled through the liturgy up at the altar a hundred yards away. The prayers beseeched God to strengthen the hands of those who campaigned for the rights of the unborn child. It was already hot, and my sleepy mind wandered, back to the small grey chapel by the river at Dunquin where islandmen would stand in the old days, on the edges of that crowded room, caps in their hands, steam rising from clothes still wet and warm from the row across the Sound. Praying for the children they had lost to America, fingering rosaries as their women were back in the island.

Before I had left Dunquin, a man from the valley had warned me that I would find a very different kind of Irishness in Springfield. 'It's a kind of a plastic culture,' he said, recalling the green beer he had been served on Saint Patrick's Day. 'They even have "Up the IRA" in places, things they don't understand. They're kind of crystallized in time. They kept their Irish dancing and they kept their Gaelic football, and they kept . . . wherever they got the shamrock from, I don't know. But they are so divorced from the people they came from, and they don't know it.'

The man, who would not thank me for naming him, said that when he visited Springfield there was a knock on the door as he lay in bed with his wife, and a voice called out that it was time to go to Mass. 'We don't go,' he replied. 'When you're here you do,' said the voice. So they did. 'It left me cold. There was a really shitty ceremony that involved people standing up talking about the favour that someone had done for them that week. There were three or four collections. Everybody was really dressed up in their finery. I kind of noticed they were all white and Irish, but I knew that the Puerto Ricans were living in this area, and they were also supposed to be Roman Catholics, so on the way out from church I asked our host, "Puerto Ricans are Catholics, aren't they?" He said, "Yeah, they are." I said, "I didn't see any Puerto Ricans in church." He said, "Sure ya didn't, they got their own goddam church."'

Those words came back to me as a baritone led the singing over a public-address system, accompanied by Spanish guitar. There were only white faces at Our Lady that morning, but then the Church had always been at the centre of the Irish community, a place where the exiles gathered and drew strength from their faith and from each other. There were black churches, and hispanic ones, and places of worship for every immigrant community, reminders of home that did not always welcome outsiders. 'That's America, I suppose,' the man in Dunquin had said. His country had few problems with racial integration because it was almost exclusively white. 'It's a melting pot but they all hate one another.'

'He's very religious,' Mike Carney told Maureen with a wink when he took me back to their house after the service. 'He was singing.' After a huge breakfast of sausages, scrambled eggs, bagels and bacon cooked to a crisp in the New England way, we went out to talk in the back garden, on loungers under the shade of a spreading tree. The Carneys were treating me with kindness and generosity. They both had a dry sense of humour that I had mistaken for rudeness at first, but Mike was also very serious about presenting the people of the Great Blasket in the best possible light. I wanted to know whether he thought of himself as an Irishman or an islander. 'I don't know if there is any difference between the two. I'm an Irishman, there's no doubt about that. Everybody thinks, "Christ, my God, that's Mike Carney the Irishman." I'm proud to be an islander, yes. I can't see any reason why I shouldn't be, even though we didn't have a hell of a lot there. I couldn't even buy myself a pair of shoes. I was in Dingle twice before I left the island, that's all.'

Growing up there had taught him to work hard, to be civilized and to listen to people, he said. 'And to do the right thing. We were always taught to do the right thing at once. See, there was no crime on the island. Did you know that? No crime, so help me God. Maybe the only time the policeman came to the island was to take a census.'

I found it hard to believe. In any community of that size there were bound to have been people who fell out, and others who did things they shouldn't. 'They had their disagreements, yes,' he said. 'But they also had the will to settle it within themselves. You don't have that today. They'd sit down and they'd talk. If two elderly men had a disagreement about sheep, or fish, or whatever it was, then they'd get together and iron it out. They shook hands and it was all over. You had a king on the island and sometimes he got involved as a judge. He had no qualifications at all. It was the responsibility of the people.' If two young hot-heads had an argument they were usually terrified of their parents finding out, he said. The island fathers were as tough as their hobnailed boots. 'If you came home with a broken nose, a split lip, a cut or something, you were asked how it happened. You had to explain it. And then so did the other fella. So the fathers got together with the boys. They were told there was no reason why it should happen.' According to this version of history, then, there were no feuds, no boycotts, and no brooding silences. 'Everybody in the island, mostly, in my day, spoke to one another. I suppose being on an island you have to do that. You have no escape. You cannot call the police. You cannot file a complaint in the court-house. You have to live together.'

It sounded like they were all saints, I said. He missed the irony completely. 'Yeah, well, there were a lot of saints in the Blaskets. They were saintly people. Very saintly people. Of course, we had a cousin who was a nun. I had a nephew who was a monsignor here.'

Mike and Maureen had four children. Kathleen, the oldest, was born in Springfield in 1952 but she went to live in New York. Her sister Maureen worked as a community developer in Springfield, while Noreen had got involved in oceanography research at Cape Cod. All three were married with children. Michael, the youngest child, was a cop in his home town. 'He doesn't intend to get married, or so he tells me,' said his father. He once took the four back to see his old house on the Great Blasket – which was when they realized he had been spinning them a yarn about having to walk six miles to school in his bare feet.

'I made sure that every one of them went to college,' he said. 'They got their degrees and they're doing well. They're all Americans but they have a total respect for Irish. I taught them Gaelic as they grew up. Being bilingual is important. It's not an extra load. I keep telling them, "Don't ever lose your heritage." The younger generation intermarry, intermix with other nationalities, and they lose their Irish connection. When I got my citizenship here, the judge said, "I do not expect you to lose your belief in your Irish culture and Irish ideals." I said, "That's very nice of you, Sir, thank you very much, 'cos I don't intend to do that."'

Mike was always going to marry an Irish girl. 'Oh yes. That was my firm belief. And even my family, here in America, I always thought it would be better for them to marry someone of Irish descent. Their relationship would be better.' He admitted that any deviation from this ideal would have been hard to take. 'I would have been totally surprised. But I would have swallowed the pill. Well, it has happened today – you know, you hear of people getting married to a black person, I know families where it has happened. It's a heart-breaker. It's a hard pill to swallow. Thank God, it hasn't happened in my family. No.'

Mike Carney was the sort of man who got involved, and liked to run things. First there was the Gaelic football side, then in 1960 he became president of the John Boyle O'Reilly, a club that had been going since the end of the last century but was down to its last fifty members. 'We built up the place, cleaned it up and started making money. We got out of the old building after ten years with $57,000. This was our initial downpayment on the new one. There was nothing there, only the walls. We had to furnish it, we had to put in heating and lighting. It wasn't easy, it took a lot of hours, but people believed in it. Today we got one of the most active clubs in America.' Being president of such a place made him a powerful man, I suggested. A politician even. 'No, I never believed in politics. I knew a lot of politicians. They wanted me to run for office here, as a city councillor or something, but I said I was interested in just what I was doing and that's it. Sixteen years as president and eight years on the board of directors, all a voluntary contribution. I had a good, understanding woman.'

The Irish were still influential in Springfield. 'Oh my God, there's forty-four thousand Irish people, out of a total of maybe seventy-four thousand altogether. Of course we have an influx of Asian people now, you can see for yourself. I always used to tell them up in the club when they had anything to say, "This is our place. This is for us. You ought to be proud of it." Last Sunday we were up there and they had a free steak for all the gold-card members. You have to be over sixty-five and have been a member for ten years to get a gold card. We got a meal, entertainments and all, free of charge, paid for by the club.' I now realized why he was so passionately involved in the John Boyle O'Reilly — the club was a way of reproducing at least a fraction of the strong sense of community that he had left behind on the Great Blasket. 'That is correct. That was an echo from the island to here. It was a follow-up to the way we were brought up on the island, and raised together in an eggshell.'

A box of papers lay open on the sofa between us, and at the top was a photograph of Mike himself in a suit and pullover, taken when he was working in Davey Byrne's during the forties. There was a Gaelic League pin in his lapel. He must have had a pretty low opinion of the English at that time, I suggested. 'No,' he said. 'I always thought that it was great to be fifty—fifty Gaelic and English. Having a couple of languages is very educational. I used to teach the kids conversational Gaelic —' I didn't mean the language, as he knew very well. 'Oh, the politics? No. As I said I had no . . . look at the hair I had that time. A head of hair. Of course we had to wear a sweater in Ireland, the cold weather, the damp. You don't wear sweaters out here, hardly. In the wintertime you do, though.'

He rubbed the tight, mottled skin on his left forearm with

the opposite hand, as was his habit when trying to think of something to say. Fingertips went up to touch his hairline, another indication of unease. I wasn't going to let him avoid the question. 'No, you seem to be very interested in politics.' There was a pause. 'I think I have stated that I never had any interest. I had an interest in other people running for politics, yes. I always want to make sure the right person gets elected.'

De Valera had visited Springfield on a tour of America in 1919, raising funds for the armed struggle. When the Sinn Fein president Gerry Adams was allowed back into the country by President Clinton, against the wishes of the British government, he received a hero's welcome at the John Boyle O'Reilly. That was before he renounced the use of force. I had heard whispers that some members of the club were enthusiastic and successful fund-raisers for Noraid. So I pressed Mike Carney again, reminding him that Irish Americans were among the most vocal and committed supporters of the idea that violence could lead to the unification of their country.

'I feel that Ireland is entitled to its unification,' he said, slowly and deliberately. Suddenly his guard was up again, as it had been that first time. 'There's no reason it shouldn't be otherwise. Unfortunately it has taken quite a time, and unfortunately it has taken an awful lot of innocent lives to do so. I don't know if we've reached an end yet.'

A few days later it was made obvious that we had not, when a bomb killed twenty-eight people and injured hundreds more in Omagh, County Tyrone. This attempt to destroy the peace process was made by a renegade group calling itself the Real IRA, which then realized it had made a serious miscalculation and announced a ceasefire like the one already being observed by the *real* IRA. Gerry Adams condemned the bombing. I rang Mike Carney, and he too was disgusted.

★

The conversation had become awkward and uncomfortable. It was as though I had abused Mike's hospitality. The tension began to disappear again, however, as my host began to reminisce about the beauty of the island and the simplicity of life there. His account of it all was so nostalgic that I was surprised when he said he would never go back and live on the Great Blasket, even if it were possible to do so. 'Everything went against us on the island. The weather was against us. The living was tough. When somebody got sick you had to go through hell, just like my brother's death. It's beautiful to look at, but scenery doesn't fill the stomach.'

After the hardships of home it had been easy to fall for the American way of life. He was fit, tanned and relaxed, comfortable in cotton clothes that did not pinch or rub like the rough garments of his youth. He felt safe in an Irish suburb of a wealthy city, in a peaceful state that was part of a powerful union. Everything seemed right in the world as far as Mike Carney could tell, and he felt sorry for those who had stayed close to the island, living in the traditional way. 'Oh poor Muiris Guithín. I dunno, he's got no life. No. Maybe he does enjoy what he's doing, but in my estimation I think he was entitled to go out and see the world, expose himself to various events, him and his brother. I think they have lost something. Whether they know it or not, maybe they don't. It's a hell of a way to live. Inside the house all day? Oh my God, I'd shoot myself. I'd hang myself. Unfortunately. I shouldn't say that, but . . .'

Surely the same could be said of his sister Céit? 'Well, the poor woman. Well, she got married. She cries the blues when I talk to her, but I keep telling her she's got family over there. She did well. She's got three boys and two girls there. Her boys, they're good guys, quiet guys. She's all alone, but she's got the dog there.'

If the government had acted earlier his brother Seáinín would not have died, he said. 'And if they had done it ten years before that, maybe half my family would still be there. My brother's death brought about the death of the island.' In those last days, when he was working in Dublin, Mike wrote as many letters and articles as he could manage to highlight what was happening on the Great Blasket. 'They were human beings. They put up with more aggravation, more hard life, more struggle, than anybody in Ireland did, trying to battle with what they had to do to survive. The government should have done something while they were still in the island – then, you see, assuming that they had put in a new pier, a new motor boat, new communication, or even a helicopter service in the wintertime, well, if that had failed I'd say the government had tried and it wasn't their fault that the people had left. But to come along when the people were over-aged, not hardly able to walk, some of them, anxious to draw their last breath in a dry bed . . . that was too late.'

By the time the evacuation took place Mike was in Springfield, but he read about it in imported Irish newspapers, and letters from Céit. 'I did cry about it. A hell of a situation, after all those years. I did feel bad about it, as an Irishman, as a cultural man, as a Gaelic man. I wish it was there today, and I like to drop a tear over it, that's the way I feel.' He looked down at the dregs of milk in his glass and shook his head slowly. Our time together was coming to an end. 'I'd like to be able to go back there and go in, and talk to the local people, to sit down and have a cup of tea, talk about the old days. You cannot do that any more. It's a sad event. It's something that should not have happened.' He sighed, and rubbed a forearm again. 'Yep.'

40

'And this here is Bottle Park,' said my guide, a small man with slicked black hair and a gravel voice as we stood by the roadside on a triangle of dusty grass with an old bench and a couple of trees. A green metal sign proclaimed that Springfield's sister city was Tralee in Ireland, 2,935 miles away, but there was no arrow to direct the lonesome exile home. Officially this pitiful patch of vegetation was named after Daniel L. Brunton, a former mayor, but it had been called Bottle Park since the days of Prohibition when the old boys used to walk down after mass at Our Lady of Hope and gather around the bench to drink from half-bottles of whiskey in brown paper bags. 'They bought them in a store across the road,' said Paddy O'Connor, who stood with his legs apart and hands in pockets like the old athlete he was. He talked through gritted teeth, even when smiling. 'He wasn't supposed to sell it, but he did anyway.'

Paddy was born in Dunquin but joined his cousins in Springfield in 1947, as soon as the immigration authorities would allow. He had agreed to show me around Hungry Hill, a place that did not exist. Everyone I had met so far talked about it, some even wore T-shirts that said 'Hungry Hill Boys' on the chest and had 'Hungry Hill – the Home of the Irish' on the back, but there was no such name on the map. They all just knew that it meant the Irish part of Springfield, a large area on the edge of the city that included Liberty Heights, where Mike Carney lived. Some said it was named after the hill in Cork, others said the cops thought it was so large that anyone patrolling it got hungry. My favourite theory was that the name came from the huge amount of groceries delivered in big red trucks from the Springfield market on pay day.

The Irish moved to the wider streets and more spacious apartments of Hungry Hill *en masse* as they became established and got better jobs, leaving the tenements in their old downtown areas to Italian immigrants and Jews arriving from Eastern Europe. Paddy worked in a paper mill by the canal then a grocery warehouse before he joined the Post Office, for which he spent the next thirty-five years sorting mail. Soon after arriving from Ireland he met his wife Mary at a dance in Springfield; she was from Ventry and they moved into a street that was entirely full of people from the Dingle peninsula. We drove past coloured lightbulbs strung across the wall of the fire station in the shape of the ubiquitous shamrock.

As Paddy talked, the nickel dropped. I remembered thinking it odd that everyone in the John Boyle O'Reilly seemed to have been born in a village west of Dingle. When they heard I was interested in the Blaskets they had smiled and said I was in the right place. Now Paddy told me directly what I had begun to suspect since arriving in Springfield: that the community of the Great Blasket island had not been shattered into a thousand pieces by the evacuation at all. I had known that Seán Team Ó Cearna's first journey in 1901 was part of a movement to America that gathered pace as the century went on, but I had no idea that they had all come to the one place. It was extraordinary to be told now that those who had travelled west in search of the Land of Youth had not scattered, nor lost their identity, but that some curious, collective instinct had brought the island people here, to settle together on the other side of the Atlantic in an obscure suburb of a landlocked industrial town in the Pioneer Valley. It was as though the magical force that preserved Oisín in *Tir na nÓg* had lifted the whole island up at once and put it down again at random thousands of miles away in Hungry Hill, where you could walk down certain streets in the fifties and see only Blasket people, and hear only Blasket Irish.

The island emptied as successive generations of sons and daughters came to Massachusetts, until it was said there were at least sixteen different families from the Great Blasket living within a few streets of each other on Hungry Hill. Paddy used the anglicized forms as he recited names I knew from the history of the island, including O'Sullivan, Keane, Sayers, Daly, and the different Kearney clans. They were young and extended families with lots of children, not the elderly and single inhabitants who were so desperate to be evacuated at the time. If each of the sixteen names was represented by four couples and each couple had four children (both conservative estimates), then there were 256 first- or second-generation islanders on Hungry Hill – ten times more than were left on the Great Blasket at the end. They were a tight knot in the wider group of people from west Kerry who had settled there, who in turn were just part of the Irish settlement in Springfield as a whole.

Nobody knew the name of the first islandman to come to Springfield, but there was a story about him, of course. It was said that he travelled to America before the Hunger, found work on the railways and made a home among the other Irish in the fledgling city. Then trouble found him, in the form of a disagreement with two of his fellow workers. They were not men of Ireland, the legend emphasized. The dispute became furious and resulted in a threat to the islander's life. Not wishing to be killed, he struck the first blows and both his adversaries died. When he realized what he had done, the Blasket man was full of remorse, and naturally in fear of the law, so he took up his possessions and struck out for the open west, where his crime would not be remembered and he could start again. Years later, when friends and relatives came to America themselves, they did not find him in Springfield. Of his path west there was no trace.

The Blasket enthusiast Ray Stagles once searched for the man with no name among the archives in Springfield Public Library, and discovered families with possible Blasket connections in the area as far back as the early 1800s. Unfortunately the names were fairly common and they could equally have come from other parts of Ireland. Stagles wondered whether the boy who started it all was Patrick J. Manning, who arrived in Boston in July 1849 with papers that said he had been born sixteen years earlier in Dingle – although this meant the whole peninsula and not just the town, so he could easily have been from the Blaskets, where his family name was known. Manning applied for naturalization at the age of twenty-six. If he was the first, and he did not disappear into the west as the legend suggested, it was highly likely that he wrote home with news from America and money for a younger brother to buy a ticket, establishing the pattern that so many would follow.

When our tour of Hungry Hill was over, Paddy O'Connor arranged for me to meet a second-generation Blasket boy, the son of an islandwoman. Sean Cahillane would be at a place called the City Line that night. We had a lot to talk about. I had come to Springfield in search of the Ó Cearna brothers, and found the entire island.

You could tell it was an Irish bar by the neon shamrock in the window. The room inside was dark and Sean Cahillane sat wedged in the corner, behind a bottle of Budweiser Lite, drumming his fingers on the table. He stood up quickly to shake my hand and I could see that he was short, blond and youthful looking, if a little heavier than the coach would have liked. His eyes roamed the room over my shoulder while he talked, and it didn't take long to sense the nervous energy crackling through this sharp little fella in the shorts and Hungry Hill T-shirt. Sean's Blasket credentials were impeccable: his mother had grown up on the island with her cousins Céit and Mike; it was his grandmother who knelt by Seáinín when he died, and who said the Act of Contrition into his ear.

'English, huh?' said Sean, looking at me out of the corner of one eye. 'We had Margaret Thatcher visit a couple of months ago. There were four hundred people protesting.' If she came tomorrow there would be four hundred and one, I said, and he nodded. It was the right answer. On the wall I noticed a small poster showing a machine-gun post on a sentry tower and barbed wire, appealing for funds to help Republican prisoners of war and their dependants. I was getting paranoid again. Did the tall man by the pool table mean to threaten when he leant towards me, or was he just drunk? I soon found out. He fell over, and lay down on the floor.

'There were three or four hundred Irish boys in our neighbourhood when I was growing up,' Sean said when he had finished asking questions about my motives and background. 'We'd get up in the summer, head out the door, have breakfast at somebody's house, have dinner at another house – and while we were doing that there was three meals being cooked at our house, and somebody was eating them. Friends of my sister stopping by, maybe. You thought nothing of it. You ended up with a lot of surrogate brothers and sisters.'

Sean's father, Maurice Cahillane, was born in Ballydavid by Smerwick Harbour and came to the United States in 1949. His nickname was the Prince. 'We heard different stories about why. I always thought it was because of his demeanour and the way he handled himself. When we grew up people would come in and out of our house like they were getting paid to show up – on a given day you'd have twenty-five or thirty immigrants stop by, say hello, sit down and chat for a while. I found out his third-grade teacher in Ballydavid gave him that name, because of the way he acted. He was funny, he could tell stories, he laughed great, and he was a warm, friendly person.'

Immigrants from every nation sometimes found a chasm opening up between boys and girls born in the new country and their mothers and fathers, who had left behind the stories, landmarks, weather patterns, habits and social structures that shaped them. Irish fathers could not offer their sons instructions for the all-American way of life, and neither could most of them explain why they felt the old ways were important. Men who had been woken at dawn to milk a cow before school, and who had worked all hours just to get by when they first arrived in America, found it hard to understand their sons' angst at having to do a little homework. Too many of them grew apart and stayed there – which was what happened to Sean and the Prince until a bad back intervened. 'Oh God, I don't think I met the man until I was about eleven,' said his son. 'He was a big strong guy, big huge forearms. He had five kids and he was newly immigrated, so he had three jobs. I was in junior high school when he became disabled. It was pretty bad in the family and all, but from another point of view he was home, so you got to know who he was. I was frightened of him, sure, but when he got hurt we became real close. You remember the good times.'

Sean, his sister and brothers were all born in the seven years leading up to 1958. Before then the Cahillanes lived down in the North End, an area close to the centre of Springfield where the old houses would be cleared to make way for glass office blocks and shopping malls. 'There were other enclaves throughout Springfield: there was the Italian South End, then the Indian Orchard Polish sections, Winchester Square became a black section and then there was Forest Park, which was for the pretty wealthy, mostly WASPs.' When they could afford it, the Cahillanes moved to Hungry Hill. 'Almost every household there had an immigrant Irish family living in it. Everything was close knit. We had no real transportation, so we never travelled too far outside the Hill until we became teenagers. We were safe as bugs in a rug. There was never anybody beaten up, or any neighbourhood domestic problems like they have today. I didn't know I was poor until I was in High School – either I was pretty slow or the neighbourhood just didn't put a real value on that. There wasn't a lot of happiness when you couldn't pay your bills, I'm sure, but the kids and the laughter and the helping each other were far more valuable than the dough was.'

Once again it all sounded too good to be true, but Sean almost convinced me with a story about the local grocery, run by a family from west of Dingle. 'Dad got hurt at work and he was five months in the hospital flat on the back. They fused his discs. A year later he had to go back again, for four months, all the heavy medicine. It took this big, strong, independent guy and really whittled him down. Well, for years I would go down to Galletti's with my list of what I was supposed to pick up – a couple of gallons of milk, all the meat, all the breads, the butter, everything we needed for the roast or whatever was going on – I'd write it up and he'd put the slip in the little folder. Everybody charged their food. End of the week, or the end of the month, I'm sure everybody paid. Well, we didn't have any money, we had nothing. The insurance company was being real tough, my parents had a mortgage and medical bills, so from the time when I was eleven to when I was about sixteen or seventeen I don't think we ever paid Galletti's. I know we didn't.'

Eventually the Prince was awarded compensation. 'The first person he went down to see was Harry Galletti. Walked in and paid five years' worth of grocery bills. You don't see that today with supermarkets. The lifestyle we had in that clan neighbourhood was a little bit better than life is today.'

The woman behind the bar had a bewitching Kerry accent that reminded me of Emma, wherever she was and whoever she had become. Behind her were posters of Gaelic football teams from various counties, above bottles of Bushmills and Jameson's. Gathering up a fistful of Buds I noticed a sheaf of green tickets for a benefit at the John Boyle O'Reilly, in aid of a young barman who was being treated for cancer. 'The whole neighbourhood was like that,' said Sean Cahillane, picking up speed and intensity. Loud Irish rock music came from hidden speakers in the dark bar, making him shout. Maybe he was fuelled by the gas in the beer that made me feel so bloated. 'If somebody got sick or was destitute or had a problem there'd be these big benefits. That's a fine example today – a young man whose father is from the peninsula. If you can pay $20 for the ticket you do that, and if you can pay more, you do that too.' The event happened the Sunday after we met and attracted more than fifteen hundred people, the biggest crowd ever assembled for a benefit at the John Boyle. So many cars were parked outside that people had to walk half a mile in the heavy heat to reach the stalls or hear the bands play. There was no hope of getting down into the basement bar and being seen alive again. It must have raised at least $30,000 for the boy's family.

'It's certainly a Blasket island thing,' said Sean. This man had been a politician, he had been around the block and knew who to tip to find his way back, but he was surprisingly romantic about his roots. 'It's also a Dingle Peninsula thing –

the Gaeltacht area and the clans.' Surely people fell out with each other, I demanded, exasperated with this apparently idyllic community, or took liberties? 'Oh, people can always leave, or people would put too many drains on it. But it was never like a formal, written thing. If you were a super immoral person and had really done some wrong to other people in the geographic area, yeah.'

This was important. No one else had come close to admitting the unspoken system of rough justice that underpinned life on the Great Blasket and on Hungry Hill. My questions were careful. What exactly did Sean mean by 'super immoral'? Did he actually remember anything like that happening? 'Yeah. There's people who were ostracized. There were people in the neighbourhood . . .' I was not surprised by the caveat he was about to issue '. . . the people I have in mind, the ones that were sort of ostracized, or kinda shunned, or put away, weren't really come-overs. They were neighbours that were in this community but that I know weren't of western Kerry roots.' Of course not, I said, more concerned to know what they did. 'Well, one individual was fooling around with some little kids.'

No wonder he had been reluctant to mention it. Child abuse was a very serious crime indeed in a community whose families were sprawling but intimate, and which cherished the vision of the little ones gathered around the maternal bosom. 'The whole family, everything, just shut right down. He couldn't play sports, couldn't be involved with anybody else. Couldn't really function at all for a while . . .'

The home that Sean Cahillane shared with his mother was a two-storey timber-framed house at a crossroads, modest but for Roman pillars on the porch. It was dark and cool inside, thanks to the polished wooden floors and a breeze from the slow-turning blades of a brass ceiling-fan. Sitting out front we watched three young black men lounging against their cars and eating from foil dishes outside the Fortune Cookie Chinese restaurant, as heavy drum-and-bass music boomed from inside one of the vehicles. It was a marking of territory as clear as the Cahillane family shield on the door of Sean's house, announcing to anyone who hadn't quite got the message yet that Hungry Hill was under new ownership. 'Every so many blocks you had your pharmacy, your soda shop, your ice-cream place, a cobbler, the old barber's,' said Sean, fortifying himself against what he was watching by recalling his youth again. 'There aren't many of them left any more, those independent contractors that were rooted right into a geographic neighbourhood of ten blocks and made their money from the people in them.'

Eating out was unheard of then, and why would anyone need to when the meals they got at home were so large? 'After my dad got hurt he was home a lot, so the breakfasts got bigger. He liked cooking. Dinner was always a roast, except maybe you'd have corned beef and cabbage. Then there was the traditional food: we used to have mutton pies for Christmas and New Year's, and St Patrick's Day, so different women would get together over the house and make pies all day long, telling stories and gossiping, much like in one of those books on the island where they all go to the well to hear stories and talk.' Every Friday was fish. 'The traditional Irish dish for New Year's, although we'd have it a lot during the year, was creamed codfish. It comes in a box, salty as can be.' The food that had been forced on Blasket fishermen by necessity, and prepared by stretching the catch out on the roof of each house, was now bought from the supermarket. 'You've gotta soak it for two days just to get enough salt out of it. Then there was this thick white cream sauce with potatoes and onions all through it. You'd know the time of year from what was being cooked, 'cos every house smelt the same. There are no Irish restaurants around, or we're not noted for it anyway, but my mother could cook with the best of 'em.'

It was food as fuel for an active life. 'The trips I've made to Ireland, they have big huge breakfasts. You're out in the fields, you're chasing sheep or you're fishing, you need it. The men here were all working one or two jobs, then they went to play Gaelic football. I remember seeing three thousand people at these games: all the kids in the strollers, the mothers showing off the new babies. The older Irish that had emigrated in the twenties and thirties were there. Everyone had their caps on, and was smoking.'

The law said nobody under the age of twenty-one should be able to buy alcohol, a triumph of legal optimism over matter of fact. Sean took his first drink at the age of fifteen in Van Horn Park after a football game. 'It was Colt 45 malt liquor. There were maybe 120 of us in the park on a cold night in October 1966. The cops came and everybody scattered in different directions but they picked us up, me and a couple of friends. Down at the police station the first person who comes in the door is an Irishman, Captain Paulie Fenton, who was later Chief of Police. Paulie read us the riot act, told us the evils of drinking, but there were never any charges. He dropped us off at the end of the street with the threat that if he heard about us again in the next year he'd tell our fathers. That was far worse. If you had a choice of getting arrested or your father findin' out, you'd take gettin' arrested. These fathers were all tough, strong guys. They had real pleasant sides to them, but they didn't want their kids crossing the line, and certainly not getting picked up by the cops. It's kind of funny in the telling, but it wasn't funny at that moment. I never drank Colt 45 since. Awful stuff.'

★

Ethereal music played in the background as we talked. 'We don't understand Gaelic, but we all got Gaelic tapes. It's soothing. The music is wonderful but so is the language. It's almost like lullabies, with that comforting effect. I hear it, I relax a little bit. I don't know a damn thing they're saying but it doesn't matter. It's a language of the womb.'

Unlike Mike Carney, most of the parents on Hungry Hill chose never to teach their children Irish. 'From inflection you would know what they were saying. If there was a sudden, loud shrieking Gaelic word coming out of his mouth it was because you were almost going to get burned, or something was gonna fall on you.' Young ears mesmerized by a foreign language in the home were also beguiled by the stories, some of which had been heard on a grandparent's knee half a century before as the night wind blew across the island. Others were made up on the spot. 'Somebody would always stop the conversation when there were eight or ten people over the house, and start telling a story about the pookees, or the banshee. They always talked about home, and growing up on the Blaskets, especially when you got the men over.'

Sean was twenty-two when he first went to Ireland, with his father. 'It really cleared my head, that trip. I wasn't a stranger: I was the Prince's son, or Eileen Pheats Team's son, and I had lots of uncles and aunts and cousins alive, so within forty-eight hours I was one of the people, like I had been born and brought up there. That was where I made up my mind I wanted to be in politics. I felt someone had to speak for the group, or do something for the older Irish.' Sean Cahillane stood for election to the Massachusetts state government in 1974, the youngest and poorest in a race – and in a country – where connections and money spoke loudest. 'I got my friends and we did a lot of work: knocked on doors, talked to people. Then the Irish – west of Dingle, Blaskets, Kearney – connection came in.'

Hungry Hill was mobilized in support of the young pretender. If the Kennedys could do it, why not the Kearneys? 'The clan thing fell into line. Every day there'd be twelve or fifteen Irish guys and ladies sitting around trying to figure out how to get votes to get me elected. I'd be going door to door to ask people would they vote for me and every now and then you'd hear, "Ma Kees has already called. You're all set son." We found out all the young people who weren't registered, got them motivated to vote, and they did the electioneering. If I didn't know them then my friends did, or my younger brothers, or my older cousins the Moores. It was systematic. It was a long campaign, and first time out I won.' He was the youngest representative in the state since the revolution. 'I liked it. I would have done the job for free. I ended up finding jobs – putting the word out on the street that there were three coming up here at the county court-house, or five somewhere else. At the time there was a high unemployment rate, but we could put a lot of people to work. That's how the first-generation Irish immigrants in Boston, New York and Springfield really got up. They got their leg-holds in politics. You take care of your own. In Springfield, just like in other communities, a lot of the police force, a lot of the fire department, a lot of City Hall employees are Irish.'

The first Irish Mayor of Springfield was William P. Hayes in 1899. A year later the Springfield Republican newspaper said Irish males were 'all the masons and plumbers', but they were also the lawyers, doctors, undertakers, streetcar conductors and cops. By 1940 the Chief of Police and half his men were Irish, and the unruly mob for whom the Paddy Wagon had been named had become the enforcers. In time it became unusual for the Mayor of Springfield not to be an Irishman.

Sean Cahillane had only been doing what came naturally to a certain kind of man on Hungry Hill. 'It was a massive education. You found out a lot about people's personal lives. Families would come to me because they had problems with mental health, or alcohol, finance, disease or illness in their family. The deep secrets. They knew that my folks came from west of Dingle and the Blaskets, and I'd keep my mouth shut.'

Five years later the number of representatives was cut and Sean Cahillane was out of a job. He joined Mass Mutual, the huge insurance company that dominated the Springfield economy, and then worked as a real-estate developer, but his real calling had been taken away. Out of this crisis had come a job as vice-chairman of his old school and a deeper appreciation of what the people of Hungry Hill had given him. 'The clannishness, the sense of community, helping each other out, all being in this life together . . . their values. As I've travelled the country, been in different businesses, met different socio-economic levels of people, I still find that what they had in the Blaskets, what they brought to Hungry Hill, is a real nice way to live. I don't find that in a lot of other communities.'

There was a catch. The immigrants pursued the American dream so successfully that their community began to die. As the first and second generations became better educated and made more money they moved out to the suburbs half an hour's drive away. 'You can't walk off the front porch and down three doors to see your first cousin, or around the block to see an old friend, you almost have to make appointments now. Clans have always had a geographic centre, and I think that's being lost on Hungry Hill through affluence. It's not over, it won't be over in my lifetime, but it's diminishing. So many of them are in the cemetery now, or in the nursing homes. They came here to be successful, to give their kids the chance to get ahead, and they got that. Every one of us had a high-school or college education. In most cases, we were the first ones in the family to get there, the first ones who didn't have to use a shovel or a mop to make a living.'

It was late now but we had come to the crunch question. What did the word home mean to his mother? 'Blasket islands.' The answer came without a pause. What did it mean to him? 'Er . . . I guess . . . I hesitate a little bit, but without being point blank on the question, for thirty years I have found myself referring to home as west of Dingle. And I wasn't born there. A lot of my friends say the same thing: they talk about home as Dingle, but when you're somewhere else, not in this community, and you're talking about home it's Hungry Hill. We're Americans, no doubt about it. But we like being Irish too.'

41

'May you fall without rising,' says Tadhg, 'if it isn't feeble your croak is! How well 'tis always the same tale from you! A curse on Death, seeing how he is leaving you in the throes for so long!' 'If he came, faith, and swept me off, wouldn't it be a blessing for me, rather than to be in this state with no life, or good, or use in me,' says Feidhlim. 'May he grant you no further delay than tomorrow evening!' says Tadhg.

Tomás Ó Criomhthain, *Island Cross-Talk*

I had been warned. The Blasket wit shown in the books was dry and savage, an adversarial humour fashioned among people who had no choice but to work together. You couldn't go to war with the family next door or punch the head of the household because you might need help to bring turf down from the mountain tomorrow; but you could let them – and everybody else – know how you felt with a cutting comment, or a joke sharpened by the truth. The island poets were feared, because if you crossed one of them there would soon be a satirical couplet or a story about you spreading through the village like sea spray through a fisherman's jersey. I had not seen much of this legendary wit among the surviving islanders on the Irish mainland, probably because Céit, Seán and Muiris had all talked to me through a translator or in their second language. They were also unsure of themselves in the company of a stranger. In Springfield the island humour was more visible. Secure in his own home or among his people at the club, Mike Carney was a terrible tease, a deadpan comedian who liked to pretend that he was offended before letting on with a smile. 'If you're not taken on then you're not part of the group, or you're not trusted yet,' said Sean Cahillane as we waited for his mother to come home. 'If you're picked on, and toyed with, then that's a form of endearment.'

Eileen Cahillane watched me and waited before revealing her true self, just as her son had done. We ate a take-out meal from a Greek restaurant and chewed the fat about life in Dunquin. Who was looking after Paddy's house? Was the Shea home really up for sale? Eileen wore royal-blue bermuda shorts printed with carrots and flowers, a white cotton T-shirt and a matching cardigan. I had expected this woman in her eighties to be frail and vague, but her loose, leathery skin concealed a mind as sharp as when she had left the island half a century before. Sharper, surely, given all that she had seen. Even now her accent was strong enough to require concentration, and our faltering conversation was punctuated by looks from behind her bifocals that said, 'Oh yes, and what have you got to offer?' She wouldn't tell me what year she was born in – 'Ah, that's a question,' – just the month, June. As for what she remembered about the island, 'Everything was so lovely.' Even in winter? 'That didn't bother us.' It must have been cold then, I suggested tamely, but her response was indignant. 'It was not! Of course, our father and mother was worrying, but we had no worry in the world. We didn't care if the weather was good or not.'

Her parents were the now familiar paragons of island virtue. 'They were nice, though. Oh, gentle. My father was very, very tough; and my mother was tall and good looking. A real lady, had a very beautiful touch. She'd never scream or holler, but she made you sit down. She'd talk to you. We had a beautiful home. Very happy.' This branch of the Ó Cearna family lived at the top of the village, past what she called 'the cement houses' built by the Congested Districts Board, out towards the fields. A good walk from the schoolhouse. Was she a good student? 'I suppose I was.' For the first time she looked directly at me and gave a throaty laugh. 'What do you think, would I tell you that I wasn't?'

This wasn't working. Eileen was the only Blasket woman I had access to in Springfield, my only chance to hear the story from a daughter, a wife and a mother. Women deferred to men in island society – they had no place among the elders, and they hardly ever went to the mainland – and yet they were so often the strong ones. They were sent to America as equals. Eileen was in better health and mind than most of her contemporaries, but unless she spoke to me frankly I would have no hope of really understanding anything. I was just about to give up when her nephew came calling with his children, in time for tea.

'You know how to boil a kettle, do you?' she asked suddenly, and everyone looked at me. This was Grandma's test. I laughed and went into the kitchen, but made the mistake of returning to the room after a few minutes while the water boiled. 'Tea's made already then, is it?' This time the look was fierce. 'So much for Blasket hospitality,' I said. 'You just sit there.' Her face split into a smile and she gave a deep, hearty chuckle. So did everyone else, even the baby. I was in.

'At that time everybody was going to America,' said Eileen when the tea was made, thinking of the years immediately before the war when she managed a small team of island women sewing jackets in her father's house. 'One night he told all us children, "You know, I hate to see any of you go. And if I had plenty money, I'd never bid you go. But you are of the age now, and you got your wings. And when you get them wings you fly, and make life for yourself." So from that day out, we watched for any chance we got. I don't know where in the name of God did he learn to say that? They knew so much, you know, when I think of it now, without reading a book or a paper. How did they know how to build houses? How did the women know how to cook? They were great cooks. And knitting? There was no such thing as anyone going in to teach them how to do it.'

I chanced my arm. Back in Muirríoch there had been just the slightest hint from Céit, her contemporary, that the love lives of the Blasket teenagers were relaxed and free, taking full advantage of the solitude the island could provide. 'No-oh!' Eileen protested. 'No! No sex like they have here. If there had been, we'd have kids like rabbits. What was going to stop us? We didn't know any better. Oh, we had boyfriends, don't worry. What do you call a boyfriend? It's somebody that'll dance you twice.' What about three times? 'Oh, that's overdoin' it. If you get two dances from someone then, good God, he's crazy about you.' There were visitors from outside, of course, who came to learn Irish or just to see the island they had read about. 'Oh, they were good-looking, some of them. Oh my God, nice.' But were they never naughty? 'If they were, we didn't notice it. Maybe we thought they were crazy or something. We thought they were nuts anyway, the way they used to get up at five o'clock to go swimming. That would kill us altogether. And they'd get up from the table running for pictures of sunset. We were so tired we didn't even take any notice of sunset. Oh my God!'

Her mother was standing by the door of their house in the winter of 1940 when she heard an unearthly roar and saw an enormous black shape swoop out of the fog and over the village. Terrifying. 'Nobody knew what it was until later.' Four days later Eileen's father came back from cutting turf with an unconscious blond teenager slumped over the back of his donkey – Willie Krupp, the pilot of the German flying boat that had been forced to land by the shore of Inis Icíleáin, the next island. His colleagues had given themselves up in the Great Blasket village. 'They looked so cute in their uniforms, and so young,' Eileen said, sharing her memories of the story Seán and Muiris had told me in Dunquin. Water was boiled and she was about to wash the unconscious pilot when her father shouted out not to waste it on him. 'Tickle his feet first, and if he moves or reacts then he's not dead.' The daughter did as she was told. 'Oh boy, he reacted then.'

The raw skin of a recently butchered sheep was spread over Krupp's burns, and the islanders gave their German guests sweaters and trousers to wear instead of the uniforms that were soaked through and torn. A patrol of Irish soldiers came to the island looking for the men, but they were hidden in ditches where the search party would be afraid to look for fear of falling, or underneath upturned canoes. 'That night was great fun,' said Eileen. Four of the flyers stayed in her house, but it was the pilot that she most admired. When he had regained consciousness and looked into the eyes of his nurse, Krupp made her a promise that she would never forget: 'If we win the war I'll take you out in Belfast.'

Once their strength was restored, the Germans gave themselves up, and were sent to a camp on the mainland where they waited for peace in comfort and freedom. Many years later Willie Krupp and two of the others returned to the Dingle Peninsula, searched out Seán Pheats Team and the remaining island lads and took them for a drink. 'My brother told me the youngest German had asked for me by name three times, and asked for my address,' said Eileen. 'But by the end of the evening my brother couldn't even remember what his own name was, let alone where I lived.' She would have loved to meet Krupp again.

Sean Cahillane was out of the room and did not hear his mother's story. Later that night, when Eileen was in bed, he gave me his own version of the tale which ended very differently and revealed where his sympathies lay. 'When the time came, they turned 'em over,' he said with the authority of someone reciting words he had heard many times over the years. He did not seem to know about Irish neutrality or the relative luxury afforded to the Germans at the Curragh camp. 'I guess the British were real, real cruel to them.'

Eileen first left home at fifteen, bound for Dublin to be trained by the company that had commissioned her team of island women to make jackets. How on earth had she managed in that great European city without a word of English? 'That's what I'd love to know now. I couldn't even think about it. It's amazing.' Inevitably, she was homesick. 'I used to hear the other kids out in the street calling their mother. Oh, good God. I didn't know about anything bad. I thought the world was going on like it was on the island. Everyone helping each other. As innocent as could be. My God!'

There was no escaping the gravitational pull of America, which grew stronger for her as for her friends after the war. 'I came here in 1948,' she said. 'We are fifty years in the country now. A lifetime.' Her first impressions of New York harbour were spoiled by seasickness, a distressing surprise to a woman who had spent her entire youth surrounded by water. 'I wouldn't mind, but myself from the Blasket island! Good God, that's what I was so mad about. Then everything was so big. That day in New York I thought, "The best thing for me now is to stay quiet and follow the crowd." The quiet life was left behind.'

Relatives arranged a job for her at Springfield Hospital, which was also a culture shock. 'I used to cry going over there every morning. I thought I was crazy coming here. Taking sick people up and down in the elevator? Good God, was I heartbroken. One day I got the kitchen all done – that was my job – and I was told to go up to the operating room and clean it. I went in the door. Somebody had been operated on, right the minute before that I think, and the blood was still living. Oh, good God I turned, and out the door. That was that.'

The American way of life was strange to her in those days, and the memory of it made her laugh. 'Everything we ate in the island was fresh. The lobsters were out of our ears. In summer we used to have a big pot of them out in the window to cool off. I came over here, and when I see the price of a lobster, I said, "Oh dear God, I didn't know how good I had it!" And the first day I went to the Cape, they were paying to go down to the beach! It was only one fee, they said – it was only one fee for me to go down the beach in the island every once in a while, and that fee was nothing. I said to myself, "Who gave it to them? It's God's creation. How come I have to pay for something God gave us?" Of course, I didn't come out with any of these things, for they'd say I was nuts.'

The man she married had grown up just along the coast from the island, but they were three thousand miles from home when they met for the first time. On her wedding day Eíbhlín Pheats Team Uí Chearna had just turned thirty, a tall woman with deep-set eyes and a wide mouth, and her white silk wedding-dress spilled over on to the floor like foam on the White Strand. The Prince was also just past the first flush of youth, a straight-backed fellow in white tie and tails with a big flower in the buttonhole. An attractive, athletic man, I said, looking at their wedding photograph. 'Naturally. I wouldn't have 'em any other way.' They met in Van Horn Park and were married at Sacred Heart, the second largest church on Hungry Hill. 'Believe me it was a party. He went to play football down in Hartford the Saturday before, and everybody he met down there, he invited them to the wedding. I wasn't told anything, or his aunt even. He came into the club where we were preparing before the day and he says, "Keep cooking – there is more coming than what you think!"'

Their first child arrived less than a year later. 'The fun started then. And the fooling stopped.' There is a special place in heaven for the mother of four sons, said a plaque on Eileen's living-room wall. Sean, Tommy, Muiris, Billy, who died in his youth, and Margaret were all given island names. 'We had lots of fun together. One day the children were sitting at the table and I said, "Now, I'm only your mother, I'm no boss over you, but I'm your best friend that you could ever get, and if there's anything wrong I want you to come to me first. If we can, we'll straighten it out together instead of drawing other people in." From that day on they were great.' This very modern approach to motherhood was 'just common sense from the island'.

Teaching them Irish would have been 'terrible', she said. 'If we wanted to say anything – myself and my husband – that we didn't want them to know, we'd be talking in Irish. They had no notion to learn it, so why would we force them?' Everyone knew that the best hope for the next generation was to become fully American – it was only once that had been established that they could afford to flirt with their other language and culture. The things she wanted for her kids as they grew up in an environment so different from her own owed more to the survival instinct of an islander than to the win-at-all-costs way of the WASPs. 'I told 'em first of all not to be too keen on getting the highest mark. Once you do that, if you lose out you'll be very upset, and you'll have to work yourself like anything. Life is not worth that. You have to have the fun of growing up too. As long as you're passing, it's the main thing. They had their fights between them but we straightened it out. They went along to college, and they left Mama then.'

They left behind Mama's idea of what it meant to be a husband or a wife, and behaved in ways she found hard to understand. 'In our times, if you were drinking – I mean drinking good, you know – nobody cared. We thought they should do it, the men, after working so hard during the week. When I see them now, the poor men can't go out at all. The woman says, "Where you go?" Give them a freedom for a while, I say. That's one thing I can't get over.' Her sons were far more demonstrative than their late father and his friends. 'They show a lot of loving to their wives and children today. And nice, kissing and hugging after your day's work. It won't hurt at all. But they'd die if they do that in Ireland. They'd never go for that.'

As Eileen held court in the armchair by an open window, her words were drowned out by brutal music from a passing car. She felt vulnerable out on the streets of Hungry Hill, and sad for the ending of the old ways. 'Ah, good God, we had a beautiful gang. Every house open, kids down on the fences, and you'd never be afraid if they'd go out, nobody was going to touch them at all. It's a different world now. You have to lock all the doors. We used to have a lot of parties, but nobody wants to leave their houses at night, they all want to stay home, for fear somebody will break in. I feel sorry for the ones that are starting with kids now. Too many sick people on the road. Robbing them and hurting them.'

Most of her friends had moved away or died. 'One time there'd be somebody knocking at the door every minute, all day long. Now there is nobody around to come. And if they are, they're too old to walk. That makes it very lonesome.' Not that Eileen Cahillane was afraid of the future. The body may have been failing but she continued to face the prospect of change with a clear eye. 'We are the kind of people that doesn't have a fright of death.' Islanders did not welcome the end, they grieved with passion, but there was seldom a sense of injustice – which made the pointless death of her cousin Seáinín in 1947 so exceptional, so painful and so decisive. In her adopted country, however, death was an enemy to be defied at all costs. 'Here they are scared stiff. I say, "You had a good life, a nice life. Why you so worried to be going and to rest in peace for yourself?"'

Her brother Seán Pheats Team, one of the *naomhóg* crew who made the mad dash to fetch a coffin for Seáinín in the winter of 1947, visited America on holiday and declared himself amazed at the amount of washing and cleaning that went on. 'They'll take the skin off themselves in the end.' Americans were scared of growing old, said Eileen, and it was easy to see her point. From anti-wrinkle creams to Viagra pills, her fellow citizens had spent billions of dollars in pursuit of the elusive Land of Youth. She was not immune from that longing herself, even though she could see no reason for anyone to be fearful. 'I'd love to be young though. I hate it, to be getting wrinkles and old.' You don't look so old to me, I said. 'Oh, you're getting very clever now. You won't get the ear.'

When she flirted like that, Eileen Cahillane seemed fifty years younger. Something in her eyes or the flash of a smile revealed the sassy, irreverent woman on the ocean liner whose determination and adaptability would see her through an American adventure. She had achieved so much and would die unafraid, without regrets. Except one: despite returning to the west coast of Ireland many times, she had never quite managed to get back on to the Great Blasket, because of the weather. 'I was not a bit lucky in that. You know it is the most lonesome thing in the world to go up the Classach, leaving for America again, and look back, and say to yourself, "I never went in."'

Still, she was happy enough at home with her memories on Hungry Hill. As we left the house this strong-hearted woman, who had been reluctant to offer precious stories up to a stranger without some fun in return, gave me a hug and a kiss on the cheek, and whispered in my ear. 'Well, boy, at least I made you hop.'

42

The expert hands of the islandman tied my four limbs together and threw me over the back of a wooden chair. His knife found my jugular and cut it with a twist, spilling blood on to the floor. His grandchildren laughed, and carried on eating their lunch.

There was no rope, no knife and no real blood, thank God, and we were all laughing as Martin Kearney held me down against the chair and demonstrated how he had been taught to kill a sheep as a boy. He wrestled one to the ground before Christmas 1946, so that his father could open its throat and let death into the house. The youth wrapped up against the cold and damp who saw his brother fall that night had become a skinny, lively old man in voluminous shorts who loved the sun and looked a decade younger than his seventy-six years. The smell and the fear of the dying animal had stayed with him always, even in America, where he went to join his brothers two years after the death of Seáinín. The best job he could find was at Handy's slaughterhouse. 'I worked on stabbing the pigs, down on North Main Street near the river, till it closed down. They didn't squeal too much.'

We were around the table at Martin's place on Hungry Hill, a large timber-frame house with a swimming-pool deck that filled the entire backyard. In his window was a traffic sign that Kerry County Council could have sworn it had put out on the road somewhere. It warned motorists to slow down, but the literal translation of the Irish phrase *tóg bog é* was 'take it easy'. Warm rolls with sesame seeds had been piled on the blue plastic tablecloth next to slices of Swiss and American cheese, salad and celery sticks, turkey and cold roast beef. No ham, though. 'They used to drive 'em up to the fifth floor to shackle 'em. They'd corner 'em in this place tiled like a bathroom, with a huge wheel going around in there all the time, with hooks on the bottom. A coloured guy used to grab her by the leg, put chains on her and hook her to that wheel. One leg up in the air, screamin' and hollerin'.' Martin loved the attention this story got him. A gold chain rose and fell on his skinny chest, in the V of a white vest, as he clucked out his tale. 'Our job was to stab her. Then she used to go right down a little hill and a Polish fella on the end would take the hook right off her, and she'd fall right into the boiling water. And she still screamin' and hollerin'.'

There were groans from the grandchildren, who had stopped eating. Martin's daughter just grinned – she had heard this all before, many times. 'She'd be going around in that hot water, bleeding away. Then she went up the conveyor and she'd go into the hairing machine. Come out nice and clean, no squeals no more. I had the blow-torch for a while, to take the hair off her head, and whatever was left underneath the neck. One shot. I had that job in the summertime. Was that hot? Jeepers creepers. That was the highest-paid place in Springfield in them days. I had a lot more than the American boys.' And in the mornings, before he went to work, Martin ate bacon for breakfast. 'Sure. If I could steal it I would have it. And pigs' heads. And a couple of crubeens, pigs' feet. I was there five years. You could leave a job on Friday and walk into one on Monday in those days.'

Máirtín Ó Cearna was one of the last pupils in the school on the Great Blasket when it closed down. His younger brothers and sisters were sent to the mainland for lessons, but he stayed at home to help Seán Team from the age of fourteen. It was hard work. 'Your father would wake you up at three o'clock in the morning to go pull the lobster-pots. You had to get up with the tide, you know. You'd be rowing out in the front of the boat and all of a sudden he would throw the salt water on you to wake you up. Then you had to shear sheep, milk the cows, get the turf, cut the turf. Save the hay for the cows and the donkeys. Everything was done by the season. It never stopped. You'd be falling asleep in the middle of the day. You would have been up all night, for crying out loud, trying to dance until one o'clock in the morning.'

'We used to go in there on a Sunday evening just to dance a set,' interrupted Paddy O'Connor, my guide to Springfield, who had brought me out visiting. 'There was a couple of nice ladies in the island. In the summer when all the college kids would be gone from Dunquin, you'd have to find something!' The impossibility of emigration during those uncertain years before and during the war gave the Great Blasket community one last, brief burst of life. 'Oh, could they dance? That's all they did. They had a couple of fiddles, accordions, harmonicas, singers.'

'When the summer would come and the visitors would go into the island all the lads would be talking about getting rid of the local girls, sending them out to Beiginis for the season. Leave 'em out there for a while,' said Martin. They were both laughing now. The two old friends had plenty of stories to tell, and since we were eating they included the one about a man on the island who took advantage of the end of Lent, when eating eggs was allowed again after a period of devotional abstinence, to devour twenty-one of them on Easter morning. And a goose egg.

'You didn't want to be in the same room as him.'

'Worse than a dog.'

'How about the woman on that TV the other night, weighed twelve hundred pounds?' said Martin. 'She's down to four hundred now. Spent over a thousand dollars a month on food for herself: four or five packets of bacon, sleeping inside in the bed and eating whole big bags of chips.'

'My God.'

The mood changed when Martin started to talk about why he left the island for good. 'I guess they all got scared after my brother died. They all wanted to leave, even the old folks.' He went to England as Peaidí had done, working in the beet fields of Norfolk and sleeping in dormitories with men from Clare and Mayo, but when the harvests were in Martin kept returning to be with his sister Céit until the letters from his brothers convinced him to emigrate. 'Shit, I had enough of it. Couldn't settle in the island, no way. No women there; plenty women in America.'

It took seven days for the *Georgic* to get from Cobh to New York via Canada, and another night before the passengers were allowed to disembark. 'We were right out in the ocean all looking at the lights, because it was after six o'clock and they wouldn't take us in. Cost too much money for the tugs then, cheaper to leave you on the boat. So we had a party in the harbour with music and dancing, movies, whatever you want.' The *craic* was so good that he didn't wake up the next morning until everyone else had gone ashore. The American who slept in the bunk below left without rousing him, as revenge for all the nights he had been kept awake by Martin's partying. 'The guy came round checking the rooms and found me still there. I had been up until three o'clock in the morning. Three ladies had bought me a pint of Irish whiskey that night for taking care of 'em all the time they were on the boat.'

Out on the pier, worrying, were his brother Billy and a

friend called Jimmy. 'There was no time to look at New York at all. I said, "Come on Jimmy, let's go, we'll stop some place have a drink." But he said, "No way, we're going straight through right now." They were in a hurry to get up to Springfield because there was a Gaelic football match being played up in the Cowflop, a field back here. It's all houses now. We got there around three o'clock in the afternoon to watch it. Paddy was playing.'

Paddy O'Connor remembered the game. 'Sure. I took a shot at the goal and Jess Sullivan was standing next to the goalpost. Instead of scoring I hit Jess right in the stomach and knocked him out. Mrs Guithín was pouring whiskey back in him. He didn't wanna get up until he had a half a pint finished.'

'There was one big party that night. And a big, big fight. They had a battle down there. Hartford was mad, they didn't like to get beat.'

In the crowd was a woman called Eleanor, whose family came from France but who liked to dance Irish sets and watch the football. She also liked what she saw of Martin that day, but it took them a while to get married. In the meantime he relished being part of a new community far more vibrant than the island had been since its prime. 'There were Kearneys everywhere, all along the Hill. Just like being home.'

There were new arrivals from all points west of Dingle, but one easy way to tell Blasket men from the others: they walked together in single file, just as they had in the island where the paths were slippery, steep and narrow. 'They had the shoes on with the big shoe-horns, a piece of steel on the heel and the nails sticking out the bottom,' said Martin. 'You got them in Dingle, and you could hear them coming down the street like horses.'

'They don't make 'em any more,' said Paddy. 'If you got a kick from one of them you'd know it.'

'Oh, Jesus Christ, yes.'

'I got thrown out of a dance at Ventry Hall on account of it. Your man saw the shoes and so he threw me out because I'd scratch all the floor with the nails. I was mad that time, but right now you could see why he'd do it.'

'They'd last for ever.'

'When the fishermen would catch the eels they'd just step on them with a hobnail shoe and they wouldn't move. The eels were so slippery, that's the only way you could catch 'em. They wouldn't get away from them nails.'

The island boys were tough, but even they found it hard to deal with summers in Springfield, when the temperature hit the nineties and the deep humidity sucked all strength from 'come-overs'. 'You got used to it after a while,' said Martin. How long did that take? 'Oh, a year.'

The highest pay available was for those who worked in the worst conditions, inside the inferno that was the Fisk Tyre & Rubber Company. During the summer ambulances waited outside all day, to help the scores of people overcome by the heat in a factory where molten rubber was poured by hand and the only air conditioning was an open window. The Fisk had long since fallen silent, like the other redundant factories and warehouses along the canal, and the broken panes all over the huge, flat face of the building were like smashed-in teeth. Soot had striped the concrete as a menacing reminder of the filthy work, but some of the employees left with their own personal scars. One man who came over from Coumeenole where the air was clean was crippled by the place. 'He had three different headbands,' said Paddy. 'Every two hours he'd have to change the headband and put it on the machine to dry out the sweat. He finished up with only part of a lung left to him, because of the dirt and the fumes. You were breathing them all day. Sometimes he would work two eight-hour shifts.

You can't imagine the heat. They didn't care about their employees. There was no such thing as unions. There was a lot of blood and sweat spilled in there.'

No parent on Hungry Hill wanted their children to have to work in a place like the Fisk or the slaughterhouse. They watched with pride as the offspring grew up, passed exams, went to college and began careers in the law, medicine and other professions that no islandman or woman had ever taken up before. Inevitably, they also had to watch the children leave. The island community had been translated almost wholesale to Hungry Hill but that was a remarkable thing, and as it grew it scattered. The young people moved on and the elders stayed behind, just as before. The third generation of island children were also Americans, and they had a continent to explore. Martin Kearney's daughter drove a people-carrier with the number-plate BLASKET, but she lived in Florida. When the factories began to close during the seventies the Irish started to drift away from the Hill. Their homes were taken over by Puerto Ricans who had come over to work in the tobacco farms of the Pioneer Valley and stayed. On the way to Martin's house I had seen Puerto Rican mothers on the balconies of several tired apartment blocks, gazing down at their children playing in the street. Only the colour of their skins seemed to distinguish these patient Catholic mothers from their Irish counterparts, but Paddy O'Connor was adamant that the upturned trash cans and overgrown gardens would never have been allowed during the old days. 'The Puerto Ricans don't wanna do nothing. They got the city ruined.' There was such rich irony in a Kerryman attacking another community for being insular, self-supportive and speaking its own language, just as his own had in order to survive, and Paddy knew very well that the language he used against these strangers had once been directed at the Irish, but he insisted that they were different. 'They're vicious, you know. They're vicious people. A lot of 'em don't work, they just hang around. They have gangs, you know. That's why the doors are not open in the churches now, because these guys would go in and steal everything that's in there. They're unbelievable.'

So Hungry Hill was no longer home in the way it had once been, in the old days when there were friends and relatives on every block. Neither was there anything left on the Great Blasket for Máirtín Ó Cearna, who had found it hard to go back after the evacuation. 'It was lonesome. You were talking to yourself up there. You'd go right up on the hill and chase the rabbits, and watch the young lambs, and sheep, take care of them. Then you'd come in and see the storms coming in, watch the boats going by. Waiting for the next boat trip to go back out to the mainland.' The dreams and memories he had of the island were more vivid and comforting than the reality of an empty and abandoned village where life would be impossible for someone who had grown soft in America. Still, he couldn't quite bring himself to let the old place go.

'Maybe some day I'll go back and build another house there.'

43

'It is three hundred years since you came to this kingdom with me,' said the Queen of Youth. 'If you must go to Erin, I'll give you this white steed to carry you; but if you come down from the steed or touch the soil of Erin with your foot, the steed will come back that minute and you'll be where he left you, a poor old man.'

'*Oisín in Tír na nÓg*' from Jeremiah Curtin, *Myths and Folklore of Ireland*

September 1998

The Arcadia hospital is a profoundly sad place. Patients lie motionless on the lawns, strapped into their beds under the sun or the shade of trees. The six-storey concrete box resembles the Fisk rubber factory, and inside the heat is so thick that one can hardly walk through it. Old men and women in their nightclothes line the nicotine-yellow corridors, waiting by the long windows for an angel to disturb the still air. Some rock back and forth, back and forth, others stare. A grey-haired woman rolls her tongue around blubbery lips and repeats words quickly under her breath, over and again. 'Howya doin'? What can I getcha? Howya doin'? What can I getcha?'

A very old lady twisted double in a wheelchair shouts out to nobody in particular, or maybe to me. 'Wha's time? Wha's time?' I don't know how to react. Time seems irrelevant here.

'Patrick Kearney? We don't know where he is,' says the Hispanic hospital orderly in the white uniform as she looks up from her ward phone with half a smile. 'One minute he's there, the next he's somewhere else. He's a free spirit.'

I have come to see the last brother. Muiris Kearney, who escaped to the merchant marine all those years ago, is out of town. Team and Billy are with Seáinín and little Seamus in an eternal place. Máirín lives down in Florida, a world away again. Peaidí Ó Cearna is a sick man somewhere in Arcadia and he is not expecting anyone.

I wade towards him through the heavy heat. Doors open on rooms with three or four beds. Long bundles of limb and clothing are motionless on the sheets, and those few faces that turn towards me are vacant. Peaidí is among them. He rises from a green woollen blanket on a bed near the door as a man surfacing from the sea, gulping air and blinking at the light.

'They told me I had visitors from Ireland,' he mumbles. There is sleep at the corner of each eye. 'I thought, "Who the hell is that?"' Paddy O'Connor has come with me. 'Remember this guy. Stayed in his house a few times.'

The man from Dunquin greets his old island companion in Gaelic, and explains that we want to chat about the past. He nods. 'I remember I was cutting turf on top of the mountain when I saw my father coming around the other side. I knew damn well there was something wrong when he was coming up to see me . . .' The words evaporate as he turns to rummage through his drawers. Jammed in beside a chest at the foot of his bed is a tall cardboard box containing clothes and newspapers. On top of the chest is an old television, and a framed photograph of Peaidí in a shiny grey morning suit with a wing collar and bow tie.

'I didn't want to come at all. No.'

Peaidí seems cloud-frail under his crumpled blue slacks and

blue shirt, with a white vest visible. His eyes are startled, and his chest whistles. 'I was happy the way I was, fishing and chasing rabbits.'

He left Cobh fifty years ago on the *George Washington*. 'That son of a gun is down under now. Huh.'

Helicopters land at Pier 69 these days, I say. He doesn't hear me.

'I didn't like New York too much. I still don't. Too busy. I like Springfield. I been here since 1948, except two years I spent in the United States Army, in Georgia. And it was no prize package down there in Georgia either.' From the bottom drawer he pulls a black-and-white photograph taken when he was drafted, only seven months after arriving in Springfield. A smiling, bashful man of twenty-seven, in uniform and shining helmet. The rest of his working life was spent at the Bay State Gas Company with Billy and Team, digging holes and laying pipes.

'I went back to Ireland for four months when I retired in 1986,' he says. 'It was nice. Four months is all the time in the world. I thought of moving back there, I was gonna live with my sister. But I didn't. I took sick. I came down with sugar diabetes.'

One version of the story of the Land of Youth, the paradise that the people of the Great Blasket associated with America, has the hero Oisín begging to return to see his old friends again after three hundred years. His wish is granted, on condition that he remains on the back of a magical white horse and does not allow his feet to touch the ground. Oisín slips as he tries to help two travellers, and his foot does go down on the earth. The horse disappears, and the hero ages instantly, so that he becomes ancient and blind. His friends, he discovers, are all long since dead.

The islanders who went west in search of their own Land

of Youth found that they also longed to go back eventually, if only for a visit. When they did return it was as though they aged instantly like Oisín. Friends and relatives in Ireland still cherished the bright youngsters who had left so many years before, and no matter how much they prepared themselves by repeating the truth that everyone grew old, it was still a shock that the lovers or companions of memory were now elderly. The returning ones found their old island haunts inaccessible and abandoned, forcing them to accept not just their mortal frailty but the death of the community that had nurtured and sustained them.

In the legend, the elderly Oisín is tended by Saint Patrick. Peaidí Ó Cearna, who never married, is cared for by the nurses in Arcadia. Our visit has confused him. We should not have arrived unannounced. We thank the ailing islandman for his time, and leave.

'I pray to God he'll take me quickly when I go,' says his friend as we walk back to the car, past the statuesque infirm. 'That's no place to stay.'

I'm still thinking of Peaidí Ó Cearna's last words to us: that he would love to go back to live with his sister, if only his health would improve a little, God willing. Leaving him, and leaving Springfield, I'm sure he knows that it will never happen.

Epilogue

For it was inside that all the magic was, the kind of magic
that only a person raised by the water's edge can understand,
who spends his days looking out across it at the base of the sky.
But this magic quickly disappears when the depths of winter
return, and one realizes that it was but a summer's dream that
did not last.

Tomás Ó Criomhthain

Surf burst on the bow as the ferry burrowed through a heavy
swell, cutting across the waves. Our blue-and-white boat the
Oileánn na n'Óg lacked the nimble elegance of the *naomhóga*
that used to skirt rocks along the coast to Dún Mór before
turning to ride into the island on the fast current. We had
guard-rails, safety notices, life preservers and diesel power.
The boatmen had waited for days to be sure that they could
go into the island and get back again safely. Far below us,
unseen under the surface of the oil-black sea, were the broken
bodies of the many ships that had succumbed to the Sound
over the centuries. There were only half a dozen passengers
on board this first ferry of the year, in the sharp air of early
spring, but wind and waves and the straining engine made
it impossible to talk during the half-hour journey from
Dunquin.

The view from the mainland had been burned into my
brain by a winter's wait, so that it was unsettling to watch the

islands shift shape and grow from sea level as we approached them. Beiginis had seemed an inconsequential table of low, flat land just in front of the main island, but close up it was a long wall of jagged rocks crowned by rich pasture. We entered the bay where Spanish Armada galleons had sought shelter, and saw the narrow channel they had passed through at speed in a storm. Even those veteran sailors must have been terrified by the reef. A dozen seals barked and bolted for the surf from the long white beach on the Great Blasket, and the island loomed over the boat as we came nearer, blocking out the sky. It was huge and dark, in a way I had never imagined, and so steep. There seemed to be no landing place, but sharp slices of algae-mottled rock were piled up against each other, all leaning in the same direction, as though the prehistoric flow of molten mountain had been flash-frozen.

The only way into the island and its ruined village was by rubber dinghy from the ferry to a hidden landing slip, then a slow climb upwards. Paths that had once been well trodden were no more than indentations in a carpet of rich, thick grass that covered every surface, slippery with drizzle and sea spray. I leaned into the slope, breathing heavily, and turned a corner to find myself in a flinty maze of walls and gables all standing up from the uneven ground, some half-hidden by its warps and furrows. These, then, were the ruins of the village, their former neatness fallen into earth. One cottage had been restored with whitewash and tar, and shone like a gold tooth. There was a padlock on the door. Close by, the stone remains of other homes were pock-marked with old plaster, and camouflaged by gorse and clumps of yellow-headed tormentil.

Rising up behind it all was the first peak of the long, hump-backed island. Set against that steep mountain and the

infinite seascape, the village seemed compact and claustropho-
bic, its houses crowded close together in the one small corner
of the Great Blasket that faced the mainland and offered shelter.
The islanders were pragmatic people. In the years after the
evacuation they returned in *naomhóga* to strip their former
homes of doors, roof beams and slates, and anything else that
might be useful in their new lives.

At the top of the village, way above, was the two-storey house
where Peig Sayers had lived. It had been modern and strong
in 1910, but the winds had punctured the slate roof and blown
out the windows. In the seventies it was bought by a rich and
eccentric pilot from Alabama called Taylor Collings, who
visited the Great Blasket on holiday and fell in love with it.
Seized with an ambition to rebuild the village as a holiday
ranch, he called on exiled islanders and bought their plots,
very cheaply. After all, who could expect big money for a
derelict house on an inaccessible island? One man sold for a
bottle of brandy, or so the rumour went. Collings was larger
than life and the people west of Dingle loved a character, so
some were sorry when his plans came to nothing.

The next time anyone thought about who owned the Great
Blasket was in the mid-eighties, when an advertisement in the
Wall Street Journal offered the island for sale for a million
dollars. That was the start of a long and complicated legal
battle between a company based in Dingle, which had acquired
Taylor Collings's share of the land, and the Irish government
– led at that time by Charles Haughey, the owner of Inis
Icíleáin – which wanted to establish a national park. The issue
was still before the Supreme Court as I crossed on that first
boat of the season, and the future was unclear. There were
signs of the island being brought back to life anyway, I had

been told, particularly in the summer, when tents were pitched among the ruins. The ferrymen stayed overnight when they could. My fellow passengers included a mother and son who ran a vegetarian café for day visitors, and an English woman who sold the tourists what she wove. The weather was so unpredictable that these new islanders could never be sure when they might be able to cross the Sound again, and the weaver often stayed alone for weeks.

'It is worth it for the beauty of the place,' she told me as she whitewashed the inside of her cottage, to make it ready for the season. 'There is a strange peace here when everyone else is gone.'

A strange peace. The wind hushed and the midges regrouped as I stood in the doorway of the house where Seáinín Ó Cearna had died. The roof was gone and the entrance was just an empty space. The earthen floor where he fell was piled with slate and stone, and overgrown with weeds. Through a hole that had once been the back window I could see the next house, the post office where Céit's husband grew up. One seal remained in the surf down below, on his back looking up at the village. Beyond him, on the distant side of the Sound, was Sybil Head. From here the end of the peninsula looked like an island itself, the mother of the one I was on. Then, as I watched, the mist descended. A cloud passed between the Great Blasket and the mainland, at sea level, so that we were alone in the world. It was quiet, suddenly, and the scent of wet grass was strong. My clothes and hair were drenched at once, and the earth between the stones of the house grew dark. A stonechat shook itself and flew away.

It was half a century since Céit had moved around within these walls and heated flour to ease her Seáinín's headache. The hearth was empty and cold. I thought of the young girl preparing her brothers and sisters for school, while their father was out in the fields. Céit lived far away behind the grey veil now, but she was still brooding over the family as she moved around her home, lonely in old age. This house seemed too small to have contained so much life. The door to the room where Seáinín died had been blocked up. There were marks on the chimney breast where the wooden floorbeams of the upstairs room had once been joined to the wall. And other marks, too, that I had not noticed at first, names scratched into the plaster with pieces of slate: Caroline, Lisa, Graine, Martin. On the mottled walls were traces of paint, a hopeful blue like the swimming pool in Máirtin Ó Cearna's backyard. I thought of the road sign in his window. *Tóg bog é.* Take it easy. I thought of Mícheál and the years he had spent trying to recreate the sense of community that had been lost here. I thought of Peaidí in Arcadia, and his longing to come back. Like Oisín, they had all tried so hard to settle in their Land of Youth, and had loved it so, and yet been surprised by the power of their desire to return. The life they had made in Hungry Hill had turned out to be temporary and was now almost over, dismantled by its own success. The young people there had grown strong on love and left the Hill, just as they had once left the Great Blasket. There was nowhere for the old ones to go but back into their memories and dreams of the island, which had never faded.

The ferry was waiting below, to take me away from this place, which was not mine, but I could leave knowing what these fallen stones on this desolate, beautiful mountain meant to brothers who had travelled so far and seen so much. There was nothing here for them any more, no possible life, and no way back, and yet the derelict cottage represented some great thing beyond itself, and always would, regardless of reality. The name of this illusion was scratched on the wall in capital letters, alongside those of all the family members who had come back to the island, trying to understand:

'THE KEARNEY HOME.'

List of Illustrations

Photograph 1. Neilí Uí Cearna, mother of ten children, with her youngest daughter Máirín.

Photograph 2. Seán Ó Guithín makes his way downhill back to the island village at dusk, after cutting turf. Picture taken by a visitor, George Chambers.

Photograph 3. Peaidí Ó Cearna, later known as Paddy Kearney, on the beach at Rhode Island in 1950.

Photograph 4. Blasket children on the White Strand. Mícheál Ó Cearna stands on the left, his brothers Team, Máirtin and Peaidí sit. Their friend Muiris Ó Guithín, who never left Ireland, stands on the far right.

All courtesy of the Great Blasket Centre, Dunquin, County Kerry, Ireland.

Jacket photographs courtesy of A. W. Turner, 1999, and the *Cork Examiner*. The main image shows islandmen, government officials and crew aboard the *St Lawrence O'Toole* on evacuation day in November 1953.

Acknowledgements

There are many people to thank for their help and encouragement, including:

In England
Jane Bradish-Ellames for an inspired chicken leg; Juliet Annan, Anya Waddington, Kate Samano and all at Penguin UK; Andy Turner, the man who was blessed; Ray & Barbara Stagles; the late Joan Stagles; Malcolm Doney; Martin Wroe; Suzi Feay and other colleagues at the *Independent on Sunday*; the late Donald Davie; Arthur & Marion Moreton; Jacob Moreton, love of my life; and his mother, Rachel, for her patience and loving support.

In Ireland
Mícheál de Mordha, for sharing his scrupulous love and knowledge of the Blasket islanders, which made this book possible; Angela de Mordha; Céit Ní Cearna; Ruth hÓgáin for her great help with the research; Fionnán hÓgáin; Diarmuid Ó Donnchadha; Breandeán Feiritéar, whose films were an inspiration; Molly O'Connor; Walter McGrath; Muiris Ó Guithín and his brother Seán, who died as the book was being edited; and the people of the Great Blasket, past and present.

In America

Kathryn Court; Laurie Walsh and all at Penguin; Mike & Maureen Carney; Martin & Eleanor Kearney; Sean Cahillane; Eileen Cahillane; Barry & Delia Donovan; Tom Moriarty; Tommy Moore; Paddy O'Connor; the late Tom Biuso; and Emma Preston, wherever and whoever she may be.

Permissions

The author and publisher gratefully acknowledge permission to reprint copyrighted material from:

Island by Brendan Behan by permission of Hutchinson;
Letters from the Great Blasket by Eibhlís Ní Shuilleabhain (Cork, 1978) by permission of Mercier Press;
An Old Woman's Reflections by Peig Sayers, translated by Seamus Ennis (1962, reissued 1978) by permission of Oxford University Press;
The Western Island by Robin Flower (1944) by permission of Oxford University Press;
The Islandman by Tomás O'Crohan, translated by Robin Flower (1951, reissued 1978) by permission of Oxford University Press;
A Day in Our Life by Seán O'Crohan, translated by Tim Enright (1992) by permission of Oxford University Press;
Island Cross-Talk by Tomás O'Crohan, translated by Tim Enright (1928, reissued 1986) by permission of Oxford University Press.
The passage from *Is Cuimhin Linn Kruger: Kruger Remembered* is by permission of An Sagart, Maynooth, County Kildare, Ireland.

Every effort has been made to obtain permission from all copyright holders whose material is included in this book. Penguin apologizes for any errors or omissions in the above list and would be grateful to be notified of any corrections that should be incorporated in the next printing of this volume.

Bibliography

Since almost all of the books by island writers were read in translation, their surnames are rendered here in the anglicized form as it appears in modern English editions.

Barrington, T. J., *Discovering Kerry* (Blackwater, Dublin, 1976)

Bayor, Ronald H. and Meagher, Timothy J., *The New York Irish* (Johns Hopkins University Press, Baltimore, 1996)

Behan, Brendan, *Brendan Behan's Island – An Irish Sketch-book* (Corgi, London, 1962)

Bourke, Edward J., *Shipwrecks of the Irish Coast 1105–1993* (published by author, Dublin, 1994)

Burns, Kathryne A., *Springfield's Ethnic Heritage: The Irish Community* (Bicentennial Committee of Springfield, 1976)

Ó Cearna, Sean Pheats Team, *Fiolar an Eireabaill Bháin* (Coiscéim, Dublin, date unknown)

Chermayeff, Ivan; Shapiro, Mary J.; & Wasserman, Fred, *Visiting Ellis Island* (Macmillan, New York, 1991)

Ó Conchúir, Doncha, *Corca Dhuibhne, Its Peoples and Their Buildings* (Cló Dhuibhne, 1977)

Connolly, S. J., ed., *The Oxford Companion to Irish History* (OUP, Oxford, 1998)

Costello, Michael, ed., *The Famine in Kerry* (Kerry Archaeological & Historical Society, Tralee, 1997)

O'Crohan, Sean, *A Day in Our Life* (Government Publications, Dublin, 1969; OUP, Oxford, 1992, trans. Timothy Enright)

O'Crohan, Tomás, *The Islandman* (Talbot Press, Dublin, 1929, and

Chatto & Windus, London, 1937, trans. Robin Flower; OUP, Oxford, 1951)

O'Crohan, Tomás, *Island Cross-Talk* (Government Publications, Dublin, 1928; OUP, Oxford, 1986, trans. Timothy Enright)

Curtin, Jeremiah, *Myths and Folklore of Ireland* (Wings, New York, 1975)

Ó Dúshláne, Tadgh, ed., *Is Cuimhin Linn Kruger: Kruger Remembered* (An Sagart, Maynooth, County Kildare, 1994)

O'Flaherty, Liam, 'Going Into Exile', from *Classic Irish Short Stories*, ed. Frank O'Connor (OUP, 1957; 1988)

Flower, Robin, *The Western Island* (OUP, Oxford, 1944)

Ní Ghaoithin, Máire, *An tOileán a Bhí* (An Clóchomhar Tta, Dublin, 1978)

O'Guiheen, Mícheál, *A Pity Youth Does Not Last* (Government Publications, Dublin, 1953; OUP, Oxford, 1986, trans. Timothy Enright)

Hamblin, B. Colin, *Ellis Island* (Companion, Santa Barbara, 1991; 1994)

O'Hanlon, Ray, *The New Irish Americans* (Roberts Rinehart, Colorado, 1998)

Haughey, Anthony, *The Edge of Europe* (Department of Arts, Culture and the Gaeltacht, Dublin, 1996)

Jackson, Kenneth, 'Scéalta ón mBlascaod', in *Béaloideas: Journal of the Folklore Society of Ireland*, volume 8, number 1 (1938)

Jones, Maldwyn A., *Destination America* (Fontana, London, 1977)

Kavanagh, P. J., *Voices in Ireland: A Traveller's Literary Companion* (John Murray, London, 1994)

Kiberd, Declan, *Inventing Ireland: The Literature of the Modern Nation* (Vintage, London, 1996)

Laxton, Edward, *The Famine Ships* (Bloomsbury, London, 1996)

MacConghail, Muiris, *The Blaskets: People and Literature* (Country House, Dublin, 1987; 1994)

MacDonogh, Steve, *The Dingle Peninsula* (Brandon, Dingle, 1993)

MacKillop, James, ed., *Dictionary of Celtic Mythology* (OUP, Oxford, 1998)

MacManus, Seumas, *The Story of the Irish Race* (Devin-Adair, Connecticut, 1921; 1990)

Mannion, Seán, *Fungie: Ireland's Friendly Dolphin* (Brandon, Dingle, 1998)

Mason, Thomas H., *The Islands of Ireland* (Mercier, Cork, 1936; 1967)

Matson, Leslie, *Méiní, the Blasket Nurse* (Mercier, Cork, 1996)

Ua Maoileoin, Pádraig, *The Blaskets* (Stationery Office, Dublin, 1993)

St Leger, Dr Alicia, *Gateway to the New World* (Cobh Heritage Trust, Cobh, no date)

Sayers, Peig, *An Old Woman's Reflections* (Government Publications, Dublin, 1939; OUP, Oxford, 1962, trans. Séamus Ennis)

Sayers, Peig, *Peig* (Talbot Press, Dublin, 1936; trans. Bryan MacMahon 1974)

Ní Shúilleabháin, Eibhlís, *Letters from the Great Blasket* (Mercier, Cork, 1978)

Simms, George Otto, *Brendan the Navigator* (O'Brien, Dublin; Irish American Book Company, 1989)

Ó Súilleabháin, Seán, *Irish Folk Custom and Belief* (Three Candles, Dublin, 1967)

O'Sullivan, Maurice, *Twenty Years A-Growing* (Chatto & Windus, London, 1933, trans. Moya Llewelyn Davies and George Thomson; Penguin, Harmondsworth, 1938; OUP, Oxford, 1953)

Stagles, Ray & Joan, *The Blasket Islands: Next Parish America* (O'Brien Press, Dublin, 1980; revised edition, 1998)

Synge, John Millington, *In Wicklow and West Kerry* (Maunsel and Co., Dublin, 1912; Mercier, Dublin, 1979)

Thomson, George, *Island Home: The Blasket Heritage* (Brandon, Dingle, 1987; 1988 with memoir by Timothy Enright)

Thomson, George, *The Prehistoric Aegean* (Lawrence & Wishart, London, 1949)

Tyers, Pádraig, ed., *Blasket Memories: The Life of an Irish Island Community* (Mercier, Cork, 1998)

Watts, J. F. & Stotsky, Sandra, *The Irish Americans* (Chelsea House, New York, 1996)

Whyte, Robert, *1847 Famine Ship Diary* (Mercier, Cork, 1994)

Wilson, Andrew J., *Irish America and the Ulster Conflict* (CUA Press, Washington, 1995)

Wyman, Mark, *Round-Trip to America* (Cornell University Press, New York, 1993)

I am particularly grateful for the information and inspiration contained in various newspaper and magazine articles by Ray Stagles, the late Professor Tom Biuso, who interviewed and wrote about many Blasket families, and Walter McGrath. The television documentaries made by Breandán Feiritéar for RTE were a source of many clues. Anthony P. Kearns of Dublin was kind enough to help with the story of the German aircraft that landed near *Inís Icíleáin*. Other sources include the *Kerryman* and *Examiner*, and the following papers from the *Journal of the Kerry Archaeological and Historical Society*: de Brún, Pádraig, 'John Windele and Father John Casey: Windele's visit to Inis Tuaisceart in 1838', no. 7 (1974); McGrath, Walter, and Rowlands, David, 'The Dingle train in the life and lore of Corkaguiny', no. 11 (1978); Stagles, Joan, 'Nineteenth-century settlements in the lesser Blasket Islands', no. 8 (1975).

The Great Blasket Heritage Centre is at Dunquin, Tralee, County Kerry, Ireland. E-mails may be sent to demordha@indigo.ie.

The author's address is colemoreton@tesco.net.